ENGLISH LITERATURE: MODERN WORLD VIEW

ENGLISH LITERATURE: MODERN WORLD VIEW

M.P. Kotter

2008

CYBER TECH PUBLICATIONS
4264/3, Ansari Road, Daryaganj, New Delhi-110002 (India)
Ph.: 011-23244078. Fax: 011-23280028
E-Mail: cyberpublicationsdelhi@yahoo.com

ENGLISH LITERATURE: MODERN WORLD VIEW

M.P. KOTTER

First Edition 2008

Published by :

G.S. Rawat for **Cyber Tech Publications**
4264/3, Ansari Road, Daryaganj, New Delhi-110002 (India)
Ph.: 011-23244078. Fax: 011-23280028
E-Mail: cyberpublicationsdelhi@yahoo.com

Printed at : **Amit Enterprises**, Maujpur, Delhi, (9810878184)

Preface

This book aims to provide a general manual of English Literature for students in colleges and universities and others beyond the high-school age. The first purposes of every such book must be to outline the development of the literature with due regard to national life, and to give appreciative interpretation of the work of the most important authors. I have written the present volume because I have found no other that, to my mind, combines satisfactory accomplishment of these ends with a selection of authors sufficiently limited for clearness and with adequate accuracy and fullness of details, biographical and other. A manual, it seems to me, should supply a systematic statement of the important facts, so that the greater part of the student's time, in class and without, may be left free for the study of the literature itself.

I hope that the book may prove adaptable to various methods and conditions of work. Experience has suggested the brief introductory statement of main literary principles, too often taken for granted by teachers, with much resulting haziness in the student's mind. The list of assignments and questions at the end is intended, of course, to be freely treated. I hope that the list of available inexpensive editions of the chief authors may suggest a practical method of providing the material, especially for colleges which can provide enough copies for class use. Poets, of course, may be satisfactorily read in volumes of, selections; but to me, at least, a book of brief extracts from twenty or a hundred prose authors is an absurdity. Perhaps I may venture to add that personally I find it advisable to pass hastily over the seventeenth and eighteenth centuries and so gain as much time as possible for the nineteenth century. Valuable suggestions of the readers is always welcome to improve this book in its forthcoming editions.

Contents

1

An Introduction

LITERATURE

Literature is literally "acquaintance with letters" as in the first sense given in the Oxford English Dictionary (from the Latin littera meaning "an individual written character (letter)"). The term has generally come to identify a collection of texts or work of art, which in Western culture are mainly prose, both fiction and non-fiction, drama and poetry. In much, if not all of the world, texts can be oral as well, and include such genres as epic, legend, myth, ballad, plus other forms of oral poetry, and the folktale.

Introduction

Nations can have literatures, as can corporations, philosophical schools or historical periods. Popular belief commonly holds that the literature of a nation, for example, comprises the collection of texts which make it a whole nation. The Hebrew Bible, Persian Shahnama, the Indian Mahabharata, Ramayana and Thirukural, the Iliad and the Odyssey, Beowulf, and the Constitution of the United States, all fall within this definition of a kind of literature.

More generally, one can equate a literature with a collection of stories, poems, and plays that revolve around a particular topic. In this case, the stories, poems and plays may or may not have nationalistic implications. The Western Canon forms one such literature.

Classifying a specific item as part of a literature (whether as American literature, advertising literature, gay and lesbian literature or Roman literature) can involve severe difficulties. To some people, the term "literature" can apply broadly to any symbolic record which can include images and sculptures, as well as letters. To others, a literature must only include examples of text composed of letters, or other narrowly defined examples of symbolic written language (Egyptian hieroglyphs, for example). Even more conservative interpreters of the concept would demand that the text have a physical form, usually on paper or some other portable form, to the exclusion of inscriptions or digital media.

Furthermore, people may perceive a difference between "literature" and some popular forms of written work. The terms "literary fiction" and "literary merit" often serve to distinguish between individual works.

For example, almost all literate people perceive the works of Charles Dickens as "literature", whereas some tend to look down on the works of Jeffrey Archer as unworthy of inclusion under the general heading of "English literature". Critics may exclude works from the classification "literature", for example, on the grounds of a poor standard of grammar and syntax, of an unbelievable or disjointed story-line, or of inconsistent or unconvincing characters. Genre fiction (for example: romance, crime, or science fiction) may also become excluded from consideration as "literature".

Frequently, the texts that make up literature crossed over these boundaries. Illustrated stories, hypertexts, cave paintings and inscribed monuments have all at one time or another pushed the boundaries of "literature".

Different historical periods have emphasized various characteristics of literature. Early works often had an overt or covert religious or didactic purpose. Moralizing or prescriptive literature stems from such sources. The exotic nature of romance flourished from the Middle Ages onwards, whereas the Age of Reason manufactured nationalistic epics and philosophical tracts. Romanticism emphasized the popular folk literature and emotive involvement, but gave way in the 19th-century West to a phase of so-called realism and naturalism, investigations into what is real. The 20th century brought demands for symbolism or psychological insight in the delineation and development of character.

The Muslim Scientist and Philosopher Imam Ja'far al-Sadiq defined Literature as follows: "Literature is the garment which one puts on what he says or writes so that it may appear more attractive."

FORMS OF LITERATURE

Poetry

A poem is commonly defined as a composition written in verse (although verse has been equally used for epic and dramatic fiction). Poems rely heavily on imagery, precise word choice, and metaphor; they may take the form of measures consisting of patterns of stresses (metric feet) or of patterns of different-length syllables (as in classical prosody); and they may or may not utilize rhyme. One cannot readily characterize poetry precisely. Typically though, poetry as a form of literature makes some significant use of the formal properties of the words it uses-the properties attached to the written or spoken form of the words, rather than to their meaning. Metre depends on syllables and on rhythms of speech; rhyme and alliteration depend on words that have similar pronunciation. Some recent poets, such as E. E. Cummings, made extensive use of words' visual form.

Poetry perhaps pre-dates other forms of literature: early known examples include the Sumerian Epic of Gilgamesh (dated from around 2700 B.C.), parts of the Bible, the surviving works of Homer (the Iliad and the Odyssey), and the Indian epics Ramayana and Mahabharata. In cultures based primarily on oral traditions the formal characteristics of poetry often have a mnemonic function, and important texts: legal, genealogical or moral, for example, may appear first in verse form.

Much poetry uses specific forms: the haiku, the limerick, or the sonnet, for example. A haiku must have seventeen syllables, distributed over three lines in groups of five, seven, and five, and should have an image of a season and something to do with nature. A limerick has five lines, with a rhyme scheme of AABBA, and line lengths of 3,3,2,2,3 stressed syllables. It traditionally has a less reverent attitude towards nature.

Language and tradition dictate some poetic norms: Persian poetry always rhymes, Greek poetry rarely rhymes, Italian or

French poetry often does, English and German can go either way (although modern non-rhyming poetry often, perhaps unfairly, has a more "serious" aura). Perhaps the most paradigmatic style of English poetry, blank verse, as exemplified in works by Shakespeare and by Milton, consists of unrhymed iambic pentameters. Some languages prefer longer lines; some shorter ones. Some of these conventions result from the ease of fitting a specific language's vocabulary and grammar into certain structures, rather than into others; for example, some languages contain more rhyming words than others, or typically have longer words. Other structural conventions come about as the result of historical accidents, where many speakers of a language associate good poetry with a verse form preferred by a particular skilled or popular poet.

Works for theatre traditionally took verse form. This has now become rare outside opera and musicals, although many would argue that the language of drama remains intrinsically poetic.

In recent years, digital poetry has arisen that takes advantage of the artistic, publishing, and synthetic qualities of digital media.

Drama

A play or drama offers another classical literary form that has continued to evolve over the years. It generally comprises chiefly dialogue between characters, and usually aims at dramatic / theatrical performance rather than at reading. During the eighteenth and nineteenth centuries, opera developed as a combination of poetry, drama, and music. Nearly all drama took verse form until comparatively recently.

Greek drama exemplifies the earliest form of drama of which we have substantial knowledge. Tragedy, as a dramatic genre, developed as a performance associated with religious and civic festivals, typically enacting or developing upon well-known historical or mythological themes. Tragedies generally presented very serious Theme.

With the advent of newer technologies, scripts written for non-stage media have been added to this form. War of the Worlds (radio) in 1938 saw the advent of literature written for radio broadcast, and many works of Drama have been adapted for film or television. Conversely, television, film, and radio literature have been adapted to printed or electronic media.

Essays

An essay consists of a discussion of a topic from an author's personal point of view, exemplified by works by Francis Bacon or by Charles Lamb.

'Essay' in English derives from the French 'essai', meaning 'attempt'. Thus one can find open-ended, provocative and/or inconclusive essays. The term "essays" first applied to the self-reflective musings of Michel de Montaigne, and even today he has a reputation as the father of this literary form.

Genres related to the essay may include:

- the memoir, telling the story of an author's life from the author's personal point of view
- the epistle: usually a formal, didactic, or elegant letter.
- the blog, an informal short rant about a particular topic or topics, usually opinion

Prose Fiction

Prose consists of writing that does not adhere to any particular formal structures (other than simple grammar); "non-poetic writing," writing, perhaps. The term sometimes appears pejoratively, but prosaic writing simply says something without necessarily trying to say it in a beautiful way, or using beautiful words. Prose writing can of course take beautiful form; but less by virtue of the formal features of words (rhymes, alliteration, metre) but rather by style, placement, or inclusion of graphics. But one need not mark the distinction precisely, and perhaps cannot do so. Note the classifications:

- "prose poetry", which attempts to convey the aesthetic richness typical of poetry using only prose
- "free verse", or poetry not adhering to any of the structures of one or another formal poetic style

Narrative fiction (narrative prose) generally favours prose for the writing of novels, short stories, graphic novels, and the like. Singular examples of these exist throughout history, but they did not develop into systematic and discrete literary forms until relatively recent centuries. Length often serves to categorize works of prose fiction. Although limits remain somewhat arbitrary, modern publishing conventions dictate the following:

- A Mini Saga is a short story of exactly 50 words
- A Flash fiction is generally defined as a piece of prose under a thousand words.
- A short story comprises prose writing of less than 10,000 to 20,000 words, but typically more than 500 words, which may or may not have a narrative arc.
- A story containing between 20,000 and 50,000 words falls into the novella category.
- A work of fiction containing more than 50,000 words falls squarely into the realm of the novel.

A novel consists simply of a long story written in prose, yet the form developed comparatively recently. Icelandic prose sagas dating from about the 11th century bridge the gap between traditional national verse epics and the modern psychological novel. In mainland Europe, the Spaniard Cervantes wrote perhaps the first influential novel: Don Quixote, the first part of which was published in 1605 and the second in 1615. Earlier collections of tales, such as Boccaccio's Decameron and Chaucer's The Canterbury Tales, have comparable forms and would classify as novels if written today. Earlier works written in Asia resemble even more strongly the novel as we now think of it-for example, works such as the Chinese Romance of the Three Kingdoms and the Japanese Tale of Genji by Lady Murasaki. Compare to The Book of One Thousand and One Nights.

Early novels in Europe did not, at the time, count as significant literature, perhaps because "mere" prose writing seemed easy and unimportant. It has become clear, however, that prose writing can provide aesthetic pleasure without adhering to poetic forms. Additionally, the freedom authors gain in not having to concern themselves with verse structure translates often into a more complex plot or into one richer in precise detail than one typically finds even in narrative poetry. This freedom also allows an author to experiment with many different literary and presentation styles-including poetry-in the scope of a single novel.

Other Prose Literature

Philosophy, history, journalism, and legal and scientific writings traditionally ranked as literature. They offer some of the oldest prose writings in existence; novels and prose stories earned the names "fiction" to distinguish them from factual writing or nonfiction, which writers historically have crafted in prose.

The "literary" nature of science writing has become less pronounced over the last two centuries, as advances and specialization have made new scientific research inaccessible to most audiences; science now appears mostly in journals. Scientific works of Euclid, Aristotle, Copernicus, and Newton still possess great value; but since the science in them has largely become outdated, they no longer serve for scientific instruction, yet they remain too technical to sit well in most programmes of literary study. Outside of "history of science" programmes students rarely read such works. Many books "popularizing" science might still deserve the title "literature"; history will tell.

Philosophy, too, has become an increasingly academic discipline. More of its practitioners lament this situation than occurs with the sciences; nonetheless most new philosophical work appears in academic journals. Major philosophers through history--Plato, Aristotle, Augustine, Descartes, Nietzsche--have become as canonical as any writers. Some recent philosophy works are argued to merit the title "literature", such as some of the works by Simon Blackburn; but much of it does not, and some areas, such as logic, have become extremely technical to a degree similar to that of mathematics.

A great deal of historical writing can still rank as literature, particularly the genre known as creative nonfiction. So can a great deal of journalism, such as literary journalism. However these areas have become extremely large, and often have a primarily utilitarian purpose: to record data or convey immediate information. As a result the writing in these fields often lacks a literary quality, although it often and in its better moments has that quality. Major "literary" historians include Herodotus, Thucydides and Procopius, all of whom count as canonical literary figures. Law offers a less clear case. Some writings of Plato and Aristotle, or even the early parts of the Bible, might count as legal literature. The law tables of Hammurabi of Babylon might count. Roman civil law as codified in the Corpus Juris Civilis during the reign of Justinian I of the Byzantine Empire has a reputation as significant literature. The founding documents of many countries, including the United States Constitution, can count as literature; however legal writing now rarely exhibits literary merit.

Game Design Scripts-In essence never seen by the player of a game and only by the developers and/or publishers, the audience for these pieces is usually very small. Still, many game scripts contain immersive stories and detailed worlds making them hidden literary gems.

Most of these fields, then, through specialization or proliferation, no longer generally constitute "literature" in the sense under discussion. They may sometimes count as "literary literature"; more often they produce what one might call "technical literature" or "professional literature".

Related Narrative Forms

- Graphic novels and comic books present stories told in a combination of sequential artwork, dialogue and text.
- Films, videos and broadcast soap operas have carved out a niche which often parallels the functionality of prose fiction.
- Interactive fiction, a term for a prose-based genre of computer games, occupies a small literary niche.
- Electronic literature is a developing literary genre meant to be read on a computer screen, often making use of hypertext.

Genres of Literature

A literary genre refers to the traditional divisions of literature of various kinds according to a particular criterion of writing.

Literary Techniques

A Literary technique or literary device may be used by works of literature in order to produce a specific effect on the reader. Literary technique is distinguished from literary genre as military tactics are from military strategy. Thus, though David Copperfield employs satire at certain moments, it belongs to the genre of comic novel, not that of satire. By contrast, Bleak House employs satire so consistently as to belong to the genre of satirical novel. In this way, use of a technique can lead to the development of a new genre, as was the case with one of the first modern novels, Pamela by Samuel Richardson, which by using the epistolary technique strengthened the tradition of the epistolary novel, a genre which had been practiced for some time already but without the same acclaim.

Literature by Country, Language, or Cultural Group

Literary Criticism

Literary criticism implies a critique and evaluation of a piece of literature and in some cases is used to improve a work in progress or classical piece. There are many types of literary criticism and each can be used to critique a piece in a different way or critique a different aspect of a piece. The major types of literary criticism are Marxism, Human studies, which umbrellas homosexual studies and feminism, historical, and Traditional, also known as New Criticism.

Themes in Literature

Theme is a broad idea in a story, or a message conveyed by a work. This message is usually about life, society or human nature. Themes are usually implied rather than explicitly stated. Deep thematic content is not required in literature; however, some readers would say that all stories inherently project some kind of outlook on life that can be taken as a theme, regardless of whether or not this is the intent of the author. Analysis of changes in dynamic characters can provide insight into a particular theme.

WESTERN CANON

The Western canon is a term used to denote a canon of books, and, more widely, music and art, that has been the most influential in shaping Western culture. It asserts a compendium of the greatest works of artistic merit. Such a canon is important to the theory of educational perennialism and the development of high culture. Although previously held in high regard, it has been the subject of increasing contention through the latter half of the

20th century. In practice, debates, and attempts to actually define the Canon in lists, are essentially restricted to books of various sorts: Literature, including Poetry, Fiction and Drama, autobiographical writings and Letters, Philosophy and History. A few accessible books on the Sciences are usually included.

Examples

Examples of shorter canonical lists include (in which the selectors have attempted to list only the most important ones):

- The Harvard Classics
- Great Books
- Great Books of the Western World
- Harold Bloom's Western Canon link

University reading lists are also good indicators of what is considered to be in the Western canon:

- St. John's College reading list
- Columbia College Core Curriculum

Longer lists (in which the selectors have attempted to be more comprehensive):

- Loeb Classical Library (Greek and Latin authors)
- I Tatti Renaissance Library (Renaissance authors)
- Everyman's Library (Modern works)

Origins

The process of listmaking-defining the boundaries of the canon-is endless. One of the notable attempts in the English-speaking world was the Great Books of the Western World program. This program, developed in the middle third of the 20th century, grew out of the curriculum at the University of Chicago. University president Robert Hutchins and his collaborator Mortimer Adler developed a program that offered reading lists, books, and organizational strategies for reading clubs to the general public. An earlier attempt, the Harvard Classics (1909) was promulgated by Harvard University president Charles W. Eliot, whose thesis was the same as Carlyle's:... The greatest university of all is a collection of books.-Thomas Carlyle

Debate

There has been an ongoing, intensely political debate over the nature and status of the canon since at least the 1960s. In the USA, in particular, it has been attacked as a compendium of books written mainly by "dead white European males", that thus do not represent the viewpoints of many others in contemporary societies around the world. Others, notably Allan Bloom in his 1987 book The Closing of the American Mind, have disagreed strongly. Authors such as Yale Professor of Humanities Harold Bloom (no relation) have also spoken strongly in favor of the canon, and in general the canon remains as a represented idea in most institutions, though its implications continue to be debated heavily.

Defenders maintain that those who undermine the canon do so out of primarily political interests, and that the measure of quality represented by the works of the canon is of an aesthetic rather than political nature. Thus, any political objections aimed at the canon are ultimately irrelevant. One of the main objections to a canon of literature is the question of authority-who should have the power to determine what works are worth reading and teaching?

Works

Works which are commonly included in the canon include works of fiction such as some epic poems, poetry, music, drama, novels, and other assorted forms of literature from the many diverse Western (and more recently non-Western) cultures. Many non-fiction works are also listed, primarily from the areas of religion, mythology, science, philosophy, economics, politics, and history. Works which directly address the canon (both for and against):

- The Western Canon: The Books and School of the Ages by Harold Bloom
- Shakespeare: The Invention of the Human by Harold Bloom
- The Dead Father by Donald Barthelme
- The History of Western Literature by Otto Maria Carpeaux (eight volumes, only available in Portuguese)

ENGLISH LITERATURE

The term English literature refers to literature written in the English language, including literature composed in English by writers not necessarily from England; Joseph Conrad was Polish, Robert Burns was Scottish, James Joyce was Irish, Dylan Thomas was Welsh, Edgar Allan Poe was American, Salman Rushdie is Indian, V.S. Naipaul is Trinidadian. In other words English literature is as diverse as the varieties and dialects of English spoken around the world. In academia, the term often labels departments and programmes practising English studies in secondary and tertiary educational systems.

MIDDLE AGES

The first works in English, written in the Anglo-Saxon dialect now called Old English, appear in the early Middle Ages (the oldest surviving text is Cædmon's Hymn). The oral tradition was very strong in early British culture and most literary works were written to be performed. Epic poems were thus very popular and many, including Beowulf, have survived to the present day in the rich corpus of Anglo-Saxon literature.

These are languages that closely resemble today's Norwegian or, better yet, Icelandic, though much Anglo-Saxon verse in the extant manuscripts is probably a "milder" adaptation of the earlier Viking and German war poems from the continent. When such poetry was brought to England it was still being handed down orally from one generation to another, and the constant presence of alliterative verse, or consonant rhyme (today's newspaper headlines and marketing abundantly uses this technique such as in Big is Better) helped the Anglo-Saxon peoples remember it. Such rhyme is a feature of Germanic languages and is opposed to vocalic or end-rhyme of Romance languages. But the first written literature dates to the early Christian monasteries founded by St. Augustine of Canterbury and his disciples and it is reasonable to believe that it was somehow adapted to suit to needs of Christian readers. Even without their crudest lines, Viking war poems still smell of blood feuds and their consonant rhymes sound like the smashing of swords under the gloomy northern sky: there is always a sense of imminent danger in the narratives. Sooner or later, all things must come to an end, as Beowulf eventually dies at the hands of the huge monster he spends his life fighting. The feelings of Beowulf that nothing lasts, that youth and joy will turn to death and sorrow entered Christianism and were to dominate the future landscape of English fiction. The "ubi sunt" theme is, for example, recurrent in Hamlet ("Alas, poor Yorick"), not to mention much Jacobean poetry. With the exception of the relatively light-hearted and optimistic Restoration and the Augustan Age, melancholia and angst remain a favorite theme with English-speaking writers, through the Gothic novel and Pre-romanticism to the birth of modern romantic sensibility.

When William the Conqueror makes England a part of the Anglo-Norman realm in 1066 bringing Norman, there is a period of Anglo-Norman literature, though Old English poetry continues to be read and its language widely spoken. It was not until the early 13th century when Albion becomes independent and severs its relations to France that the language really changes. As the Normans are assimilated into mainstream culture, their French penetrates the lower orders of society changing much of the grammar and lexicon of Old English. Though it does not become a Romance language, Chaucer's English is much closer to present-day English than the language that people spoke a century before. The average English-speaker cannot read Chaucer (Middle English) without difficulty but can nonetheless grasp the gist of the story, while he needs to read Beowulf in modern English--in translation.

In the late medieval period (1200-1500), the ideals of courtly love entered England and authors began to write romances, either in verse or prose. Especially popular were tales of King Arthur and his court. The poem Sir Gawain and the Green Knight shows many of the key features of literature at this time: a setting in the legendary time of King Arthur, an emphasis on chivalry and knightly behavior, and religious overtones.

English drama at this time was overtly religious. Mystery plays were enacted in cities and towns to celebrate major holidays, and the less formal mummers plays also conveyed Christian themes.

England's first great author, Geoffrey Chaucer (1340-1400), wrote in Middle English. His most famous work is The Canterbury

Tales, a collection of stories in a variety of genres, ostensibly told by a group of pilgrims on their way to Canterbury. Remarkably, they are from all walks of life, which is reflected as much in the language they use as in the content of their stories. But, though Chaucer is most certainly an English author, he was inspired by literary developments taking place elsewhere in Europe, especially in Italy. Chaucer's The Canterbury Tales are quite indebted to Giovanni Boccaccio's Decameron. The Renaissance was making its way to Britain.

EARLY MODERN RENAISSANCE

Following the introduction of a printing press into England by William Caxton in 1476, vernacular literature flourished. The Reformation inspired the production of vernacular liturgy which led to the Book of Common Prayer, a lasting influence on literary English language. The poetry, drama, and prose produced under both Queen Elizabeth I and King James I constitute what is today labelled as Early modern (or Renaissance). This literature is noted for its interest in the human being as a worthy subject (due in large part to the importation of humanism from Italy). Unlike the literature of Medieval England, which was almost entirely religious in nature, Early modern literature offered readers a more secular literature; though it should be noted, Early modern literature does appear overtly religious in many ways when compared with modern secularism.

Elizabethan Literature

The Elizabethan era saw a great flourishing of literature, especially in the field of drama. The Italian Renaissance had rediscovered the ancient Greek and Roman theatre, which was then beginning to evolve apart from the old mystery and miracle plays of the Middle Ages. The Italians were particularly inspired by Seneca (a major tragic playwright and philosopher, the tutor of Nero) and Plautus (its comic clichés, especially that of the boasting soldier had a powerful influence on the Renaissance and after). However, the Italian tragedies embraced a principle contrary to Seneca's ethics: showing blood and violence on the stage. In Seneca's plays such scenes were only acted by the characters. But the English playwrights were intrigued by Italian model: a conspicuous community of Italian actors had settled in London and Giovanni Florio had brought much of the Italian language and culture to England.

It is also true that the Elizabethan Era was a very violent age and that the high incidence of political assassinations in Renaissance Italy (embodied by Niccolò Machiavelli's The Prince) did little to calm fears of popish plots. As a result, representing that kind of violence on the stage was probably more cathartic for the Elizabethan spectator. Following earlier Elizabethan plays such as Gorboduc by Sackville & Norton and The Spanish Tragedy by Kyd that was to provide much material for Hamlet, William Shakespeare stands out in this period as a poet and playwright as yet unsurpassed. Shakespeare was not a man of letters by profession, and probably had only some grammar school education. He was neither a lawyer, nor an aristocrat as the "university wits" that had monopolised the English stage when he started writing. But he was very gifted and incredibly versatile, and he surpassed "professionals" as Greene who mocked this "shake-scene" of low origins. Though most dramas met with great success, it is in his later years (marked by the early reign of James I) that he wrote what have been considered his greatest plays: Hamlet, Othello, King Lear, Macbeth, Antony and Cleopatra, and The Tempest, a tragicomedy that inscribes within the main drama a brilliant pageant to the new king. This 'play within a play' takes the form of a masque, an interlude with music and dance colored by the novel special effects of the new indoor theaters.

Critics have shown that this masterpiece, which can be considered a dramatic work in its own right, was written for James's court, if not for the monarch himself. The magic arts of Prospero, on which depend the outcome of the plot, hint at the fine relationship between art and nature in poetry. Significantly for those times (the arrival of the first colonists in America), The Tempest is (though not apparently) set on a Bermudan island, as research on the Bermuda Pamphlets (1609) has shown, linking Shakespeare to the Virginia Company itself. The "News from the New World", as Frank Kermode points out, were already out and Shakespeare's interest in this respect is remarkable. Shakespeare also popularized the English sonnet which made significant changes to Petrarch's model.

The sonnet was introduced into English by Thomas Wyatt in the early 16th century. Poems intended for to be set to music as songs, such as by Thomas Campion, became popular as printed literature was disseminated more widely in households. Other important figures in Elizabethan theatre include Christopher Marlowe, Thomas Dekker, John Fletcher and Francis Beaumont. Had Marlowe (1564-1593) not been stabbed at twenty-nine in a tavern brawl, says Anthony Burgess, he might have rivalled, if not equalled Shakespeare himself for his poetic gifts. Remarkably, he was born only a few weeks before Shakespeare and must have known him well. Marlowe's subject matter, though, is different: it focuses more on the moral drama of the renaissance man than any other thing. Marlowe was fascinated and terrified by the new frontiers opened by modern science. Drawing on German lore, he introduced Dr. Faustus to England, a scientist and magician who is obsessed by the thirst of knowledge and the desire to push man's technological power to its limits.

He acquires supernatural gifts that even allow him to go back in time and wed Helen of Troy, but at the end of his twenty-four years' covenant with the devil he has to surrender his soul to him. His dark heroes may have something of Marlowe himself, whose untimely death remains a mystery. He was known for being an atheist, leading a lawless life, keeping many mistresses, consorting with ruffians: living the 'high life' of London's underworld. But many suspect that this might have been a cover-up for his activities as a secret agent for Elizabeth I, hinting that the 'accidental stabbing' might have been a premeditated assassination by the enemies of The Crown. Beaumont and Fletcher are less-known, but it is almost sure that they helped Shakespeare write some of his best dramas, and were quite popular at the time. It is also at this time that the city comedy genre develops. In the later 16th century English poetry was characterised by elaboration of language and extensive allusion to classical myths. The most important poets of this era include Edmund Spenser and Sir Philip Sidney.

Jacobean Literature

After Shakespeare's death, the poet and dramatist Ben Jonson was the leading literary figure of the Jacobean era (The reign of James I). However, Jonson's aesthetics harks back to the

Middle Ages rather than to the Tudor Era: his characters embody the theory of humors. According to this contemporary medical theory, behavioral differences result from a prevalence of one of the body's four "humors" (blood, phlegm, black bile, and yellow bile) over the other three; these humors correspond with the four elements of the universe, air, water, fire, and earth. This leads Jonson to exemplify such differences to the point of creating types, or clichés.

Jonson is a master of style, and a brilliant satirist. His Volpone shows how a group of scammers are fooled by a top con-artist, vice being punished by vice, virtue meeting its reward.

Others who followed Jonson's style include Beaumont and Fletcher, who wrote the brilliant comedy, The Knight of the Burning Pestle, a mockery of the rising middle class and especially of those nouveau riches who pretend to dictate literary taste without knowing much literature at all. In the story, a couple of grocers wrangle with professional actors to have their illiterate son play a leading role in a drama. He becomes a knight-errant wearing, appropriately, a burning pestle on his shield. Seeking to win a princess's heart, the young man is ridiculed much in the way Don Quixote was, although Don Quixote had not yet been written. One of Beaumont and Fletcher's chief merits was that of realising how feudalism and chivalry had turned into snobbery and make-believe and that new social classes were on the rise.

Another popular style of theatre during Jacobean times was the revenge play, popularized by John Webster and Thomas Kyd. George Chapman wrote a couple of subtle revenge tragedies, but must be remembered chiefly on account of his famous translation of Homer, one that had a profound influence on all future English literature, even inspiring John Keats to write one of his best sonnets.

The King James Bible, one of the most massive translation projects in the history of English up to this time, was started in 1604 and completed in 1611. It represents the culmination of a tradition of Bible translation into English that began with the work of William Tyndale. It became the standard Bible of the Church of England, and some consider it one of the greatest literary works of all time. This project was headed by James I himself, who supervised the work of forty-seven scholars. Although many other translations into English have been made, some of which are widely considered more accurate, many aesthetically prefer the King James Bible, whose meter is made to mimic the original Hebrew verse.

Besides Shakespeare, whose figure towers the early 1600s, the major poets of the early 17th century included John Donne and the other Metaphysical poets. Influenced by continental Baroque, and taking as his subject matter both Christian mysticism and eroticism, metaphysical poetry uses unconventional or "unpoetic" figures, such as a compass or a mosquito, to reach surprise effects. For example, in one of Donne's Songs and Sonnets, the points of a compass represent two lovers, the woman who is home, waiting, being the center, the farther point being her lover sailing away from her. But the larger the distance, the more the hands of the compass lean to each other: separation makes love grow fonder. The paradox or the oxymoron is a constant in this poetry whose fears and anxieties also speak of a world of spiritual certainties shaken by the modern discoveries of geography and science, one that is no longer the center of the universe.

Apart from the metaphysical poetry of Donne, the 17th century is also celebrated for its Baroque poetry. Baroque poetry served the same ends as the art of the period; the Baroque style is lofty, sweeping, epic, and religious. Many of these poets have an overtly Catholic sensibility (namely Richard Crashaw) and wrote poetry for the Catholic counter-Reformation in order to establish a feeling of supremacy and mysticism that would ideally persuade newly emerging Protestant groups back toward Catholicism.

Caroline and Cromwellian Literature

The turbulent years of the mid-17th century, during the reign of Charles I and the subsequent Commonwealth and Protectorate, saw a flourishing of political literature in English. Pamphlets written by sympathisers of every faction in the English civil war ran from vicious personal attacks and polemics, through many forms of propaganda, to high-minded schemes aiming to reform the nation. Of the latter type Leviathan by Thomas Hobbes would prove to be one of the most important works of British political philosophy. Hobbes' writings are some of the only political works from the era which are still regularly published whilst John Bramhall, who was Hobbes' chief critic, is mostly forgotten. The period also saw a flourishing of news books, the precursors to the British newspaper, with journalists such as Henry Muddiman, Marchamont Needham, John Birkenhead representing the views and activities of the contending parties. The frequent arrests of authors and the suppression of their works, with the consequence of foreign or underground printing, led to the idea of licensing being proposed. The Areopagitica, a political pamphlet by John Milton, was written in opposition to licensing and is regarded as one of the most eloquent defences of press freedom ever written.

Other forms of literature written during this period are usually ascribed political subtexts or their authors' are grouped along political lines. The cavalier poets, active mainly before the civil war, owed much to the earlier school of metaphysical poets. The forced retirement of royalist officials after the execution of Charles I was a good thing in the case of Izaak Walton as it gave him time to work on his book The Compleat Angler. Published in 1653 the book, ostensibly a guide to fishing, is much more; being a meditation on life, leisure and contentment. The two most important poets of Oliver Cromwell's England were Andrew Marvell and John Milton with both producing works praising the new government; such as Marvell's An Horatian Ode upon Cromwell's Return from Ireland. Despite their republican beliefs they escaped punishment upon the Restoration of Charles II after which Milton wrote some of his greatest poetical works with any possible political message hidden under allegory. Thomas Browne was another writer of the period; a learned man with an extensive library, he wrote prolifically on science, religion, medicine and the esoteric.

Restoration Literature

Restoration literature includes both Paradise Lost and the Earl of Rochester's Sodom, the high spirited sexual comedy of The Country Wife and the moral wisdom of Pilgrim's Progress. It saw Locke's Treatises on Government, the founding of the Royal Society, the experiments of Robert Boyle and the holy meditations of Boyle, the hysterical attacks on theaters from Jeremy Collier, the pioneering of literary criticism from Dryden, and the first newspapers. The official break in literary culture caused by censorship and radically moralist standards under Cromwell's Puritan regime created a gap in literary tradition, allowing a seemingly fresh start for all forms of literature after the Restoration. During the Interregnum, the royalist forces attached to the court of Charles I went into exile with the twenty-year old Charles II. The nobility who travelled with Charles II were therefore lodged for over a decade in the midst of the continent's literary scene. Charles spent his time attending plays in France, and he developed a taste for Spanish plays. Those nobles living in Holland began to learn about mercantile exchange as well as the tolerant, rationalist prose debates that circulated in that officially tolerant nation.

The largest and most important poetic form of the era was satire. In general, publication of satire was done anonymously. There were great dangers in being associated with a satire. On the one hand, defamation law was a wide net, and it was difficult for a satirist to avoid prosecution if he were proven to have written a piece that seemed to criticize a noble. On the other hand, wealthy individuals would respond to satire as often as not by having the suspected poet physically attacked by ruffians. John Dryden was set upon for being merely suspected of having written the Satire on Mankind. A consequence of this anonymity is that a great many poems, some of them of merit, are unpublished and largely unknown.

Prose in the Restoration period is dominated by Christian religious writing, but the Restoration also saw the beginnings of two genres that would dominate later periods: fiction and journalism. Religious writing often strayed into political and economic writing, just as political and economic writing implied or directly addressed religion. Thomas Sprat wrote his The Dead Poet's Society in 1667 and set forth, in a single document, the goals of empirical science ever after. The Restoration was also the time when John Locke wrote many of his philosophical works. Locke's empiricism was an attempt at understanding the basis of human understanding itself and thereby devising a proper manner for making sound decisions.

These same scientific methods led Locke to his three Treatises on Government, which later inspired the thinkers in the American Revolution. As with his work on understanding, Locke moves from the most basic units of society toward the more elaborate, and, like Thomas Hobbes, he emphasizes the plastic nature of the social contract. For an age that had seen absolute monarchy overthrown, democracy attempted, democracy corrupted, and limited monarchy restored, only a flexible basis for government could be satisfying.

The Restoration moderated most of the more strident sectarian writing, but radicalism persisted after the Restoration. Puritan authors such as John Milton were forced to retire from public life or adapt, and those Digger, Fifth Monarchist, Leveller, Quaker, and Anabaptist authors who had preached against monarchy and who had participated directly in the regicide of Charles I were partially suppressed. Consequently, violent writings were forced underground, and many of those who had served in the Interregnum attenuated their positions in the Restoration. John Bunyan stands out beyond other religious authors of the period. Bunyan's The Pilgrim's Progress is an allegory of personal salvation and a guide to the Christian life. Instead of any focus on eschatology or divine retribution, Bunyan instead writes about how the individual saint can prevail against the temptations of mind and body that threaten damnation.

The book is written in a straightforward narrative and shows influence from both drama and biography, and yet it also shows an awareness of the grand allegorical tradition found in Edmund Spenser. During the Restoration period, the most common manner of getting news would have been a broadsheet publication. A single, large sheet of paper might have a written, usually partisan, account of an event. However, the period saw the beginnings of the first professional and periodical (meaning that the publication was regular) journalism in England. Journalism develops late, generally around the time of William of Orange's claiming the throne in 1689. Coincidentally or by design, England began to have newspapers just when William came to court from Amsterdam, where there were already newspapers being published.

It is impossible to satisfactorily date the beginning of the novel in English. However, long fiction and fictional biographies began to distinguish themselves from other forms in England during the Restoration period. An existing tradition of Romance fiction in France and Spain was popular in England. The "Romance" was considered a feminine form, and women were taxed with reading "novels" as a vice. One of the most significant figures in the rise of the novel in the Restoration period is Aphra Behn. She was not only the first professional female novelist, but she may be among the first professional novelists of either sex in England. Behn's most famous novel was Oroonoko in 1688. This was a biography of an entirely fictional African king who had been enslaved in Suriname. Behn's novels show the influence of tragedy and her experiences as a dramatist.

As soon as the previous Puritan regime's ban on public stage representations was lifted, the drama recreated itself quickly and abundantly. The most famous plays of the early Restoration period are the unsentimental or "hard" comedies of John Dryden, William Wycherley, and George Etherege, which reflect the atmosphere at Court, and celebrate an aristocratic macho lifestyle of unremitting sexual intrigue and conquest. After a sharp drop in both quality and quantity in the 1680s, the mid-90s saw a brief second flowering of the drama, especially comedy. Comedies like William Congreve's Love For Love (1695) and The Way of the World (1700), and John Vanbrugh's The Relapse (1696) and The Provoked Wife (1697) were "softer" and more middle-class in ethos, very different from the aristocratic extravaganza twenty years earlier, and aimed at a wider audience. The playwrights of the 1690s set out to appeal to more socially mixed audiences with a strong middle-class element, and to female spectators, for instance by moving the war between the sexes from the arena of intrigue into that of marriage. The focus in comedy is less on young lovers outwitting the older generation, more on marital relations after the wedding bells.

Diarists John Evelyn and Samuel Pepys depicted everyday London life and the cultural scene of the times.

Augustan Literature

The term Augustan literature derives from authors of the 1720's and 1730's themselves, who responded to a term that George I of England preferred for himself. While George I meant the title to reflect his might, they instead saw in it a reflection of Ancient Rome's transition from rough and ready literature to highly political and highly polished literature. Because of the aptness of the metaphor, the period from 1689-1750 was called "the Augustan Age" by critics throughout the 18th century (including Voltaire and Oliver Goldsmith). The literature of the period is overtly political and thoroughly aware of critical dictates for literature. It is an age of exuberance and scandal, of enormous energy and inventiveness and outrage, that reflected an era when English, Scottish, and Irish people found themselves in the midst of an expanding economy, lowering barriers to education, and the stirrings of the Industrial Revolution.

The most outstanding poet of the age is Alexander Pope, but Pope's excellence is partially in his constant battle with other poets, and his serene, seemingly neo-Classical approach to poetry is in competition with highly idiosyncratic verse and strong competition from such poets as Ambrose Philips. It was during this time that James Thomson produced his melancholy The Seasons and Edward Young wrote Night Thoughts. It is also the era that saw a serious competition over the proper model for the pastoral. In criticism, poets struggled with a doctrine of decorum, of matching proper words with proper sense and of achieving a diction that matched the gravity of a subject. At the same time, the mock-heroic was at its zenith. Pope's Rape of the Lock and The Dunciad are still the greatest mock-heroic poems ever written.

In prose, the earlier part of the period was overshadowed by the development of the English essay. Joseph Addison and Richard Steele's The Spectator established the form of the British periodical essay, inventing the pose of the detached observer of human life who can meditate upon the world without advocating any specific changes in it. However, this was also the time when the English novel, first emerging in the Restoration, developed into a major artform. Daniel Defoe turned from journalism and writing criminal lives for the press to writing fictional criminal lives with Roxana and Moll Flanders. He also wrote a fictional treatment of the travels of Alexander Selkirk called Robinson Crusoe (1719). The novel would benefit indirectly from a tragedy of the stage, and in mid-century many more authors would begin to write novels.

If Addison and Steele overawed one type of prose, then Jonathan Swift did another. Swift's prose style is unmannered and direct, with a clarity that few contemporaries matched. He was a profound skeptic about the modern world, but he was similarly profoundly distrustful of nostalgia. He saw in history a record of lies and vanity, and he saw in the present a madness of vanity and lies. Core Christian values were essential, but these values had to be muscular and assertive and developed by constant rejection of the games of confidence men and their gullies. Swift's A Tale of a Tub announced his skeptical analysis of the claims of the modern world, and his later prose works, such as his war with Patridge the astrologer, and most of all his derision of pride in Gulliver's Travels left only the individual in constant fear and humility safe. After his "exile" to Ireland, Swift reluctantly began defending the Irish people from the predations of colonialism. His A Modest Proposal and the Drapier Letters provoked riots and arrests, but Swift, who had no love of Irish Roman Catholics, was outraged by the abuses and barbarity he saw around him.

Drama in the early part of the period featured the last plays of John Vanbrugh and William Congreve, both of whom carried on the Restoration comedy with some alterations. However, the majority of stagings were of lower farces and much more serious and domestic tragedies. George Lillo and Richard Steele both produced highly moral forms of tragedy, where the characters and the concerns of the characters were wholly middle class or working class. This reflected a marked change in the audience for plays, as royal patronage was no longer the important part of theatrical success. Additionally, Colley Cibber and John Rich began to battle each other for greater and greater spectacles to present on stage.

The figure of Harlequin was introduced, and pantomime theater began to be staged. This "low" comedy was quite popular, and the plays became tertiary to the staging. Opera also began to be popular in London, and there was significant literary resistance to this Italian incursion. This trend was broken only by a few attempts at a new type of comedy. Pope and John Arbuthnot and John Gay attempted a play entitled Three Hours After Marriage that failed. In 1728, however, John Gay returned to the playhouse with The Beggar's Opera. Gay's opera was in English and retold the story of Jack Sheppard and Jonathan Wild. However, it seemed to be an allegory for Robert Walpole and the directors of the South Sea Company, and so Gay's follow up opera was banned without performance. In 1737, 18th century drama almost ends, for that was the year of the Licensing Act. At that point, there was official state censorship of all plays.

An effect of the Licensing Act was to cause more than one aspiring playwright to switch over to writing novels. Henry Fielding began to write prose satire and novels after his plays could not pass the censors. Henry Brooke also turned to novels. In the interim, Samuel Richardson had produced a novel intended to counter the deleterious effects of novels in Pamela, or Virtue Rewarded (1749). Henry Fielding attacked the absurdity of this novel with two of his own works, Joseph Andrews and Shamela, and then countered Richardson's Clarissa with Tom Jones. Brooke wrote The Man of Feeling and indirectly began the sentimental novel.

Laurence Sterne attempted a Swiftian novel with a unique perspective on the impossibility of biography (the model for most novels up to that point) and understanding with Tristram Shandy, even as his detractor Tobias Smollett elevated the picaresque novel with his works. Each of these novels represents a formal and thematic divergence from the others. Each novelist was in dialog and competition with the others, and, in a sense, the novel established itself as a diverse and open-formed genre in this explosion of creativity. The most lasting effects of the experimentation would be the psychological realism of Richardson, the bemused narrative voice of Fielding, and the sentimentality of Brooke.

18th Century During the Age of Sensibility, literature reflected the worldview of the Age of Enlightenment (or Age of Reason)- a rational and scientific approach to religious, social, political, and economic issues that promoted a secular view of the world and a general sense of progress and perfectibility. Led by the philosophers who were inspired by the discoveries of the previous century (Newton) and the writings of Descartes, Locke and Bacon. They sought to discover and to act upon universally valid principles governing humanity, nature, and society. They variously attacked spiritual and scientific authority, dogmatism, intolerance, censorship, and economic and social restraints. They considered the state the proper and rational instrument of progress. The extreme rationalism and skepticism of the age led naturally to deism; the same qualities played a part in bringing the later reaction of romanticism. The Encyclopédie of Denis Diderot epitomized the spirit of the age. Increased emphasis on instinct and feeling, rather than judgment and restraint. A growing sympathy for the Middle Ages during the Age of Sensibility sparked an interest in medieval ballads and folk literature.

The Romanticism

The changing landscape of Britain brought about by the steam engine has two major outcomes: the boom of industrialism with the expansion of the city, and the consequent depopulation of the countryside as a result of the enclosures, or privatisation of pastures. Most peasants poured into the city to work in the new factories.

This abrupt change is revealed by the change of meaning in five key words: industry (once meaning "creativity"), democracy (once disparagingly used as "mob-rule"), class (from now also used with a social connotation), art (once just meaning "craft"), culture (once only belonging to farming).

But the poor condition of workers, the new class-conflicts and the pollution of the environment causes a reaction to urbanism and industrialisation prompting poets to rediscover the beauty and value of nature. Mother earth is seen as the only source of wisdom, the only solution to the ugliness caused by machines.

The superiority of nature and instinct over civilisation had been preached by Jean Jacques Rousseau and his message was picked by almost all European poets. The first in England were the Lake Poets, a small group of friends including William Wordsworth and Samuel Taylor Coleridge.

These early Romantic Poets brought a new emotionalism and introspection, and their emergence is marked by the first romantic Manifesto in English literature, the "Preface to the Lyrical Ballads". This collection was mostly contributed by Wordsworth, although Coleridge must be credited for his long and impressive Rime of the Ancient Mariner, a tragic ballad about the survival of one sailor through a series of supernatural events on his voyage through the south seas which involves the slaying of an albatross, the death of the rest of the crew, a visit from Death and his mate, Life-in-Death, and the eventual redemption of the Mariner.

Coleridge and Wordsworth, however, understood romanticism in two entirely different ways: while Coleridge sought to make the supernatural "real" (much like sci-fi movies use special effects to make unlikely plots believable), Wordsworth sought to stir the imagination of readers through his down-to-earth characters taken from real life (for eg. in "The Idiot Boy"), or the beauty of the Lake District that largely inspired his production (as in "Lines Composed a Few Miles Above Tintern Abbey").

The "Second generation" of Romantic Poets includes Lord Byron, Percy Bysshe Shelley, Mary Shelley and John Keats. Byron, however, was still influenced by 18th-century satirists and was, perhaps the least 'romantic' of the three. His amours with a number of prominent but married ladies was also a way to voice his dissent on the hypocrisy of a high society that was only apparently religious but in fact largely libertine, the same that had derided him for being physically impaired. His first trip to Europe resulted in the first two cantos of Childe Harold's Pilgrimage, a mock-heroic epic of a young man's adventures in Europe but also a sharp satire against London society.

Despite Childe Harold's success on his return to England, accompanied by the publication of The Giaour and The Corsair his alleged incestuous affair with his half-sister Augusta Leigh in 1816 actually forced him to leave England for good and seek asylum on the continent. Here he joined Percy Bysshe Shelley, his wife Mary, with his secretary Dr. John Polidori on the shores of Lake Geneva during the 'year without a summer' of 1816.

Although his is just a short story, Polidori must be credited for introducing The Vampyre, conceived from the same competition which spawned Mary Shelley's Frankenstein, to English literature. Percy, like Mary, had much in common with Byron: he was an aristocrat from a famous and ancient family, had embraced atheism and free-thinking and, like him, was fleeing from scandal in England.

Shelley had been expelled from college for openly declaring his atheism. He had married a 16-year-old girl, Harriet Westbrook whom he had abandoned soon after for Mary (Harriet took her own life after that). Harriet did not embrace his ideals of free love and anarchism, and was not as educated as to contribute to literary debate. Mary was different: the daughter of philosopher and revolutionary William Godwin, she was intellectually more of an equal, shared some of his ideals and was a feminist like her late mother, Mary Wollstonecraft, author of Vindication of the Rights of Women.

One of Shelley's best works is the Ode to the West Wind. Despite his apparent refusal to believe in God, this poem is considered a homage to pantheism, the recognition of a spiritual presence in nature.

Mary Shelley did not go down in history for her poetry, but for giving birth to science fiction: the plot for the novel is said to have come from a nightmare during stormy nights on Lake Geneva in the company of Percy Shelley, Lord Byron, and John Polidori. Her idea of making a body with human parts stolen from different corpses and then animating it with electricity was perhaps influenced by Alessandro Volta's invention and Luigi Galvani's experiments with dead frogs. Frankenstein's chilling tale also suggests modern organ transplants, tissue regeneration, reminding us of the moral issues raised by today's medicine. But the creature of Frankenstein is incredibly romantic as well. Although "the monster" is intelligent, good and loving, he is shunned by everyone because of his ugliness and deformity, and the desperation and envy that result from social exclusion turn him against the very man who created him.

John Keats did not share Byron's and Shelley's extremely revolutionary ideals, but his cult of pantheism is as important as Shelley's. Keats was in love with the ancient stones of the Parthenon that Lord Elgin had brought to England from Greece, also known as the Elgin Marbles). He celebrates ancient Greece: the beauty of free, youthful love couples here with that of classical art. Keats's great attention to art, especially in his Ode on a Grecian Urn is quite new in romanticism, and it will inspire Walter Pater's and then Oscar Wilde's belief in the absolute value of art as independent from aesthetics.

The most popular novelist of the era was Sir Walter Scott, whose grand historical romances inspired a generation of painters, composers, and writers throughout Europe. By contrast, Jane Austen wrote novels about the life of the landed gentry, seen from a woman's point of view, and wryly focused on practical social issues, especially marriage and money.

Victorian Literature

It was in the Victorian era (1837-1901) that the novel became the leading form of literature in English. Most writers were now more concerned to meet the tastes of a large middle class reading public than to please aristocratic patrons. The best known works of the era include the emotionally powerful works of the Brontë sisters; the satire Vanity Fair by William Makepeace Thackeray; the realist novels of George Eliot; and Anthony Trollope's insightful portrayals of the lives of the landowning and professional classes.

Charles Dickens emerged on the literary scene in the 1830s, confirming the trend for serial publication. Dickens wrote vividly about London life and the struggles of the poor, but in a good-humoured fashion which was acceptable to readers of all classes. His early works such as the Pickwick Papers are masterpieces of comedy. Later his works became darker, without losing his genius for caricature.

An interest in rural matters and the changing social and economic situation of the countryside may be seen in the novels of Thomas Hardy, Elizabeth Cleghorn Gaskell, and others.

Leading poetic figures of the Victorian era included Alfred Tennyson, Robert Browning and his wife, Elizabeth Barrett Browning, Matthew Arnold and Dante Gabriel Rossetti and his sister, Christina Rossetti.

Literature for children was published during the Victorian period, some of which has become globally well-known, such as the work of Lewis Carroll who was a proponent of nonsense verse, as was Edward Lear.

MODERNISM

The movement known as English literary modernism grew out of a general sense of disillusionment with Victorian era attitudes of certainty, conservatism, and objective truth. The movement was greatly influenced by the ideas of Romanticism, Karl Marx's political writings, and the psychoanalytic theories of Sigmund Freud. The continental art movements of Impressionism, and later Cubism, were also important inspirations for modernist writers.

Although literary modernism reached its peak between the First and Second World Wars, the earliest examples of the movement's attitudes appeared in the mid to late nineteenth century. Gerard Manley Hopkins, A. E. Housman, and the poet and novelist Thomas Hardy represented a few of the major early modernists writing in England during the Victorian period.

The first decades of the twentieth century saw several major works of modernism published, including the seminal short story collection Dubliners by James Joyce, Joseph Conrad's Heart of Darkness, and the poetry and drama of William Butler Yeats.

Important novelists between the World Wars included Virginia Woolf, E. M. Forster, Evelyn Waugh, P.G. Wodehouse, D. H. Lawrence and T. S. Eliot, the preeminent English poet of the period. Across the Atlantic writers like William Faulkner, Ernest Hemingway, and the poets Wallace Stevens and Robert Frost developed a more American take on the modernist aesthetic in their work.

Perhaps the most contentiously important figure in the development of the modernist movement was the American poet Ezra Pound. Credited with "discovering" both T. S. Eliot and James Joyce, whose stream of consciousness novel Ulysses is considered to be one of the century's greatest literary achievements, Pound also advanced the cause of imagism and free verse, forms which would dominate English poetry into the twenty-first century.

Other notable writers of the period included W. H. Auden, Vladimir Nabokov, William Carlos Williams, Ralph Ellison, Dylan Thomas, R.S. Thomas and Graham Greene. However, some of these writers are more closely associated with what has become known as post-modernism, a term often used to encompass the diverse range of writers who succeeded the modernists.

POSTMODERNISM

Postmodernism is an idea that has been extremely controversial and difficult to define among scholars, intellectuals, and historians, because the term implies to many that the modern historical period has passed. Nevertheless, most agree that postmodern ideas have influenced philosophy, art, critical theory, literature, architecture, design, marketing/business, interpretation of history, and culture since the late 20th century. Postmodernity, a separate term, describes social and cultural conditions connected to the era in which postmodernism arose.

An Overview

Scholars and historians most commonly hold postmodernism to be a movement of ideas contrary to modernism. Modernism places a great deal of importance on ideals such as rationality, objectivity, and progress--as well as other ideas rooted in the Enlightenment, and as positivist and realist movements from the late 19th century. Postmodernism questions whether these ideals can actually exist at all.

In a nutshell, the pro-postmodernism argument runs that economic and technological conditions of our age have given rise to a decentralized, media-dominated society in which ideas are simulacra and only inter-referential representations and copies of each other, with no real original, stable or objective source for communication and meaning. Globalization, brought on by innovations in communication, manufacturing and transportation, is often cited as one force which has driven the decentralized modern life, creating a culturally pluralistic and interconnected global society lacking any single dominant center of political power, communication, or intellectual production.

Postmodernism's adherents often argue that their ideals have arisen as the result of particular economic and social conditions, including what is described as "late capitalism" and the growth of broadcast media, and that such conditions have pushed society into a new historical period. However, a large number of thinkers and writers hold that postmodernism is at best simply a period, variety, or extension of modernism and not actually a separate period or idea.

Postmodern scholars argue that such a decentralized society inevitably creates responses/perceptions that are described as post-modern, such as the rejection of what are seen as the false, imposed unities of meta-narrative and hegemony; the breaking of traditional frames of genre, structure and stylistic unity; and the overthrowing of categories that are the result of logocentrism and other forms of artificially imposed order.

Scholars who accept the division of post-modernity as a distinct period believe that society has collectively eschewed modern ideals and instead adopted ideas that are rooted in the reaction to the restrictions and limitations of those ideas, and that the present is therefore a new historical period. While the characteristics of postmodern life are sometimes difficult to grasp, most postmodern scholars point to concrete and visible technological and economic changes that they claim have brought about the new types of thinking.

Critics of the idea claim that it does not represent liberation, but rather a failure of creativity, and the supplanting of organization with syncreticism and bricolage. They argue that post-modernity is obscurist, overly dense, and makes assertions about the sciences that are demonstrably false.

There are often strong political overtones to this debate, with conservative commentators often being the harshest critics of post-modernism. There is a great deal of disagreement over whether or not recent technological and cultural changes represent a new historical period, or merely an extension of the modern one. Complicating matters further, others have argued that even the postmodern era has already ended, with some commentators asserting culture has entered a post-postmodern period. Alan Kirby has argued, in his essay "The Death of Postmodernism, and Beyond", that we now inhabit an entirely new cultural landscape, which he calls "pseudo-modernism".

Meaning and Definitions

As with many other divisions, the use of the term is subject to the lumpers and splitters problem. There are those who use very small and exact definitions of postmodernism, often for theories perceived as relativist, nihilist, counter-Enlightenment or antimodern. Others believe the world has changed so profoundly that the term applies to nearly everything, and use postmodernism in a broad cultural sense. People who believe postmodernism is really just an aspect of the modern period may instead use terms such as "late modernism".

"Postmodernism is incredulity towards metanarratives."

Jean-Francois Lyotard: "The theory of rejecting theories."

Tony Cliff: "A generation raised on channel-surfing has lost the capacity for linear thinking and analytical reasoning."

Chuck Colson: "Postmodernist fiction is defined by its temporal disorder, its disregard of linear narrative, its mingling of fictional forms and its experiments with language."

Barry Lewis, Kazuo Ishiguro: "Weird for the sake of being weird."

Moe Szyslak, of The Simpsons: "It's the combination of narcissism and nihilism that really defines postmodernism,"

Al Gore: "Post-modernism swims, even wallows, in the fragmentary and the chaotic currents of change as if that is all there is."

David Harvey, The Condition of Postmodernity, Oxford: Basil Blackwell, 1989.: "We could say that every age has its own post-modern, just as every age has its own form of mannerism (in fact, I wonder if postmodern is not simply the modern name for *Manierismus*...). I believe that every age reaches moments of crisis like those described by Nietzsche in the second of the Untimely Considerations, on the harmfulness of the study of history (Historiography). The sense that the past is restricting, smothering, blackmailing us."

Development of Postmodernism

From Modernism

Modernity is defined as a period or condition loosely identified with the Industrial Revolution, or the Enlightenment. One "project" of modernity is said to have been the fostering of progress, which was thought to be achievable by incorporating principles of rationality and hierarchy into aspects of public and artistic life.

Although useful distinctions can be drawn between the modernist and postmodernist eras, this does not erase the many continuities present between them. (These continuities are the reason that some refer to post-modernism as both the continuation as well as the cessation of modernism.) One of the most significant differences between modernism and postmodernism is its interest in universality or totality. While modernist artists aimed to capture universality or totality in some sense, postmodernists have rejected these ambitions as "metanarratives." This usage is ascribed to the philosophers Jean-François Lyotard and Jean Baudrillard.

Lyotard understood modernity as a cultural condition characterized by constant change in the pursuit of progress, and postmodernity as the culmination of this process, where constant change has become a status quo and the notion of progress, obsolete. Following Ludwig Wittgenstein's critique of the possibility of absolute and total knowledge, Lyotard also further argued that the various "master-narratives" of progress, such as positivist science, Marxism, and Structuralism, were defunct as a method of achieving progress.

Writers such as John Ralston Saul among others have argued that postmodernism represents an accumulated disillusionment with the promises of the Enlightenment project and its progress of science, so central to modern thinking.

Notable Philosophical Contributors

Thinkers in the mid and late 19th century and early 20th century, like Søren Kierkegaard and Friedrich Nietzsche, through their arguments against objectivity, and emphasis on skepticism (especially concerning social morals and norms), laid the groundwork for the existentialist movement of the 20th century. Writers such as Jean-Paul Sartre, Albert Camus, and Samuel Beckett, drew heavily from Kierkegaard and Nietzsche, and other previous thinkers, and brought about a new sense of subjectivity, and forlornness, which greatly influenced contemporary thinkers, writers, and artists.

Karl Barth's fideist approach to theology and lifestyle, brought an irreverence for reason, and the rise of subjectivity. Post-colonialism after World War II contributed to the idea that one cannot have an objectively superior lifestyle or belief. This idea was taken further by the anti-foundationalist philosophers: Heidegger, then Ludwig Wittgenstein, then Derrida, who examined the fundamentals of knowledge; they argued that rationality was neither as sure nor as clear as modernists or rationalists assert.

Features of postmodern culture begin to arise in the 1920s with the emergence of the Dada art movement. Both World Wars contributed to postmodernism; it is with the end of the Second World War that recognizably post-modernist attitudes begin to emerge. Some identify the burgeoning anti-establishment movements of the 1960s as an early trend toward postmodernism. The theory gained some of its strongest ground early on in French academia. In 1979 Jean-François Lyotard wrote a short but influential work The Postmodern Condition: A report on knowledge. Also, Richard Rorty wrote Philosophy and the Mirror of Nature (1979). Jean Baudrillard, Michel Foucault, and Roland Barthes are also influential in 1970s postmodern theory.

Marxist critics argue that postmodernism is symptomatic of "late capitalism" and the decline of institutions, particularly the nation-state. The literary critic Fredric Jameson and the geographer David Harvey have also identified post-modernity with "late capitalism" or "flexible accumulation". This situation, called finance capitalism, is characterized by a high degree of mobility of labor and capital, and what Harvey called "time and space compression." They suggest that this coincides with the breakdown of the Bretton Woods system which they believe defined the economic order following the Second World War. Other thinkers assert that post-modernity is the natural reaction to mass broadcasting and a society conditioned to mass production and mass politics. Related to this critical perspective on the economic, political and ideological realities of capitalist modernity is the work of Alasdair MacIntyre, who informs the versions of postmodernism elaborated by such authors as Murphy and Bielskis. On their account, MacIntyre's postmodern revision of Aristotelianism poses a challenge to the kind of consumerist ideology that now promotes capital accumulation.

The movement has had diverse political ramifications: its anti-ideological ideas appear to have been conducive to, and strongly associated with, the feminist movement, racial equality movements, gay rights movements, most forms of late 20th century anarchism, and even the peace movement, as well as various hybrids of these in the current anti-globalization movement. Unsurprisingly, none of these institutions entirely embraces all aspects of the postmodern movement in its most concentrated definition, but they reflect, or borrow from, some of its core ideas.

DECONSTRUCTION

Deconstruction is a term which is used to denote the application of post-modern ideas of criticism, or theory, to a "text" or "artifact". A deconstruction is meant to undermine the frame of reference and assumptions that underpin the text or the artifact.

In its original use, a "deconstruction" is an important textual "occurrence" described and analyzed by many postmodern authors and philosophers. They argue that aspects in the text itself would undermine its own authority or assumptions and that internal contradictions would erase boundaries or categories which the work relied on or asserted. Post-structuralists beginning with Jacques Derrida, who coined the term, argued that the existence of deconstructions implied that there was no intrinsic essence to a text, merely the contrast of difference. This is analogous to the scientific idea that only the variations are real, that there is no established norm to a genetic population, or the idea that the difference in perception between black and white is the context. A deconstruction is created when the "deeper" substance of text opposes the text's more "superficial" form.

This idea too is not isolated to post-structuralists, but is related to the idea of hermeneutics in literature, intellectuals as early as Plato asserted it, and so did modern thinkers such as Leo Strauss. Derrida's argument is that deconstruction proves that texts have multiple meanings, and the "violence" between the different meanings of text may be elucidated by close textual analysis. Popularly, close textual analyses describing deconstruction within a text are often themselves called deconstructions. Derrida argued, however, that deconstruction is not a method or a tool, but an occurrence within the text itself. Writings about deconstruction are therefore referred to in academic circles as deconstructive readings.

Deconstruction is far more important to postmodernism than its seemingly narrow focus on text might imply. According to Derrida, one consequence of deconstruction is that the text may be defined so broadly as to encompass not just written words, but the entire spectrum of symbols and phenomena within Western thought. To Derrida, a result of deconstruction is that no Western philosopher has been able to escape successfully from this large web of text and reach that which is "signified", which they imagined to exist "just beyond" the text. The more common use of the term is the more general process of pointing to contradictions between the intent and surface of a work, and the assumptions about it. A work then "deconstructs" assumptions when it places them in context. For example, someone who can pass as the opposite sex is said to "deconstruct" gender identity, because there is a conflict between the superficial appearance, and the reality of the person's gender.

Social Construction, Structuralism, Post-structuralism

Often opposed to deconstruction are social constructionists, labelled as such within the analytic tradition, but not usually in the case of the continental tradition. The term was first used in Peter Berger and Thomas Luckmann's book The Social Construction of Reality. Usually in the continental tradition, the terms structuralism or post-structuralism are used. Maurice Merleau-Ponty is seen as the biggest contributor to structuralism, which is epitomized in the philosophy of Claude Levi-Strauss. Michel Foucault was also a structuralist, but then turned to what would be termed post-structuralism, although he himself disputed that his views had been post-structuralist.

Structuralism historically gave way to post-structuralism, often the role of postmodernism within the analytic tradition is played down, although works by major figures of the analytic tradition in the 20th century, including those of Thomas Kuhn, and Willard Van Orman Quine, show a similarity with works in the continental tradition for their lack of belief in absolute truth as well as in the pliability of language. In the continental tradition, most works argue that power dissimulates, and that society constructs reality, while its individuals remain powerless or almost powerless. Often, both continental and analytic sources argue for a renewed subjectivity, borrowing heavily from Immanuel Kant, while they largely reject his a priori/a posteriori distinction. They both minimize discussions of practical ethics, instead borrowing heavily from post-Holocaust accounts of the need for an ethics of responsibility, which is very rarely practically defined.

One of the large differences between analytic postmodern sources and continental postmodern sources is that the analytic tradition by and large guards at least some of the tenets of liberalism, while many continental sources flirt with, or completely immerse themselves in, Marxism.

Criticism

The term post-modernism is often used pejoratively to describe tendencies perceived as Relativist, Counter-enlightenment or antimodern, particularly in relation to critiques of Rationalism, Universalism or Science. It is also sometimes used to describe tendencies in a society that are held to be antithetical to traditional systems of morality. The criticisms of postmodernism are often complicated by the still fluid nature of the term, and in many cases the criticisms are clearly directed at poststructuralism and the philosophical and academic movements that it has spawned rather than the broader term postmodernism.

As Political

Michel Foucault rejected the label of postmodernism explicitly in interviews but is seen by many to advocate a form of critique that is "postmodern" as it breaks with the utopian and transcendental nature of "modern" critique by calling universal norms of the Enlightenment into question. Giddens (1990) rejects this characterisation of modern critique by pointing out that a critique of Enlightenment universals were central to philosophers of the modern period, most notably Nietzsche.

What counts as "postmodern" is a stake in political struggles where the method of critique is at stake. The recurring themes of these debates are between essentialism and anti-foundationalism, universalism and relativism, where modernism is seen to represent the former and postmodernism the latter. This is why theorists as diverse as Nietzsche, Lacan, Foucault, Derrida and Butler have been labelled "postmodern", not because they formed an historical intellectual grouping but because they are seen by their critics to reject the possibility of universal, normative and ethical judgments.

As Intellectually and Artistically Disingenuous

Charles Murray, a critic of postmodernism, defines the term: By contemporary intellectual fashion, I am referring to the constellation of views that come to mind when one hears the words multicultural, gender, deconstruct, politically correct, and Dead White Males. In a broader sense, contemporary intellectual fashion encompasses as well the widespread disdain in certain circles for technology and the scientific method. Embedded in this mind-set is hostility to the idea that discriminating judgments are appropriate in assessing art and literature, to the idea that hierarchies of value exist, hostility to the idea that an objective truth exists. Postmodernism is the overarching label that is attached to this perspective.

Charles Murray: Central to the debate is the concept of "objectivity" and what it means. Denial of the practical possibility of objectivity is held to be the postmodern position, and a hostility towards claims advanced on the basis of objectivity its defining feature. It is this underlying hostility towards the concept of objectivity, evident among many contemporary critical theorists, that is the common point of attack for critics of postmodernism. Many critics characterise postmodernism as an ephemeral phenomenon that cannot be adequately defined simply because, as a philosophy at least, it represents nothing more substantial than a series of disparate conjectures allied only in their distrust of modernism.

The most prominent recent criticism of postmodern art is that of John Gardner. Gardner wrote that the classification "post-modern" / "modern" applied to the art of his time was an evasion, a stab at nothing-i.e., a move to elude the basic function of criticism, which, according to Gardner, is to judge art's moral value.

The Stuckist art movement has issued a series of manifestos denouncing postmodernism for what they see as its "scientific materialism, nihilism and spiritual bankruptcy".

As a False Distinction

The antipathy of postmodernists towards modernism, and their consequent tendency to define themselves against it, has also attracted criticism. It has been argued that modernity was not actually a lumbering, totalizing monolith at all, but in fact was itself dynamic and ever-changing; the evolution, therefore, between "modern" and "postmodern" should be seen as one of degree, rather than of kind-a continuation rather than a "break." One theorist who takes this view is Marshall Berman, whose book All That is Solid Melts into Air (1982) (a quote from Marx) reflects in its title the fluid nature of "the experience of modernity."

Some theorists such as Habermas argue that the supposed distinction between the "modern" and the "postmodern" does not exist, but that the latter is no more than a development within a larger, still-current, "modern" framework.

Many who make this argument are academics with Marxist leanings, such as Seyla Benhabib, Terry Eagleton, Fredric Jameson, and David Harvey (social geographer), who are concerned that postmodernism's undermining of Enlightenment values makes a progressive cultural politics difficult, if not impossible. That is, "How can 'we' effect any change in people's poor living conditions, in inequality and injustice, if 'we' don't accept the validity of underlying universals such as the 'real world' and 'justice' in the first place?" How is any progress to be made through a philosophy so profoundly skeptical of the very notion of progress, and of unified perspectives?

These critics argue that the postmodern vision of a tolerant, pluralist society in which every political ideology is perceived to be as valid, or as redundant, as the other, may encourage individuals to lead lives of a rather disastrous apathetic quietism. This reasoning leads Habermas to compare postmodernism with conservatism and the preservation of the status quo. Such critics often argue that, in fact, such postmodern premises are rarely, if ever, actually embraced-that if they were, we would be left with nothing more than a crippling radical subjectivism. They point to the continuity of the projects of the Enlightenment and modernity as alive and well, as can be seen in science, in political rights movements and in the very idea of universities.

To some critics, there seems to be a glaring contradiction between maintaining the death of objectivity and privileged position on one hand, while the scientific community continues a project of unprecedented scope to unify various scientific disciplines into a theory of everything, on the other. Hostility toward hierarchies of value and objectivity becomes problematic to them when postmodernity itself attempts to analyse such hierarchies with, apparently, some measure of objectivity and make categorical statements concerning them.

As Empty Rhetoric

The criticism of Postmodernism as ultimately meaningless rhetorical gymnastics was demonstrated in the Sokal Affair, where Alan Sokal, a physicist, wrote a deliberately nonsensical article purportedly about interpreting physics and mathematics in terms of postmodern theory, which was nevertheless published by the Social Text, a journal which he and most of the scientific community considered postmodernist. Interestingly, Social Text never acknowledged that the article's publication was a mistake, but supported a counter-argument defending the "interpretative validity" of Sokal's false article, despite the author's rebuttal of his own article.

2

British Literature

British literature is literature from the United Kingdom, the Isle of Man and the Channel Islands. By far the largest part of this literature is written in the English language, but there are also separate literatures in Welsh, Scottish Gaelic, Scots, Cornish, Manx, Jèrriais, Dgèrnésiais and other languages. Northern Ireland is the only part of Ireland still part of the United Kingdom and it possesses literature in English, Ulster Scots and Irish. Irish writers have also played an important part in the development of English-language literature.

OLD CELTIC LITERATURE

Literature in the Celtic languages of the islands is the oldest surviving vernacular literature in Europe. The Welsh literary tradition stretches from the 6th century to the 21st century. The oldest Welsh literature does not belong to the territory we know as Wales today, but rather to northern England and southern Scotland. But though it is dated to be from the 6th, 7th, and 8th centuries, it has survived only in 13th and 14th century manuscript copies. Irish poetry represents a more or less unbroken tradition from the 6th century to the present day.

OLD ENGLISH LITERATURE

The earliest form of English literature developed after the settlement of the Saxons and other Germanic tribes in England after the withdrawal of the Romans and is known as Old English or Anglo-Saxon. The most famous work in Old English is the epic poem Beowulf. (The oldest surviving text in English is Caedmon's hymn of creation.) The precise date of the manuscript is debated, but most estimates place it close to AD 1000. Chronicles contained a range of historical and literary accounts, for example: Historia ecclesiastica gentis Anglorum by Bede and the Anglo-Saxon Chronicle.

LATE MEDIEVAL LITERATURE IN ENGLAND

Latin literature circulated among the educated classes.

Following the Norman conquest, the development of Anglo-Norman literature in the Anglo-Norman realm introduced literary trends from Continental Europe such as the chanson de geste.

In the later medieval period a new form of English now known as Middle English evolved. This is the earliest form which is comprehensible to modern readers and listeners, albeit not easily.

The most significant Middle English author was the poet Geoffrey Chaucer who was active in the late 14th Century. His main works were The Canterbury Tales and Troilus and Criseyde.

The multilingual audience for literature in the 14th century can be illustrated by the example of John Gower, who wrote in Latin, Middle English and Anglo-Norman.

Religious literature, such as hagiographies enjoyed popularity.

Women writers such as Marie de France and Julian of Norwich were also active.

- Sir Gawain and the Green Knight
- Morte d'Arthur by Sir Thomas Malory

OTHER MEDIEVAL LITERATURES

For a comparatively small country, Ireland has made a large contribution to world literature in all its branches. The Irish literature that is best known outside the country is in English, but the Irish language also has the most significant body of written literature, both ancient and recent, in any Celtic language, in addition to a strong oral tradition of legends and poetry.

In Medieval Welsh literature the period before 1100 is known as the period of Y Cynfeirdd ("The earliest poets") or Yr Hengerdd

("The old poetry"). It roughly dates from the birth of the Welsh language until the arrival of the Normans in Wales towards the end of the eleventh century.

Geoffrey of Monmouth's Historia Regum Britanniae spread Celtic motifs to a wider audience.

The Jersey poet Wace is considered the founder of Jersey literature and contributed to the development of the Arthurian legend in British literature. His Brut showed the interest of Norman patrons in the mythologising of the new English territories of the Anglo-Norman realm. His Rou placed the Dukes of Normandy within an epic context.

Since at least the 14th century, poetry in English has been written in Ireland and by Irish writers abroad. The earliest poem in English by a Welsh poet dates from about 1470.

Among the earliest Lowland Scots literature is Barbour's Brus (14th century). Whyntoun's Kronykil and Blind Harry's Wallace (15th century) From the 13th century much literature based around the Royal Court in Edinburgh and the University of St. Andrews was produced by writers such as Henrysoun, Dunbar, Douglas and Lyndsay.

In the Cornish language Passhyon agan Arloedh (The Passion of our Lord), a poem of 259 eight-line verses written in 1375, is one of the earliest surviving works of Cornish literature. The most important work of literature surviving from the Middle Cornish period is An Ordinale Kernewek (The Cornish Ordinalia), a 9000-line religious drama composed around the year 1400. The longest single surviving work of Cornish literature is Bywnans Meriasek (The Life of Meriasek), a play dated 1504, but probably copied from an earlier manuscript.

- Mabinogion
- Ulster Cycle
- Early English Jewish literature.

EARLY MODERN ENGLISH LITERATURE TO 1660

The sonnet form and other Italian literary influences arrived in English literature. The sonnet was introduced into English by Thomas Wyatt in the early 16th century.

In the later 16th century English poetry was characterised by elaboration of language and extensive allusion to classical myths. The most important poets of this era include Edmund Spenser and Sir Philip Sidney.

The most important literary achievements of the English Renaissance were in drama. William Shakespeare wrote over thirty-five plays in several genres, including tragedy, comedy, history and romance. Other leading playwrights of the time included Ben Jonson, and Christopher Marlowe.

- Elizabethan theatre

At the Reformation the translation of liturgy and Bible into vernacular languages provided new literary models. The Anglican Book of Common Prayer and the Authorised Version of the Bible have been influential on the literatures of the islands.

The major poets of the 17th century included John Donne and the other Metaphysical poets, and John Milton, the author of the religious epic Paradise Lost.

- Metaphysical poets

English Language Literature from 1660 to the late 18th Century

The position of Poet Laureate was formalised in this period.

The early 18th century is known as the Augustan Age of English literature. The poetry of the time was highly formal, as exemplified by the works of Alexander Pope.

Although the documented history of Irish theatre began at least as early as 1601, the earliest Irish dramatists of note were William Congreve, one of the most interesting writers of Restoration comedies, and Oliver Goldsmith and Richard Brinsley Sheridan, who were two of the most successful playwrights on the London stage in the 18th century.

The English novel developed during the 18th century, partly in response to an expansion of the middle class reading public. One of the major early works in this genre was Robinson Crusoe by Daniel Defoe. The 18th century novel tended to be loosely structured and semi-comic. Major novelists of the middle and later part of the century included Henry Fielding, Laurence

Sterne and Tobias Smollett, who was a great influence on Charles Dickens.

Although the epics of Celtic Ireland were written in prose and not verse, most people would probably consider that Irish fiction proper begins in the 18th century with the works of Jonathan Swift (especially Gulliver's Travels) and Oliver Goldsmith (especially The Vicar of Wakefield).

- First novel in English
- Cavalier poet

Non English-language Literatures from the 16th Century to the 19th Century

As the Norman nobles of Scotland assimilated to indigenous culture they commissioned Scots versions of popular continental romances, for example: Launcelot o the Laik and The Buik o Alexander. In the early 16th century, Gavin Douglas produced a Scots translation of the Aeneid. Chaucerian, classical and French literary language continued to influence Scots literature up until the Reformation. The Complaynt of Scotland shows the interplay of language and ideas between the kingdoms of Scotland and England in the years leading up to the Union of the Crowns.

The earliest datable text in Manx (preserved in 18th century manuscripts), a poetic history of the Isle of Man from the introduction of Christianity, dates to the 16th century at the latest.

The first book to be printed in Welsh was published in 1546. From the Reformation until the 19th century most literature in the Welsh language was religious in character.

The earliest surviving examples of Cornish prose are Pregothow Treger (The Tregear Homilies), a set of 66 sermons translated from English by John Tregear around 1555-1557.

The Book of Common Prayer and Bible were translated into Manx in the 17th and 18th centuries. A tradition of carvals, religious songs or carols, developed. Religious literature was common, but secular writing much rarer.

In Scotland, after the 17th century, anglicisation increased, though Lowland Scots was still spoken by the vast majority of the population. At the time, many of the oral ballads from the borders and the North East were written down. Writers of the period include Robert Sempill (c.1595-1665), Lady Wardlaw and Lady Grizel Baillie.

The first printed work in Manx dates from 1707: a translation of a Prayer Book catechism in English by Bishop Thomas Wilson.

In the Scots-speaking areas of Ulster there was traditionally a considerable demand for the work of Scottish poets, often in locally printed editions. Alexander Montgomerie's The Cherrie and the Slae in 1700, shortly over a decade later an edition of poems by Sir David Lindsay, nine printings of Allan Ramsay's The Gentle shepherd between 1743 and 1793, and an edition of Robert Burns' poetry in 1787, the same year as the Edinburgh edition, followed by reprints in 1789, 1793 and 1800. Among other Scottish poets published in Ulster were James Hogg and Robert Tannahill.

In the 18th century, Scottish writers such as Ramsay, Robert Fergusson, Robert Burns and Sir Walter Scott continued to use Lowland Scots. Scott introduced vernacular dialogue to his novels. The Habbie stanza was developed as a poetic form.

The first printed Jèrriais literature appears in the first newspapers following the introduction of the printing press at the end of the 18th century. The earliest identified dated example of printed poetry in Jèrriais is a fragment by Matchi L'Gé (Matthew Le Geyt 1777-1849) dated 1795.

Some 60 to 70 volumes of Ulster rhyming weaver poetry were published between 1750 and 1850, the peak being in the decades 1810 to 1840. These weaver poets, such as James Orr, looked to Scotland for their cultural and literary models and were not simple imitators but clearly inheritors of the same literary tradition following the same poetic and orthographic practices; it is not always immediately possible to distinguish traditional Scots writing from Scotland and Ulster.

The importance of translation in spreading the influence of English literature to other cultures of the islands can be exemplified by the abridged Manx version of Paradise Lost by John Milton published in 1796 by Thomas Christian. The influence also went the other way as Romanticism discovered inspiration in the literatures and legends of the Celtic countries of the islands. The Ossian hoax typifies the growth of this interest.

Increased literacy in rural and outlying areas and wider access to publishing through, for example, local newspapers encouraged regional literary development as the 19th century progressed. Some writers in lesser-used languages and dialects of the islands gained a literary following outside their native regions, for example William Barnes in Dorset, George Métivier (1790-1881) in Guernsey and Robert Pipon Marett in Jersey. George Métivier published Rimes Guernesiaises, a collection of poems in Dgèrnésiais and French in 1831. The poems had first appeared in newspapers from 1813 onward. The first printed anthology of Jèrriais poetry, Rimes Jersiaises, was published in 1865.

Scots was used in the narrative by Ulster novelists such as W. G. Lyttle (1844-1896). Scots also regularly appeared in Ulster newspaper columns.

Scottish authors as Robert Louis Stevenson, William Alexander, George MacDonald and J. M. Barrie also wrote in Lowland Scots or used it in dialogue.

The first major novelist in the Welsh language was Daniel Owen, author of works such as Rhys Lewis (1885) and Enoc Huws (1891).

Edward Faragher (1831-1908) has been considered the last important native writer of Manx. He wrote poetry, reminiscences of his life as a fisherman, and translations of selected Aesop's Fables.

19th Century English Language Literature

The Romantics

Major political and social changes at the end of the eighteenth century, particularly the French Revolution, prompted a new breed of writing now known as Romanticism. William Wordsworth and Samuel Taylor Coleridge began the trend for bringing emotionalism and introspection to English literature, with a new concentration on the individual and the common man. The reaction to urbanism and industrialisation prompted poets to explore nature, for example the Lake Poets.

The major "Second generation" Romantic Poets were Lord Byron, Percy Bysshe Shelley and John Keats. They flouted social convention and often used poetry as a political voice.

The 19th Century Novel

At the same time Jane Austen was writing highly polished novels about the life of the landed gentry, seen from a woman's point of view, and wryly focused on practical social issues, especially marriage and money.

Charles Dickens emerged on the literary scene in the 1830s, confirming the trend for serial publication. Dickens wrote vividly about London life and the struggles of the poor, but in a good-humoured fashion which was acceptable to readers of all classes. His early works such as the Pickwick Papers are masterpieces of comedy. Later his works became darker, without losing his genius for caricature.

It was in the Victorian era (1837-1901) that the novel became the leading form of literature in English. Most writers were now more concerned to meet the tastes of a large middle class reading public than to please aristocratic patrons. The best known works of the era include the emotionally powerful works of the Brontë sisters; the satire Vanity Fair by William Makepeace Thackeray and Anthony Trollope's insightful portrayals of the lives of the landowning and professional classes. George Eliot's novels are frequently held in the highest regard for their combination of high Victorian literary detail combined with an intellectual breadth that removes them from the narrow confines they often depict.

An interest in rural matters and the changing social and economic situation of the countryside may be seen in the novels of Thomas Hardy and others.

Literature for children was published during the Victorian period, some of which has become globally well-known, such as the work of Lewis Carroll.

Victorian Poets

Leading poetic figures of the Victorian era included Alfred Tennyson, Robert Browning (and his wife, Elizabeth Barrett Browning), and Matthew Arnold, whilst multi-disciplinary talents such as John Ruskin and Dante Gabriel Rossetti were also famous for their poetry.

Nonsense verse, such as by Edward Lear, taken with the work of Lewis Carroll, is regarded as a precursor of surrealism.

Ireland

In the 19th century, the Irish playwright Dion Boucicault was an extremely popular writer of comedies. However, it was in the last decade of the century that the Irish theatre finally came of age with the emergence of George Bernard Shaw and Oscar Wilde. All of these writers lived mainly in England and wrote in English.

The Celtic Revival (c. 1890), also known as the Irish Literary Revival, was begun by William Butler Yeats, Lady Gregory, John M. Synge, Sean O'Casey, James Joyce and others. The Revival stimulated new appreciation of traditional Irish literature. The movement also encouraged the creation of works written in the spirit of Irish culture, as distinct from English culture.

Wales

Anglo-Welsh literature is a term used to describe works written in the English language by Welsh writers, especially if they either have subject matter relating to Wales or (as in the case of Anglo-Welsh poetry in particular) are influenced by the Welsh language in terms of patterns of usage or syntax. It has been recognised as a distinctive entity only since the 20th century. The need for a separate identity for this kind of writing arose because of the parallel development of modern Welsh literature, ie. literature in the Welsh language.

Scotland

The Kailyard school of Scottish writers presented an idealised version of society.

English Language Literature since 1900

The major lyric poet of the first decades of the 20th century was Thomas Hardy, who concentrated on poetry after the harsh response to his last novel, Jude the Obscure.

The most widely popular writer of the early years of the 20th century was arguably Rudyard Kipling, a highly versatile writer of novels, short stories and poems, often based on his experiences of British ruled India. Kipling was closely associated with imperialism and this has damaged his reputation in more recent times.

From around 1910, the Modernist Movement began to influence English literature. Whereas their Victorian predecessors had usually been happy to cater to mainstream middle class taste, 20th century writers often felt alienated from it, and responded by writing more intellectually challenging works or by pushing the boundaries of acceptable content.

The major poets of this period included the American born T. S. Eliot and the Irishman William Butler Yeats. Free verse and other stylistic innovations came to the forefront in this era.

The experiences of the First World War were reflected in the work of war poets such as Wilfred Owen, Rupert Brooke, Isaac Rosenberg, Edmund Blunden and Siegfried Sassoon. Many writers turned away from patriotic and imperialist themes as a result of the war, notably Kipling.

Important novelists between the two World Wars included the Irish writer James Joyce, D.H. Lawrence and Virginia Woolf.

Joyce's increasingly complex works included Ulysses, an interpretation of the Odyssey set in Dublin, and culminated in the famously obscure Finnegans Wake. Lawrence wrote with understanding about the social life of the lower and middle classes, and the personal life of those who could not adapt to the social norms of his time. He attempted to explore human emotions more deeply than his contemporaries and challenged the boundaries of the acceptable treatment of sexual issues in works such as Lady Chatterley's Lover. Virginia Woolf was an influential feminist, and a major stylistic innovator associated with the stream of consciousness technique. Her novels included To the Lighthouse, Mrs Dalloway, and The Waves.

Novelists who wrote in a more traditional style, such as John Galsworthy and Arnold Bennett continued to receive great acclaim in the interwar period. At the same time the Georgian poets maintained a more conservative approach to poetry.

The leading poets of the middle and later 20th century included the traditionalist John Betjeman, Philip Larkin, Ted Hughes and the Northern Irish Catholic Seamus Heaney, who lived in the Republic of Ireland for much of his later life.

Major novelists of the middle and later 20th century included the satirist Evelyn Waugh, William Golding, Anthony Burgess, Grahame Greene and Iris Murdoch.

In drama, the drawing room plays of the post war period were challenged in the 1950s by the Angry Young Men, exemplified by as John Osborne's iconic play Look Back in Anger. Also in the 1950s, the bleak absurdist play Waiting for Godot, by the Southern Irish playwright Samuel Beckett profoundly affected British drama. The theatre of the absurd influenced playwrights of the later decades of the 20th century, including Harold Pinter, whose works are often characterised by menace or claustrophia, and Tom Stoppard. Stoppard's works are however also notable for their high-spirited wit and the great range of intellectual issues which he tackles in different plays.

- Georgian poets
- Anthology of Twentieth-Century British and Irish Poetry
- British Poetry Revival
- Kitchen sink drama

Non English Language Literatures since 1900

In the late 19th and early 20th century, Welsh literature began to reflect the way the Welsh language was increasingly becoming a political symbol. Two important literary nationalists were Saunders Lewis and Kate Roberts.

In the early 20th century in Scotland, a renaissance in the use of Lowland Scots occurred, its most vocal figure being Hugh MacDiarmid. Other contemporaries were Douglas Young, Sidney Goodsir Smith, Robert Garioch and Robert McLellan. However, the revival was largely limited to verse and other literature.

The end of the First World War saw a decline in the quantity of poetry published in Jèrriais and Dgèrnésiais in favour of short-story-like newspaper columns in prose, some being collected in book or booklet form-this being a common genre in the Norman mainland. The imported eisteddfod tradition in the Channel Islands encouraged recitation and performance, a tradition that continues today. The German military occupation of the Channel Islands 1940-1945 encouraged increased use of the vernacular languages among those who remained, but the German censorship permitted little original writing to be published. Within the restrictions, Les Chroniques de Jersey, the only surviving French language newspaper in the Islands, republished considerable quantities of older Jèrriais literature for purposes of morale and the assertion of identity. The post-Liberation social changes meant, however, that vernacular literature has never regained the situation it had enjoyed previously.

Sorley MacLean's work in Scottish Gaelic in the 1930s gave new value to modern literature in that language.

Highly anglicised Lowland Scots is often used in contemporary Scottish fiction, for example, the Edinburgh dialect of Lowland Scots in Trainspotting by Irvine Welsh. Edwin Morgan is the current Makar (Scottish national poet) and also produces translations of world literature.

Translations are an important feature of the literatures of the regional languages of the islands, for example: Contoyryssyn Ealish ayns Cheer ny Yindyssyn a Manx translation of Alice in Wonderland by Brian Stowell, published in 1990, or the 2004 Scots version of the Rubaiyat of Omar Khayyam by Rab Wilson. Alexander Hutchison has translated the poetry of Catullus into Scots, and in the 1980s Liz Lochhead produced a Scots translation of Tartuffe by Molière. Original literature continues to be promoted by organisations and institutions such as the Eisteddfod or the Mod.

With the revival of Cornish there have been newer works written in the language. The bard Pol Hodge is an example of a poet writing in Cornish.

3

English Poetry

The history of English poetry stretches from the middle of the 7th century to the present day. Over this period, English poets have written some of the most enduring poems in European culture, and the language and its poetry have spread around the globe. Consequently, the term English poetry is unavoidably ambiguous. It can mean poetry written in England, or poetry written in the English language.

The earliest surviving poetry from the area currently known as England was likely transmitted orally and then written down in versions that do not now survive; thus, dating the earliest poetry remains difficult and often controversial. The earliest surviving manuscripts date from the 10th century. Poetry written in Latin, Brythonic (a predecessor language of Welsh) and Old Irish survives which may date as early as the 6th century. The earliest surviving poetry written in Anglo-Saxon, the most direct predecessor of modern English, may have been composed as early as the seventh century.

With the growth of trade and the British Empire, the English language had been widely used outside England. In the twenty-first century, only a small percentage of the world's native English speakers live in England, and there is also a vast population of non-native speakers of English who are capable of writing poetry in the language. A number of major national poetries, including the American, Australian, New Zealand and Canadian poetry have emerged and developed. Since 1922, Irish poetry has also been increasingly viewed as a separate area of study.

This article focuses on poetry written in English by poets born or spending a significant part of their lives in England.

However, given the nature of the subject, this guideline has been applied with common sense, and reference is made to poetry in other languages or poets who are not primarily English where appropriate.

THE EARLIEST ENGLISH POETRY

The earliest known English poem is a hymn on the creation; Bede attributes this to Cædmon (fl. 658-680), who was, according to legend, an illiterate herdsman who produced extemporaneous poetry at a monastery at Whitby. This is generally taken as marking the beginning of Anglo-Saxon poetry.

Much of the poetry of the period is difficult to date, or even to arrange chronologically; for example, estimates for the date of the great epic Beowulf range from AD 608 right through to AD 1000, and there has never been anything even approaching a consensus. It is possible to identify certain key moments, however. The Dream of the Rood was written before circa AD 700, when excerpts were carved in runes on the Ruthwell Cross. Some poems on historical events, such as The Battle of Brunanburh (937) and the Battle of Maldon (991), appear to have been composed shortly after the events in question, and can be dated reasonably precisely in consequence. By and large, however, Anglo-Saxon poetry is categorised by the manuscripts in which it survives, rather than its date of composition. The most important manuscripts are the four great poetical codices of the late tenth and early eleventh centuries, known as the Caedmon manuscript, the Vercelli Book, the Exeter Book, and the Beowulf manuscript.

While the poetry that has survived is limited in volume, it is wide in breadth. Beowulf is the only heroic epic to have survived in its entirety, but fragments of others such as Waldere and the Finnsburg Fragment show that it was not unique in its time. Other genres include much religious verse, from devotional works to biblical paraphrase; elegies such as The Wanderer, The Seafarer, and The Ruin (often taken to be a description of the ruins of Bath); and numerous proverbs, riddles, and charms.

With one notable exception (Rhyming Poem), Anglo-Saxon poetry depends on alliterative verse for its structure and any rhyme included is merely ornamental.

The Elizabethans

The Elizabethan period (1558 to 1603) in poetry is characterised by a number of frequently overlapping developments. The introduction and adaptation of themes, models and verse forms from other European traditions and classical literature, the Elizabethan song tradition, the emergence of a courtly poetry often centred around the figure of the monarch and the growth of a verse-based drama are among the most important of these developments.

Elizabethan Song

A wide range of Elizabethan poets wrote songs, including Nicholas Grimald, Thomas Nashe and Robert Southwell. There are also a large number of extant anonymous songs from the period. Perhaps the greatest of all the songwriters was Thomas Campion. Campion is also notable because of his experiments with metres based on counting syllables rather than stresses. These quantitative metres were based on classical models and should be viewed as part of the wider Renaissance revival of Greek and Roman artistic methods.

The songs were generally printed either in miscellanies or anthologies such as Richard Tottel's 1557 Songs and Sonnets or in songbooks that included printed music to enable performance. These performances formed an integral part of both public and private entertainment. By the end of the 16th century, a new generation of composers, including John Dowland, William Byrd, Orlando Gibbons, Thomas Weelkes and Thomas Morley were helping to bring the art of Elizabethan song to an extremely high musical level.

Courtly Poetry

With the consolidation of Elizabeth's power, a genuine court sympathetic to poetry and the arts in general emerged. This encouraged the emergence of a poetry aimed at, and often set in, an idealised version of the courtly world.

Among the best known examples of this are Edmund Spenser's The Faerie Queene, which is effectively an extended hymn of praise to the queen, and Philip Sidney's Arcadia. This courtly

THE RENAISSANCE IN ENGLAND

The Renaissance was slow in coming to England, with the generally accepted start date being around 1509. It is also generally accepted that the English Renaissance extended until the Restoration in 1660. However, a number of factors had prepared the way for the introduction of the new learning long before this start date. A number of medieval poets had, as already noted, shown an interest in the ideas of Aristotle and the writings of European Renaissance precursors such as Dante.

The introduction of movable-block printing by Caxton in 1474 provided the means for the more rapid dissemination of new or recently rediscovered writers and thinkers. Caxton also printed the works of Chaucer and Gower and these books helped establish the idea of a native poetic tradition that was linked to its European counterparts. In addition, the writings of English humanists like Thomas More and Thomas Elyot helped bring the ideas and attitudes associated with the new learning to an English audience.

Three other factors in the establishment of the English Renaissance were the Reformation, Counter Reformation, and the opening of the era of English naval power and overseas exploration and expansion.

The establishment of the Church of England in 1535 accelerated the process of questioning the Catholic world-view that had previously dominated intellectual and artistic life. At the same time, long-distance sea voyages helped provide the stimulus and information that underpinned a new understanding of the nature of the universe which resulted in the theories of Nicolaus Copernicus and Johannes Kepler.

EARLY RENAISSANCE POETRY

With a small number of exceptions, the early years of the 16th century are not particularly notable. The Douglas Aeneid was completed in 1513 and John Skelton wrote poems that were transitional between the late Medieval and Renaissance styles. The new king, Henry VIII, was something of a poet himself. The most significant English poet of this period was Thomas Wyatt, who was among the first poets to write sonnets in English.

THE ANGLO-NORMAN PERIOD AND THE LATER MIDDLE AGES

With the Norman conquest of England, beginning in 1066, the Anglo-Saxon language rapidly diminished as a written literary language. The new aristocracy spoke French, and this became the standard language of courts, parliament, and polite society. As the invaders integrated, their language and literature mingled with that of the natives: the French dialect of the upper classes became Anglo-Norman, and Anglo-Saxon underwent a gradual transition into Middle English.

While Anglo-Norman or Latin was preferred for high culture, English literature by no means died out, and a number of important works illustrate the development of the language. Around the turn of the thirteenth century, Layamon wrote his Brut, based on Wace's twelfth century Anglo-Norman epic of the same name; Layamon's language is recognisably Middle English, though his prosody shows a strong Anglo-Saxon influence remaining. Other transitional works were preserved as popular entertainment, including a variety of romances and lyrics. With time, the English language regained prestige, and in 1362 it replaced French and Latin in Parliament and courts of law. It was with the fourteenth century that major works of English literature began once again to appear; these include the so-called Pearl Poet's Pearl, Patience, Cleanness, and Sir Gawain and the Green Knight; Langland's political and religious allegory Piers Plowman; Gower's Confessio Amantis; and, of course, the works of Chaucer, the most highly regarded English poet of the middle ages, who was seen by his contemporaries as a successor to the great tradition of Virgil and Dante. The reputation of Chaucer's successors in the 15th century has suffered in comparison with him, though Lydgate and Skelton are widely studied.

However, the century really belongs to a group of remarkable Scottish writers. The rise of Scottish poetry began with the writing of The Kingis Quair by James I of Scotland. The main poets of this Scottish group were Robert Henryson, William Dunbar and Gavin Douglas. Henryson and Douglas introduced a note of almost savage satire, which may have owed something to the Gaelic bards, while Douglas' version of Virgil's Aeneid is one of the early monuments of Renaissance literary humanism in English.

trend can also be seen in Spenser's Shepheardes Calender. This poem marks the introduction into an English context of the classical pastoral, a mode of poetry that assumes an aristocratic audience with a certain kind of attitude to the land and peasants. The explorations of love found in the sonnets of William Shakespeare and the poetry of Walter Raleigh and others also implies a courtly audience.

Elizabethan verse Drama

Elizabethan verse drama is widely considered to be one of the major achievements of literature in English, and its most famous exponent, William Shakespeare, is revered as the greatest poet in the language. This drama, which served both as courtly masque and popular entertainment, deals with all the major themes of contemporary literature and life.

There are plays on European, classical, and religious themes reflecting the importance of humanism and the Reformation. There are also a number of plays dealing with English history that may be read as part of an effort to strengthen the British national myth and as artistic underpinnings for Elizabeth's resistance to the Spanish and other foreign threats. A number of the comic works for the stage also use bucolic themes connected with the pastoral genre.

In addition to Shakespeare, other notable dramatists of the period include Christopher Marlowe, Thomas Dekker and Ben Jonson.

CLASSICISM

Gavin Douglas' Aeneid, Thomas Campion's metrical experiments, and Spenser's Shepheardes Calender and plays like Shakespeare's Antony and Cleopatra are all examples of the influence of classicism on Elizabethan poetry. It remained common for poets of the period to write on themes from classical mythology; Shakespeare's Venus and Adonis and the Christopher Marlowe/ George Chapman Hero and Leander are examples of this kind of work.

Translations of classical poetry also became more widespread, with the versions of Ovid's Metamorphoses by Arthur Golding

(1565-7) and George Sandys (1626), and Chapman's translations of Homer's Iliad (1611) and Odyssey (c.1615), among the outstanding examples.

Jacobean and Caroline Poetry

English Renaissance poetry after the Elizabethan poetry can be seen as belonging to one of three strains; the Metaphysical poets, the Cavalier poets and the school of Spenser. However, the boundaries between these three groups are not always clear and an individual poet could write in more than one manner.

The Metaphysical Poets

The early 17th century saw the emergence of this group of poets who wrote in a witty, complicated style. The most famous of the Metaphysicals is probably John Donne. Others include George Herbert, Henry Vaughan, Andrew Marvell and Richard Crashaw. John Milton in his Comus falls into this group. The Metaphysical poets went out of favour in the 18th century but began to be read again in the Victorian era. Donne's reputation was finally fully restored by the approbation of T. S. Eliot in the early 20th century.

The Cavalier Poets

The Cavalier poets wrote in a lighter, more elegant and artificial style than the Metaphysical poets. Leading members of the group include Ben Jonson, Richard Lovelace, Robert Herrick, Edmund Waller, Thomas Carew and John Denham. The Cavalier poets can be seen as the forerunners of the major poets of the Augustan era, who admired them greatly.

The School of Spenser

The early 17th century also saw a group of poets who were interested in Giles]] and Phineas Fletcher. Although these poetsto John Milton's great mythic long poem, Paradise Lost.

THE RESTORATION AND 18TH CENTURY

It is perhaps ironic that Paradise Lost, a story of fallen pride, was the first major poem to appear in England after the Restoration. The court of Charles II had, in its years in France, learned a worldliness and sophistication that marked it as distinctively different from the monarchies that preceded the Republic. Even if Charles had wanted to reassert the divine right of kingship, the -Protestantism and taste for power of the intervening years would have rendered it impossible.

Satire

It is hardly surprising that the world of fashion and scepticism that emerged encouraged the art of satire. All the major poets of the period, Samuel Butler, John Dryden, Alexander Pope and Samuel Johnson, and the Irish poet Jonathan Swift, wrote satirical verse. What is perhaps more surprising is that their satire was often written in defence of public order and the established church and government. However, writers such as Pope used their gift for satire to create scathing works responding to their detractors or to criticise what they saw as social atrocities perpetrated by the government. Pope's "The Dunciad" is a satirical slaying of two of his literary adversaries (Lewis Theobald, and Colley Cibber in a later version), expressing the view that British society was falling apart morally, culturally, and intellectually.

18th Century Classicism

The 18th century is sometimes called the Augustan age, and contemporary admiration for the classical world extended to the poetry of the time. Not only did the poets aim for a polished high style in emulation of the Roman ideal, they also translated and imitated Greek and Latin verse. Dryden translated all the known works of Virgil, and Pope produced versions of the two Homeric epics. Horace and Juvenal were also widely translated and imitated, Horace most famously by John Wilmot, Earl of Rochester and Juvenal by Samuel Johnson's Vanity of Human Wishes.

WOMEN POETS IN THE 18TH CENTURY

A number of women poets of note emerged during the period of the Restoration, including Aphra Behn, Margaret Cavendish, Mary Chudleigh, Anne Finch, Anne Killigrew, and Katherine Philips. Nevertheless, print publication by women poets was still relatively scarce when compared to that of men, though manuscript evidence indicates that many more women poets were practicing than was previously thought. Disapproval of feminine "forwardness," however, kept many out of print in the early part of the period, and even as the century progressed women authors still felt the need to justify their incursions into the public sphere by claiming economic necessity or the pressure of friends. Women writers were increasingly active in all genres throughout the eighteenth century, and by the 1790s women's poetry was flourishing. Notable poets later in the period include Anna Laetitia Barbauld, Joanna Baillie, Susanna Blamire, Felicia Hemans, Mary Leapor, Lady Mary Wortley Montagu, Hannah More, and Mary Robinson. In the past decades there has been substantial scholarly and critical work done on women poets of the long eighteenth century: first, to reclaim them and make them available in contemporary editions in print or online, and second, to assess them and position them within a literary tradition.

The Late 18th Century

Towards the end of the 18th century, poetry began to move away from the strict Augustan ideals and a new emphasis on sentiment and the feelings of the poet. This trend can perhaps be most clearly seen in the handling of nature, with a move away from poems about formal gardens and landscapes by urban poets and towards poems about nature as lived in. The leading exponents of this new trend include Thomas Gray, William Cowper, George Crabbe, Christopher Smart and Robert Burns as well as the Irish poet Oliver Goldsmith. These poets can be seen as paving the way for the Romantic movement.

THE ROMANTIC MOVEMENT

The last quarter of the 18th century was a time of social and political turbulence, with revolutions in the United States, France, Ireland and elsewhere. In Great Britain, movement for social change and a more inclusive sharing of power was also growing. This was the backdrop against which the Romantic movement in English poetry emerged.

The main poets of this movement were William Blake, William Wordsworth, Samuel Taylor Coleridge, Percy Bysshe Shelley, Lord Byron, and John Keats. The birth of English Romanticism is often dated to the publication in 1798 of Wordsworth and Coleridge's Lyrical Ballads. However, Blake had been publishing since the early 1780s. However, much of the focus on Blake only came about during the last century when Northrap Frye discussed his work in his book "The Anatomy of Criticism."

In poetry, the Romantic movement emphasised the creative expression of the individual and the need to find and formulate new forms of expression. The Romantics, with the partial exception of Byron, rejected the poetic ideals of the eighteenth century, and each of them returned to Milton for inspiration, though each drew something different from Milton. They also put a good deal of stress on their own originality. To the Romantics, the moment of creation was the most important in poetic expression and could not be repeated once it passed. Because of this new emphasis, poems that were not complete were nonetheless included in a poet's body of work (such as Coleridge's "Kubla Khan" and "Christabel").

Additionally, the Romantic movement marked a shift in the use of language. Attempting to express the "language of the common man", Wordsworth and his fellow Romantic poets focused on employing poetic language for a wider audience, countering the mimetic, tightly constrained Neo-Classic poems (although it's important to note that the poet wrote first and foremost for his own creative, expression). In Shelley's "Defense of Poetry", he contends that poets are the "creators of language" and that the poet's job is to refresh language for their society.

The Romantics were not the only poets of note at this time. In the work of John Clare the late Augustan voice is blended with a peasant's first-hand knowledge to produce arguably some of the finest nature poetry in the English language. Another contemporary poet who does not fit into the Romantic group was Walter Savage Landor. Landor was a classicist whose poetry forms a link between the Augustans and Robert Browning, who much admired it.

Victorian Poetry

The Victorian era was a period of great political, social and economic change. The Empire recovered from the loss of the American colonies and entered a period of rapid expansion. This expansion, combined with increasing industrialisation and mechanisation, led to a prolonged period of economic growth. The Reform Act 1832 was the beginning of a process that would eventually lead to universal suffrage.

High Victorian Poetry

The major High Victorian poets were Alfred, Lord Tennyson, Robert Browning, Elizabeth Barrett Browning, Matthew Arnold and Gerard Manley Hopkins. Tennyson was, to some degree, the Spenser of the new age and his Idylls of the Kings can be read as a Victorian version of The Faerie Queen, that is as a poem that sets out to provide a mythic foundation to the idea of empire.

The Brownings spent much of their time out of England and explored European models and matter in much of their poetry. Robert Browning's great innovation was the dramatic monologue, which he used to its full extent in his long novel in verse, The Ring and the Book. Elizabeth Barrett Browning is perhaps best remembered for Sonnets from the Portuguese but her long poem Aurora Leigh is one of the classics of 19th century feminist literature.

Matthew Arnold was much influenced by Wordsworth, though his poem Dover Beach is often considered a precursor of the modernist revolution. Hopkins wrote in relative obscurity and his work was not published until after his death. His unusual style (involving what he called "sprung rhythm" and heavy reliance on rhyme and alliteration) had a considerable influence on many of the poets of the 1940s.

Pre-Raphaelites, Arts and Crafts, Aestheticism, and the "Yellow" 1890s

The Pre-Raphaelite Brotherhood was a mid-19th century arts movement dedicated to the reform of what they considered the sloppy Mannerist painting of the day. Although primarily concerned with the visual arts, two members, the brother and sister Dante Gabriel Rossetti and Christina Rossetti, were also poets of some ability. Their poetry shares many of the concerns of the painters; an interest in Medieval models, an almost obsessive attention to visual detail and an occasional tendency to lapse into whimsy.

Dante Rossetti worked with, and had some influence on, the leading Arts and Crafts painter and poet William Morris. Morris shared the Pre-Raphaelite interest in the poetry of the European Middle Ages, to the point of producing some illuminated manuscript volumes of his work. Towards the end of the century, English poets began to take an interest in French symbolism and Victorian poetry entered a decadent fin-de-siecle phase. Two groups of poets emerged, the Yellow Book poets who adhered to the tenets of Aestheticism, including Algernon Charles Swinburne, Oscar Wilde and Arthur Symons and the Rhymer's Club group that included Ernest Dowson, Lionel Johnson and W. B. Yeats.

THE 20TH CENTURY

The First three Decades

The Victorian era continued into the early years of the 20th century and two figures emerged as the leading representative of the poetry of the old era to act as a bridge into the new. These were Yeats and Thomas Hardy. Yeats, although not a modernist, was to learn a lot from the new poetic movements that sprang up around him and adapted his writing to the new circumstances. Hardy was, in terms of technique at least, a more traditional figure and was to be a reference point for various anti-modernist reactions, especially from the 1950s onwards.

The Georgian poets and World War I

The Georgian poets were the first major grouping of the post-Victorian era. Their work appeared in a series of five anthologies called Georgian Poetry which were published by Harold Monro and edited by Edward Marsh. The poets featured included Edmund Blunden, Rupert Brooke, Robert Graves, D. H. Lawrence, Walter de la Mare and Siegfried Sassoon. Their poetry represented something of a reaction to the decadence of the 1890s and tended towards the sentimental.

Brooke and Sassoon were to go on to win reputations as war poets and Lawrence quickly distanced himself from the group and was associated with the modernist movement. Other notable poets who wrote about the war include Isaac Rosenberg, Edward Thomas, Wilfred Owen, May Cannan and, from the home front, Hardy and Rudyard Kipling. Although many of these poets wrote socially-aware criticism of the war, most remained technically conservative and traditionalist.

MODERNISM

The early decades of the 20th century saw the United States begin to overtake the United Kingdom as the major economic power. In the world of poetry, this period also saw American writers at the forefront of avant-garde practices. Among the foremost of these poets were T.S. Eliot, H.D. and Ezra Pound, each of whom spent an important part of their writing lives in England.

Pound's involvement with the Imagists marked the beginning of a revolution in the way poetry was written. English poets involved with this group included D. H. Lawrence, Richard Aldington, T. E. Hulme, F. S. Flint, E. E. Cummings, Ford Madox Ford, Allen Upward and John Cournos. Eliot, particularly after the publication of The Waste Land, became a major figure and influence on other English poets.

In addition to these poets, other English modernists began to emerge. These included the London-Welsh poet and painter David Jones, whose first book, In Parenthesis, was one of the very few experimental poems to come out of World War I, the Scot Hugh MacDiarmid, Mina Loy and Basil Bunting.

The Thirties

The poets who began to emerge in the 1930s had two things in common; they had all been born too late to have any real experience of the pre-World War I world and they grew up in a period of social, economic and political turmoil. Perhaps as a consequence of these facts, themes of community, social (in)justice and war seem to dominate the poetry of the decade.

The poetic landscape of the decade was dominated by four poets; W. H. Auden, Stephen Spender, Cecil Day-Lewis and Louis MacNeice, although the last of these belongs at least as much to the history of Irish poetry. These poets were all, in their early days at least, politically active on the Left. Although they admired Eliot, they also represented a move away from the technical innovations of their modernist predecessors. A number of other, less enduring, poets also worked in the same vein. One of these was Michael Roberts, whose New Country anthology both introduced the group to a wider audience and gave them their name.

The 1930s also saw the emergence of a home-grown English surrealist poetry whose main exponents were David Gascoyne, Hugh Sykes Davies, George Barker, and Philip O'Connor. These poets turned to French models rather than either the New Country poets or English-language modernism, and their work was to prove of importance to later English experimental poets as it broadened the scope of the English avant-garde tradition.

John Betjeman and Stevie Smith, who were two of the most significant poets of this period, stood outside all schools and groups. Betjeman was a quietly ironic poet of Middle England with a fine command of a wide range of verse techniques. Smith was an entirely unclassifiable one-off voice.

The Forties

The 1940s opened with the United Kingdom at war and a new generation of war poets emerged in response. These included Keith Douglas, Alun Lewis, Henry Reed and F. T. Prince. As with the poets of the First World War, the work of these writers can be seen as something of an interlude in the history of 20th century poetry. Technically, many of these war poets owed something to the 1930s poets, but their work grew out of the particular circumstances in which they found themselves living and fighting.

The main movement in post-war 1940s poetry was the New Romantic group that included Dylan Thomas, George Barker, W. S. Graham, Kathleen Raine, Henry Treece and J. F. Hendry. These writers saw themselves as in revolt against the classicism of the New Country poets. They turned to such models as Gerard Manley Hopkins, Arthur Rimbaud and Hart Crane and the word play of James Joyce. Thomas, in particular, helped Anglo-Welsh poetry to emerge as a recognisable force.

Other significant poets to emerge in the 1940s include Lawrence Durrell, Bernard Spencer, Roy Fuller, Norman Nicholson, Vernon Watkins, R. S. Thomas and Norman McCaig.

These last four poets represent a trend towards regionalism and poets writing about their native areas; Watkins and Thomas in Wales, Nicholson in Cumberland and MacCaig in Scotland.

The Fifties

The 1950s were dominated by three groups of poets, The Movement, The Group and a number of poets that gathered around the label Extremist Art. The Movement poets as a group came to public notice in Robert Conquest's 1955 anthology New Lines. The core of the group consisted of Philip Larkin, Elizabeth Jennings, D. J. Enright, Kingsley Amis, Thom Gunn and Donald Davie. They were identified with a hostility to modernism and internationalism, and looked to Hardy as a model. However, both Davie and Gunn later moved away from this position. As befits their name, the Group were much more formally a group of poets, meeting for weekly discussions under the chairmanship of Philip Hobsbaum and Edward Lucie-Smith. Other Group poets included Martin Bell, Peter Porter, Peter Redgrove, George MacBeth and David Wevill. Hobsbaum spent some time teaching in Belfast, where he was a formative influence on the emerging Northern Ireland poets including Seamus Heaney.

The term Extremist Art was first used by the poet A. Alvarez to describe the work of the American poet Sylvia Plath. Other poets associated with this group included Plath's one-time husband Ted Hughes, Francis Berry and Jon Silkin. These poets are sometimes compared with the Expressionist German school. A number of young poets working in what might be termed a modernist vein also started publishing during this decade. These included Charles Tomlinson, Gael Turnbull, Roy Fisher and Bob Cobbing. These poets can now be seen as forerunners of some of the major developments during the following two decades.

The 1960s and 1970s

In the early part of the 1960s, the centre of gravity of mainstream poetry moved to Ireland, with the emergence of Seamus Heaney, Tom Paulin, Paul Muldoon and others. In England, the most cohesive groupings can, in retrospect, be seen to cluster around what might loosely be called the modernist tradition and draw on American as well as indigenous models.

The British Poetry Revival was a wide-reaching collection of groupings and subgroupings that embraces performance, sound and concrete poetry as well as the legacy of Pound, Jones, MacDiarmid, Loy and Bunting, the Objectivist poets, the Beats and the Black Mountain poets, among others. Leading poets associated with this movement include J. H. Prynne, Eric Mottram, Tom Raworth, Denise Riley and Lee Harwood.

The Mersey Beat poets were Adrian Henri, Brian Patten and Roger McGough. Their work was a self-conscious attempt at creating an English equivalent to the Beats. Many of their poems were written in protest against the established social order and, particularly, the threat of nuclear war. Although not actually a Mersey Beat poet, Adrian Mitchell is often associated with the group in critical discussion. Contemporary poet Steve Turner has also been compared with them.

English Poetry Now

The last three decades of the 20th century saw a number of short-lived poetic groupings such as the Martians. There was a growth in interest in women's writing and in poetry from England's ethnic groupings, especially the West Indian community. Poets who emerged include Carol Ann Duffy, Andrew Motion, Craig Raine, Wendy Cope, James Fenton, Blake Morrison, Liz Lochhead, Linton Kwesi Johnson and Benjamin Zephaniah. There was also a growth in performance poetry fuelled by the Poetry Slam movement. A new generation of innovative poets has also sprung up in the wake of the Revival grouping. Further activity focussed around poets in Bloodaxe Books The New Poetry including Simon Armitage, Kathleen Jamie, Glyn Maxwell, Selima Hill, Maggie Hannan, and Michael Hofmann. The New Generation movement flowered in the 1990s and early twenty first century producing poets such as Don Paterson, Julia Copus, John Stammers, Jacob Polley, David Morley and Alice Oswald.

Despite all of this activity, major publishers dropped their poetry lists and both young and established writers became increasingly reliant on small and medium sized presses, generally dependent on State funding. As of 2004, it appears that a still thriving literature is faced with an ever-decreasing audience.

4

The English Drama

Drama was introduced to England from Europe by the Romans, and auditoriums were constructed across the country for this purpose. By the medieval period, the mummers' plays had developed, a form of early street theatre associated with the Morris dance, concentrating on themes such as Saint George and the Dragon and Robin Hood. These were folk tales re-telling old stories, and the actors travelled from town to town performing these for their audiences in return for money and hospitality. The medieval mystery plays and morality plays, which dealt with Christian themes, were performed at religious festivals.

The period known as the English Renaissance, approximately 1500-1660, saw a flowering of the drama and all the arts. The most famous example of the mystery play, Everyman, and the two candidates for the earliest comedy in English Nicholas Udall's Ralph Roister Doister and the anonymous Gammer Gurton's Needle, all belong to the 16th century.

During the reign of Elizabeth I in the late 16th and early 17th century, a London-centred culture that was both courtly and popular produced great poetry and drama. Perhaps the most famous playwright in the world, William Shakespeare from Stratford-upon-Avon, wrote plays that are still performed in theatres across the world to this day. He was himself an actor and deeply involved in the running of the theatre company that performed his plays. Other important playwrights of this period include Christopher Marlowe, Ben Jonson, and John Webster. Various types of plays were popular. Ben Jonson, for example, was often engaged to write courtly masques, ornate plays where the actors wore masks. The three types that seem most often studied today are the histories, the comedies, and the tragedies. Most playwrights tended to specialise in one or another of these, but Shakespeare is remarkable in that he produced all three types. His 38 plays include tragedies such as Hamlet (1603), Othello (1604), and King Lear (1605); comedies such as A Midsummer Night's Dream (1594-96) and Twelfth Night (1602); and history plays such as Henry IV, part 1-2. Some have hypothesized that the English Renaissance paved the way for the sudden dominance of drama in English society, arguing that the questioning mode popular during this time was best served by the competing characters in the plays of the Elizabethan dramatists.

During the Interregnum 1649-1660, English theatres were kept closed by the Puritans for religious and ideological reasons. When the London theatres opened again with the Restoration of the monarchy in 1660, they flourished under the personal interest and support of Charles II. Wide and socially mixed audiences were attracted by topical writing and by the introduction of the first professional actresses (in Shakespeare's time, all female roles had been played by boys). New genres of the Restoration were heroic drama, pathetic drama, and Restoration comedy. Notable heroic tragedies of this period include John Dryden's All for Love (1677) and (Aureng-Zebe) (1675), and Thomas Otway's Venice Preserved (1682). The Restoration plays that have best retained the interest of producers and audiences today are the comedies, such as George Etherege's The Man of Mode (1676), William Wycherley's The Country Wife (1676), John Vanbrugh's The Relapse (1696), and William Congreve's The Way of the World (1700). This period saw the first professional woman playwright, Aphra Behn, author of many comedies including The Rover (1677). Restoration comedy is famous or notorious for its sexual explicitness, a quality encouraged by Charles II (1660-1685) personally and by the rakish aristocratic ethos of his court.

In the 18th century, the highbrow and provocative Restoration comedy lost favour, to be replaced by sentimental comedy, domestic tragedy such as George Lillo's The London Merchant (1731), and by an overwhelming interest in Italian opera. Popular entertainment became more dominant in this period than ever before. Fair-booth burlesque and musical entertainment, the ancestors of the English music hall, flourished at the expense of legitimate English drama, which went into a long period of decline. By the early 19th century, the drama was no longer represented by stage plays at all, but by closet drama, plays written to be privately read in a "closet" (a small domestic room).

A change came in the later 19th century with the plays on the London stage by the Irishmen George Bernard Shaw and Oscar Wilde and the Norwegian Henrik Ibsen, all of whom influenced domestic English drama and vitalised it again.

Postmodernism had a pround effect on English Drama in the latter half of the 20th Century. This can be seen particularly in the work of Samuel Beckett (most notably in Waiting for Godot), who in turn influenced writers such as Harold Pinter and Tom Stoppard.

Today the West End of London has a large number of theatres, particularly centred around Shaftesbury Avenue. A prolific writer of music for musicals of the 20th century, Andrew Lloyd Webber, has dominated the West End for a number of years, and his works have travelled to Broadway in New York and around the world, as well as being turned into film.

The Royal Shakespeare Company operates out of Stratford-upon-Avon, producing mainly but not exclusively Shakespeare's plays.

IRISH THEATRE

The history of Irish theatre begins with the rise of the English administration in Dublin at the start of the 17th century. Over the next 400 years this small country was to make a disproportionate contribution to drama in English.

In the early days of its history, theatrical productions in Ireland tended to serve the political purposes of the administration, but as more theatres opened and the popular audience grew, a more diverse range of entertainments were staged. Many Dublin-based theatres developed links with their London equivalents and performers and productions from the British capital frequently found their way to the Irish stage. However, most Irish playwrights from William Congreve to George Bernard Shaw found it necessary to go abroad to establish themselves.

At the beginning of the 20th century, theatres and theatre companies dedicated to the staging of Irish plays and the development of indigenous writers, directors and performers began to emerge. This allowed many of the most significant Irish dramatists to learn their trade and establish their reputations at home rather than in Britain or the United States.

Small Beginnings

Although there would appear to have been performances of plays on religious themes in Ireland from as early as the 14th century, the first well-documented instance of a theatrical production in Ireland is a 1601 staging of Gorboduc presented by Lord Mountjoy Lord Deputy of Ireland in the Great Hall in Dublin Castle. The play had been written by Thomas Sackville and Thomas Norton for the 1561/2 Christmas festivities at the Inner Temple in London and appears to have been selected because it was a story of a divided kingdom descending into anarchy that was applicable to the situation in Ireland at the time of the performance. Mountjoy started a fashion, and private performances became quite commonplace in great houses all over Ireland over the following thirty years.

The Court in Kilkenny

In 1642, as a result of the English Civil War, Dublin Royalists were forced to flee the city. Many of them went tc Kilkenny to join a confederacy of Old English and Irish that formed in that city. Kilkenny had a tradition of dramatic performance going back to 1366, and the Dublin company, much attenuated, set up in their new home. At least one new play was published in Kilkenny; A Tragedy of Cola's Fury, OR, Lirenda's Misery, a blatantly political work with the Lirenda of the title being an anagram of Ireland.

With the restoration of the monarchy in 1661, John Ogilby was commissioned to design the triumphal arches and write masques for the new king's entrance into London. Ogilby was reinstated as Master of the Revels and returned to Dublin to open a new theatre in Smock Alley. Although starting well, this new theatre was essentially under the control of the administration in Dublin castle and staged mainly pro-Stuart works and

Shakespearean classics. As a result, Irish playwrights and actors of real talent were drawn to London.

The Restoration

An early example of this trend is William Congreve, one of the most important writers for the late 18th London stage. Although born in Yorkshire, Congreve grew up in Ireland and studied with Jonathan Swift in Kilkenny and at Trinity College, Dublin. After graduating, Congreve moved to London to study law at the Temple and pursue a literary career. His first play, The Old Bachelor (1693) was sponsored by John Dryden, and he went on to write at least four more plays. The last of these, The Way of the World (1700) is the one Congreve work regularly revived on the modern stage. However, at the time of its creation, it was a relative failure and he wrote no further works for the theatre.

With the accession to the throne of William of Orange, the whole ethos of Dublin Castle, including its attitude to the theatre, changed. Smock Alley stayed in existence until 1811 and new theatres, such as the Theatre Royal, Queens' Theatre, and The Gaiety Theatre opened during the 19th century. However, the one constant for the next 200 years was that the main action in the history of Irish theatre happened abroad, mainly in London.

The 18th Century

The 18th century saw the emergence of two major Irish dramatists, Oliver Goldsmith and Richard Brinsley Sheridan, who were two of the most successful playwrights on the London stage in the 18th century. Goldsmith (1728-1774) was born in Roscommon and grew up in extremely rural surroundings. He entered Trinity College in 1745 and graduated in 1749. He returned to the family home, and in 1751, began to travel, finally settling in London in 1756, where he published poetry, prose and two plays, The Good-Natur'd Man 1768 and She Stoops to Conquer 1773. This latter was a huge success and is still regularly revived.

Sheridan (1751-1816) was born in Dublin into a family with a strong literary and theatrical tradition. His mother was a writer and his father was manager of Smock Alley Theatre. The family moved to England in the 1750s, and Sheridan attended Harrow Public School. His first play, The Rivals 1775, was performed at Covent Garden and was an instant success. He went on to become the most significant London playwright of the late 18th century with plays like The School for Scandal and The Critic. He was owner of the Drury Lane Theatre, which he bought from David Garrick. The theatre burned down in 1809, and Sheridan lived out the rest of his life in reduced circumstances. He is buried in Poets' Corner at Westminster Abbey.

The 19th Century

After Sheridan, the next Irish dramatist of historical importance was Dion Boucicault (1820-1890). Boucicault was born in Dublin but was sent to England to complete his education. At school, he began writing dramatic sketches and soon took up acting under the stage name of Lee Moreton. His first play was Legend of Devil's Dyke 1838 in which he acted himself in Brighton. His first London production was London Assurance 1841. This was a great success and he seemed set to become the major writer of comedies of his day. However, his next few plays were not as successful and Boucicault found himself in debt. He recovered some of his reputation with The Corsican Brothers (1852), a well constructed melodrama.

In 1853, he moved to New York, where he soon became a hit with plays like The Poor of New York (1857), Dot (1859, based on Charles Dickens's The Cricket on the Hearth) and The Octoroon (1859). These plays tackled issues such as urban poverty and slavery. Boucicault was also involved in getting the 1856 law on copyright passed through Congress. His last New York play was The Colleen Bawn (1860). In that year, Boucicault returned to London to stage The Colleen Bawn and the play ran for 247 performances at The Adelphi Theatre. He wrote several more successful plays, including The Shaughran (1875) and Robert Emmet (1884). These later plays helped perpetuate the stereotype of the drunken, hotheaded, garrulous Irishman that had been common on the British stage since the time of Shakespeare. Other Irish dramatists of the period include John Banim and Gerald Griffin, whose novel The Collegians formed the basis for The Colleen Bawn.

Boucicault is widely regarded as the wittiest Irish dramatist between Sheridan and Oscar Wilde (1845-1900). Wilde was born in Dublin into a literary family and studied at Trinity College, where he had a brilliant career. In 1874 he won a scholarship to Magdalen College, Oxford. Here he began his career as a writer, winning the Newdigate Prize for his poem Ravenna. His studies were cut short during his second year at Oxford when his father died leaving large debts.

During a short but glittering literary career, Wilde wrote poetry, short stories, criticism and a novel, but his plays probably represent his most enduring legacy. Wilde's first stage success came with Lady Windemere's Fan (1892), which resulted in his becoming the most talked about dramatist in London. He followed this up with A Woman of No Importance (1893), An Ideal Husband (1895) and his most famous play The Importance of Being Earnest that same year.

With these plays, Wilde came to dominate late-Victorian era British theatre. His plays are noted for the lightness of their wit, but he also contrived to address some serious issues around sexual and class roles and identity, as he wrote himself 'treating the serious things lightly and the light things seriously'. Events in Wilde's personal life were to overtake his literary success and he died in Paris in 1900. He remains one of the great figures in the history of Irish theatre and his plays are frequently performed all over the English-speaking world.

Wilde's contemporary George Bernard Shaw (1856-1950) was a very different kind of writer. Born in Dublin, Shaw moved to London in 1876 intending to become a novelist. Here he became active in socialist politics and became a member of the Fabian Society. He was also a very public vegetarian. His writing for the stage was influenced by Henrik Ibsen. His early political plays were not popular, but he made a breakthrough with John Bull's Other Island (1904). Shaw was extremely prolific, and his collected writings filled 36 volumes. Many of his plays are now forgotten, but a number, including Major Barbara, Saint Joan (usually considered his masterpiece) and Pygmalion are still regularly performed. Pygmalion was the basis for the movie My Fair Lady, a fact which benefitted the National Gallery of Ireland as Shaw had left the royalties of the play to the gallery. A statue to the playwright now stands outside the gallery entrance. He won the Nobel Prize for Literature in 1924.

The Abbey and After

A sea change in the history of the Irish theatre came with the establishment in Dublin in 1899 of the Irish Literary Theatre, later to become the Abbey Theatre. The history of this theatre is well documented, and its importance can be seen from the list of writers whose plays were first performed here in the early days of the 20th century. These included W.B. Yeats, Lady Gregory, John Millington Synge, George Moore, and Sean O'Casey. Equally importantly, through the introduction by Yeats, via Ezra Pound, of elements of the Noh theatre of Japan, a tendency to mythologise quotidian situations, and a particularly strong focus on writings in dialects of Hiberno-English, the Abbey was to create a style that held a strong fascination for future Irish dramatists. Indeed, it could almost be said that the Abbey created the basic elements of a national theatrical style.

This period also saw a rise in the writing of plays in Irish, especially after the formation, in 1928, of An Taidhbhearc, a theatre dedicated to the Irish language. The Gate Theatre, also founded in 1928 under the direction of Hilton Edwards and Micheál MacLiammoir, introduced Irish audiences to many of the classics of the European stage.

Mid 20th Century

The twentieth century saw a number of Irish playwrights come to prominence. Samuel Beckett is probably the most significant of these. Beckett had a long career as a novelist and poet before his first play, Waiting for Godot (1953) made him famous. This play, along with his second, Endgame, is one of the great works of absurdist theatre. Beckett was awarded for the Nobel Prize in 1969.

The Lyric Theatre, founded in 1944 by Austin Clarke was based in the Abbey until 1951 and produced many of Clarke's own verse plays. From the mid 1950s, the Unitarian Church at St Stephen's Green, Dublin was home to Amharclann an Damer/ The Damer Theatre. The Damer produced both professional and amateur Irish language theatre. The world premier of Brendan

Behan's An Giall (The Hostage) took place here in 1957. The theatre closed in the late 1970s. Behan went on to be an extremely popular dramatist, particularly through his work with Joan Littlewood's Theatre Royal in Stratford, East London.

Other important Irish dramatists of this period include: Denis Johnston, Thomas Kilroy, Tom Murphy, Hugh Leonard, and John B. Keane.

RECENT DEVELOPMENTS

In general, the Abbey was the dominant influence in theatre in Ireland across the 20th century. Beckett's example has been almost entirely ignored, although his plays are regularly performed on the Irish stage. Behan, in his use of song and direct address to the audience, was influenced by, Bertolt Brecht and Denis Johnston used modernist techniques including found texts and collage, but their works had little impact on the dramatists who came after them. Since the 1970s, a number of companies have emerged to challenge the Abbey's dominance and introduce different styles and approaches. These include Focus Theatre, The Children's T Company, the Project Theatre Company, Mangled Ferret, Druid Theatre, TEAM and Field Day. These companies have nurtured a number of writers, actors, and directors who have since gone on to be successful in London, Broadway and Hollywood or in other literary fields. These include Roddy Doyle, Peter Sheridan, Brian Friel, Stephen Rea, Garry Hynes, Martin McDonagh and Gabriel Byrne.

5

Indian English Literature

EARLY HISTORY

Indian English Literature (IEL) refers to the body of work by writers in India who write in the English language and whose native or co-native language could be one of the numerous languages of India. It is also associated with the works of members of the Indian diaspora, especially people like Salman Rushdie who was born in India. As a category, this production comes under the broader realm of postcolonial literature-the production from previously colonised countries such as India.

IEL has a relatively recent history, it is only one and a half centuries old. The first book written by an Indian in English was by Sake Dean Mahomet, titled Travels of Dean Mahomet; Mahomet's travel narrative was published in 1793 in England. In its early stages it was influenced by the Western art form of the novel. Early Indian writers used English unadulterated by Indian words to convey an experience which was essentially Indian. Raja Rao's Kanthapura is Indian in terms of its storytelling qualities. Rabindranath Tagore wrote in Bengali and English and was responsible for the translations of his own work into English. Dhan Gopal Mukerji was the first Indian author to win a literary award in the United States.

Nirad C. Chaudhuri, a writer of non-fiction, is best known for his The Autobiography of an Unknown Indian where he relates his life experiences and influences. He was a self-confessed Anglophile. P. Lal, a poet, translator, publisher and essayist, is the epitome of the literateur, and besides translating the entire Mahabharata into English, has written many essays in defense of Indian literature in English. He also sponsors a press, Writers Workshop, that has published over 3000 volumes of Indian writing in English.

R.K. Narayan is a writer who contributed over many decades and who continued to write till his death recently. He was discovered by Graham Greene in the sense that the latter helped him find a publisher in England. Graham Greene and Narayan remained close friends till the end. Similar to Thomas Hardy's Wessex, Narayan created the fictitious town of Malgudi where he set his novels. Some criticise Narayan for the parochial, detached and closed world that he created in the face of the changing conditions in India at the times in which the stories are set. Others, such as Graham Greene, however, feel that through Malgudi they could vividly understand the Indian experience. Narayan's evocation of small town life and its experiences through the eyes of the endearing child protagonist Swaminathan in Swami and Friends is a good sample of his writing style.

LATER HISTORY

Among the later writers, the most notable is Salman Rushdie, born in India, now living in the United States. Rushdie with his famous work Midnight's Children (Booker Prize 1981, Booker of Bookers 1992) ushered in a new trend of writing. He used a hybrid language-English generously peppered with Indian terms-to convey a theme that could be seen as representing the vast canvas of India. He is usually categorised under the magic realism mode of writing most famously associated with Gabriel García Márquez. Bharati Mukherjee, author of Jasmine (1989), has spent much of her career exploring issues involving immigration and identity with a particular focus upon the United States and Canada.

Vikram Seth, author of A Suitable Boy (1994) is a writer who uses a purer English and more realistic themes. Being a self-confessed fan of Jane Austen, his attention is on the story, its details and its twists and turns.

Shashi Tharoor, in his The Great Indian Novel (1989), follows a story-telling (though in a satirical) mode as in the Mahabharata drawing his ideas by going back and forth in time. His work as

UN official living outside India has given him a vantage point that helps construct an objective Indianness.

Other authors include Anita Desai, Kiran Desai, Arundhati Roy, Bapsi Sidhwa, Chitra Banerjee Divakaruni, Raj Kamal Jha, Jhumpa Lahiri, Bharti Kirchner, Prakash Kona, Rohinton Mistry and Moncy Pothen.

DEBATES

It would be useful at this point to bring in the recent debates on Indian Writing in English ("IWE").

One of the key issues raised in this context is the superiority/ inferiority of IWE as opposed to the literary production in the various languages of India. Key polar concepts bandied in this context are superficial/authentic, imitative/creative, shallow/deep, critical/uncritical, elitist/parochial and so on.

The views of Rushdie and Amit Chaudhuri expressed through their books The Vintage Book of Indian Writing and The Picador Book of Modern Indian Literature respectively essentialise this battle.

Rushdie's statement in his book-"the ironic proposition that India's best writing since independence may have been done in the language of the departed imperialists is simply too much for some folks to bear"-created a lot of resentment among many writers, including writers in English. In his book, Amit Chaudhuri questions-"Can it be true that Indian writing, that endlessly rich, complex and problematic entity, is to be represented by a handful of writers who write in English, who live in England or America and whom one might have met at a party?"

Chaudhuri feels that after Rushdie, IWE started employing magical realism, bagginess, non-linear narrative and hybrid language to sustain themes seen as microcosms of India and supposedly reflecting Indian conditions. He contrasts this with the works of earlier writers such as Narayan where the use of English is pure, but the deciphering of meaning needs cultural familiarity. He also feels that Indianness is a theme constructed only in IWE and does not articulate itself in the vernacular literatures. (It is probable that the level of Indianness constructed is directly proportional to the distance between the writer and

India.) He further adds "the post-colonial novel, becomes a trope for an ideal hybridity by which the West celebrates not so much Indianness, whatever that infinitely complex thing is, but its own historical quest, its reinterpretation of itself".

Some of these arguments form an integral part of what is called postcolonial theory. The very categorisation of IWE-as IWE or under post-colonial literature-is seen by some as limiting. Amitav Ghosh made his views on this very clear by refusing to accept the Eurasian Commonwealth Writers Prize for his book The Glass Palace in 2001 and withdrawing it from the subsequent stage.

The renowned writer V.S. Naipaul, a third generation Indian from Trinidad and Tobago and a Nobel prize laureate, is a person who belongs to the world and usually not classified under IWE. Naipaul evokes ideas of homeland, rootlessness and his own personal feelings towards India in many of his books.

Jhumpa Lahiri, a Pulitzer prize winner from the U.S., is a writer uncomfortable under the label of IWE.

Recent writers in India such as Arundhati Roy and David Davidar show a direction towards contextuality and rootedness in their works. Arundhati Roy, a trained architect and the 1997 Booker prize winner for her The God of Small Things, calls herself a "home grown" writer. Her award winning book is set in the immensely physical landscape of Kerala. Davidar sets his The House of Blue Mangoes in Southern Tamil Nadu. In both the books, geography and politics are integra the narrative. In his novel Lament of Mohini (2000), Shreekumar Varma touches up he unique matriarchal system and the sammandham system of marriage as he writes about the Namboodiris and the aristocrats of Kerala.

Moncy Pothen, an overseas Indian, who lives in the Persian Gulf for more than two de s, in his novel,] Beneath the clouds and coconut leaves, portrays a cross section of the Kerala society. He uses the Naxalite moment, the political extremist outfit, which dominated Kerala during 1970s, to express the ordinary, Indian, citizen's dissatisfaction to the existing, corrupted, political system. He,in his novel, symbolizes Ahalya, a character in Ramayana, for the curse befallen society, who expects her liberation by the touch of a strong, integrated male. This novel is poetic because the rain and the nature are inseparably visualized in it.

As the number of Indian writers in English keeps increasing, with everyone with a story to tell trying to tell a story, and as publishing houses in India vie am themselves to discover the next new whiz-kid who will land up with world fame, it could become increasingly difficult to separate the wheat from the chaff. Research, debates and seminars on IWE continue with increasing frequency. However,it might be too early a stage in the history of Indian writing in English to pass any final judgement.

POETRY

A much over-looked category of Indian writing in English is poetry. Rabindranath Tagore wrote in Bengali and English and was responsible for the translations of his own work into English. Other early notable poets English include Derozio, Michael Madhusudan Dutt, Joseph Furtado, Armando Menezes, Toru Dutt, Romesh Chandra Dutt, Sarojini Naidu and her brother Harendranath Chattopadhyaya.

In modern times, Indian poetry in English was typified by two very different poets. Dom Moraes, winner of the Hawthornden Prize at the precocious age of 19 for his first book of poems "A Beginning" went on to occupy a pre-eminent position among Indian poets writing in English. Nissim Ezekiel, who came from India's tiny Jewish community, created a voice and place for Indian poets writing in English and championed their work.

Their contemporaries in English poetry in India were Arvind Mehrotra, Jayanta Mahapatra, Gieve Patel, A. K. Ramanujan, Rajagopal Parthasarathy, Keki Daruwala, Adil Jussawala, Arun Kolatkar, Dilip Chitre, Eunice De Souza, Kersi Ka, P. Lal and Kamala Das among several others.

A generation of exiles also sprang from the Indian diaspora. Among these are names like Agha Shahid Ali, Sujata Bhatt, Melanie Silgardo and Vikram Seth.

The current generation of Indian poets writi n English includes Ranjit Hoskote, Jeet Thayil, Tabish Khair, Vijay Nambisan, H. Masud Taj, Rukmini Bhaya Nair, C.P. Surendran, Moniza Alvi, Imtiaz Dharker, Gayatri Mazumdar, Vivek Narayanan,

Meena Kandasamy, Sharanya Manivannan, Gavin Barrett, Anjum Hasan, Jerry Pinto, Shreekumar Varma, Smita Agarwal, Arundhathi Subramaniam, Anand Thakore, Meena Alexander, Gayatri Majumdar, Thachom Poyil Rajeevan, Mary Anne Mohanraj, Kumar Vikram and Reetika Vazirani (deceased).

INDO-NOSTALGIC WRITING

Indo-Nostalgic writing is a s hat loosely defined term encompassing writings, in the English language, wherein nostalgia regarding the Indian Subcontinent, typically regarding India, represent a dominant theme or strong undercurrent. The writings may be memoirs, or quasi-fictionalized memoirs, travelogues, or inspired in part by real-life experiences and in part by the writer's imagination. This would include both mass-distributed "Indo-Anglian" literature put out by major publishing houses and also much shorter articles (e.g. feature pieces in mainstream or literary magazines) or poetry, including material published initially or solely in webzines.

Certainly, Indo-Nostalgic writings have much overlap with post-colonial literature but are generally not about 'heavy' topics such as cultural identity, conflicted identities, multilingualism or rootlessness. The writings are often less self-conscious and more light-hearted, perhaps dealing with impressionistic memories of places, people, cuisines, Only-in-India situations, or simply vignettes of "the way things were". Of late, a few Indo-nostalgic writers are beginning to show signs of "long-distance nationalism", concomitant with the rise of nationalism within India against the backdrop of a booming economy.

Typically, the authors are either Western-based writers of Indian origin (e.g. Salman Rushdie, Rohinton Mistry), or Western writers who have spent long periods of time in the Subcontinent, possibly having been born or raised in India, perhaps as the children of British Raj-era European expatriates or missionaries (e.g. Jim Corbett, Stephen Alter). Or, they may even be Anglo-Indians who have emigrated from the Subcontinent to the West. Third Culture Kids (TCKs) often grow up to produce Indo-Nostalgic writings that exhibit palpably dee nd perhaps somewhat romanticized) feelings for their childhoods in the Subcontinent. Accordingly, another common theme in Indo-Nostalgic writing is "rediscovery" or its cousin, "reconnection". Of course, for mass-distributed authors, Indo-Nostalgic writings may not necessarily represent all of their literary output, but certainly would represent a high percentage; it-is their sweet spot, after all. Finally, it is worth noting that the markets for such writers are almost entirely in the West; despite the rapid growth in the incomes of urban Indians, the sales of English-language literature within India (other than books required for educational degrees or professional purposes) are uscule compared to sales in the West, even if one includes pirated copies.

ANGLO-NORMAN LITERATURE

Anglo-Norman literature is literature composed in the Anglo-Norman language developed during the period 1066-1204 when the Duchy of Normandy and England were united in the Anglo-Norman realm.

Introduction

The Norman language came over to England with William the Conqueror. During the whole of the 12th century the variety often known as Norman French shared with Latin the distinction of being the literary language of England, and it was in use at the court until the 14th century. It was not until the reign of Henry VII that English became the native tongue of the kings of England. After the loss of the French provinces, schools for the teaching of French were established in England, among the most celebrated of which we may quote that of Marlborough. The language had undergone certain changes which distinguished it m the Old French spoken in France; but, except for some graphical characteristics, from which certain rules of pronunciation are to be inferred, the changes to which the language was subjected were the individual modifications of the various authors, so that, while we may still speak of Anglo-Norman writers, an Anglo-Norman language, properly so called, gradually ceased to exist. Great prestige was enjoyed by the French language; in the 14th century, the author of the Manière de language calls French:

...le plus bel et le plus gracious language et plus noble parler, apres latin d'escole, qui soit au monde et de touz genz mieulx prisée et amée que nul autre (quar Dieux le fist si douce et amiable

principalement à l'oneur et loenge de luy mesmes. Et r ce il peut comparer au parler des angels du ciel, pour la grand doulceur et biaultée d'icel).

which means:

...the most beautiful and gracious language, and the most noble one in the world to speak, after the latin of our schooldays. All genz (could mean nobles, could mean everyone-trans.) love it more than any other (for God made it so sweet and lovable mainly for his own honor and praise. And due to this, it can be compared to the angels' speech in heaven, due to its great sweetness and beauty).

It was not till 1363 that the chancellor opened the parliamentary session with an English speech, and not until the reign of Henry VII that Statute law ceased to be written in Anglo-Norman. And although the Hundred Years' War led to a decline in the study of French and the disappearance of Anglo-Norman literature, the French language continued, through some vicissitudes, to be the classical language of the courts of justi ntil the 17th century. French, alongside Latin, remained the language of government until the mid-1480s. It is still an official language in the Channel Islands, though English has become dominant since 1901.

The most flourishing period of Anglo-Norman literature was from the beginning of the 12th century to the end of the first quarter of the 13th. The end of this period is generally said to coincide with the loss of the French provinces to Philip Augustus, but literary and political history do not correspond quite so precisely, and the end of the first period would be more accurately denoted by the appearance of the history of William the Marshal in 1225 (published for the Société de l'histoire de France, by Paul Meyer, 3 vols., 1891-1901). It owes its brilliancy largely to the protection accorded by Henry II of England to the men of letters of his day.

"He could speak French and Latin well, and is said to have known something of every tongue between the Bay of Biscay and the Jordan. He was probably the most highly educated sovereign of his day, and amid all his busy active life he never lost his interest in literature and intellectual discussion; his hands were never empty, they always had either a bow or a book" (Dict. of Nat. Biog.).

Wace and Benoît de Sainte-More compiled their histories at his bidding, and it was in his reign that Marie de France composed her poems. An event with which he was closely connected, viz. the murder of Thomas Becket, gave rise to a whole series of writings, some of which are purely Anglo-Norman. In his time appeared the works of Béroul and Thomas of Britain respectively, as well as some of the most celebrated of the Anglo-Norman romans d'aventure. It is important to keep this fact in mind when studying the different works which Anglo-Norman literature has left us. We will examine these works briefly, grouping them into narrative, didactic, hagiographic, lyric, satiric and dramatic literature.

NARRATIVE LITERATURE

Epic and Romance

The French epic came over to England at an early date. It is believed that the Chanson de Roland was sung at the battle of Hastings, and we possess Anglo-Norman MSS. of a few chansons de geste. The Pélerinage de Charlemagne (Eduard Koschwitz, Altfranzösische Bibliothek, 1883) was, for instance, only preserved in an Anglo-Norman manuscript of the British Museum (now lost), although the author was certainly a Parisian. The oldest manuscript of the Chanson de Roland that we possess is also a manuscript written in England, and amongst the others of less importance we may mention La Chançun de Willame, the MS. of which has (June 1903) been published in facsimile at Chiswick (cf. Paul Meyer, Romania, xxxii. 597-618).

Although the diffusion of epic poetry in England did not actually inspire any new chansons de geste, it developed the taste for this class of literature, and the epic style in which the tales of the Romance of Horn, of Bovon de Hampton, of Guy of Warwick (still unpublished), of Waldef (still unpublished), and of Fulk Fitz Warine are treated, is certainly partly due to this circumstance. Although the last of these works has come down to us only in a prose version, it contains unmistakable signs of a previous poetic form, and what we possess is really only a rendering into prose similar to the transformations undergone by many of the chansons de geste.

The interinfluence of French and English literature can be studied in the Breton romances and the romans d'aventure even better than in the epic poetry of the period. The Lay of Orpheus is known to us only through an English imitation, Sir Orfeo; the Lai du cor was composed by Robert Biket, an Anglo-Norman poet of the 12th century (Wulff, Lund, 1888). The lais of Marie de France were written in England, and the greater number of the romances composing the matière de Bretagne seem to have passed from England to France through the medium of Anglo-Norman.

The legends of Merlin and Arthur, collected in the Historia Regum Britanniae by Geoffrey of Monmouth (died c. 1154), passed into French literature, bearing the character which the bishop of St Asaph had stamped upon them. Chrétien de Troyes's Perceval (c. 1175) is doubtless based on an Anglo-Norman poem. Robert de Boron (c. 1215) took the subject of his Merlin (published by G. Paris and J. Ulrich, 1886, 2 vols., Société des Anciens Textes) from Geoffrey of Monmouth.

Finally, the most celebrated love-legend of the middle ages, and one of the most beautiful inventions of world-literature, the story of Tristan and Iseult, tempted two authors, Béroul and Thomas, the first of whom is probably, and the second certainly, Anglo-Norman. One Folie Tristan was composed in England in the last years of the 12th century.

Less fascinating than the story of Tristan and Iseult, but nevertheless of considerable interest, are the two romans d'aventure of Hugh of Rutland, Ipomedon (published by Kölbing and Koschwitz, Breslau, 1889) and Protesilaus (still unpublished) written about 1185. The first relates the adventures of a knight who married the young duchess of Calabria, niece of King Meleager of Sicily, but was loved by Medea, the king's wife.

The second poem is the sequel to Ipomedon, and deals with the wars and subsequent reconciliation between Ipomedon's sons, Daunus, the elder, lord of Apulia, and Protesilaus, the younger, lord of Calabria. Protesilaus defeats Daunus, who had expelled him from Calabria. He saves his brother's life, is reinvested with the dukedom of Calabria, and, after the death of Daunus, succeeds to Apulia. He subsequently marries Medea, King Meleager's widow, who had helped him to seize Apulia, having transferred her affection for Ipomedon to his younger son (cf. Ward, Cat. of Rom., i. 728).

To these two romances by an Anglo-Norman author, Amadas et Idoine, of which we only possess a continental version, is to be added. Gaston Paris has proved indeed that the original was composed in England in the 12th century (An English Miscellany presented to Dr. Furnivall in Honour of his Seventy-fifth Birthday, Oxford, 1901, 386-394).

The Anglo-Norman poem on the Life of Richard Coeur de Lion is lost, and an English version only has been preserved. About 1250 Eustace of Kent introduced into England the roman d'Alexandre in his Roman de toute chevalerie, many passages of which have been imitated in one of the oldest English poems on Alexander, namely, King Alisaunder (P. Meyer, Alexandre le grand, Paris, 1886, ii. 273, and Weber, Metrical Romances, Edinburgh).

Fableaux, Fables and Religious Tales

In spite of the incontestable popularity enjoyed by this class of literature, we have only some half-dozen fableaux written in England, viz.

- Le chevalier à la corbeille,
- Le chevalier qui faisait parler les muets,
- Le chevalier, sa dame et un clerc,
- Les trois dames,
- La gageure,
- Le prêtre d'Alison,
- La bourgeoise d'Orléans (Bédier, Les Fabliaux, 1895).

As to fables, one of the most popular collections in the middle ages was that written by Marie de France, which she claimed to have translated from King Alfred. In the Contes moralisés, written by Nicole Bozon shortly before 1320 (Soc. Anc. Textes, 1889), a few fables bear a strong resemblance to those of Marie de France. The religious tales deal mostly with the Mary Legends, and have been handed down to us in three collections:

1. The Adgar's collection. Most of these were translated from William of Malmesbury by Adgar in the 12th century ("Adgar's Marien-Legenden," Altfr. Biblioth. ix.; J. A. Herbert, Rom. xxxii. 394).
2. The collection of Everard of Gateley, a monk of St. Edmund at Bury, who wrote c. 1250 three Mary Legends (Rom. xxix. 27).
3. An anonymous collection of sixty Mary Legends composed c. 1250 (Brit. Museum Old Roy. 20 B, xiv.), some of which have been published in Suchier's Bibliotheca Normannica; in the Altf. Bibl. See also Mussafia, "Studien zu den mittelalterlichen Marien-legenden" in Sitzungsh. der Wien. Akademie (t. cxiii., cxv., cxix., cxxiii., cxxix.).

Another set of religious and moralizing tales is to be found in Chardri's Set dormans and Josaphat, c. 1216 (Koch, Altfr. Bibl., 1880; G. Paris, Poèmes et légendes du moyen âge).

History

Of far greater importance, however, are the works which constitute Anglo-Norman historiography. The first Anglo-Norman historiographer is Geoffrey Gaimar, who wrote his Estorie des Angles (between 1147 and 1151) for Dame Constance, wife of Robert Fitz-Gislebert (The Anglo-Norman Metrical Chronicle, Hardy and Martin, i. ii., London, 1888). This history comprised a first part (now lost), which was merely a translation of Geoffrey of Monmouth's Historia Regum Britanniae, preceded by a history of the Trojan War, and a second part which carries us as far as the death of William Rufus. For this second part he has consulted historical documents, but he stops at the year 1087, just when he has reached the period about which he might have been able to give us some first-hand information. Similarly, Wace in his Roman de Rou (ed. Anthony Holden, Paris, 1970-1973), written 1160-1174, stops at the battle of Tinchebray in 1107 just before the period for which he would have been so useful. His Brut or Geste des Bretons (Le Roux de Lincy, 1836-1838, 2 vols.), written in 1155, is merely a translation of Geoffrey of Monmouth.

"Wace," says Gaston Paris, speaking of the Roman de Rou, "traduit en les abrégeant des historiens latins que nous possédons; mais çà et là il ajoute soit des contes populaires, par exemple sur Richard 1er, sur Robert 1er, soit des particularités qu'il savait par tradition (sur ce même Robert le magnifique, sur l'expédition de Guillaume, &c.) et qui donnent à son oeuvre un réel intérêt historique. Sa langue est excellente; son style clair, serré, simple, d'ordinaire assez monotone, vous plaît par sa saveur archaïque et quelquefois par une certaine grâce et une certaine malice."

The History of the Dukes of Normandy by Benoît de Sainte-More is based on the work of Wace. It was composed at the request of Henry II. about 1170, and takes us as far as the year 1135 (ed. by Francisque Michel, 1836-1844, Collection de documents inédits, 3 vols.). The 43,000 lines which it contains are of but little interest to the historian; they are too evidently the work of a romancier courtois, who takes pleasure in recounting love-adventures such as those he has described in his romance of Troy. Other works, however, give us more trustworthy information, for example, the anonymous poem on Henry II.'s Conquest of Ireland in 1172 (ed. Francisque Michel, London, 1837), which, together with the Expugnatio hibernica of Giraud de Barri, constitutes our chief authority on this subject. The Conquest of Ireland was republished in 1892 by Goddard Henry Orpen, under the title of The Song of Dermot and the Earl (Oxford, Clarendon Press).

Similarly, Jourdain Fantosme, who was in the north of England in 1174, wrote an account of the wars between Henry II., his sons, William the Lion of Scotland and Louis VII., in 1173 and 1174 (Chronicle of the reigns of Stephen... III., ed. by Joseph Stevenson and Fr. Michel, London, 1886, pp. 202-307). Not one of these histories, however, is to be compared in value with The History of William the Marshal, Count of Striguil and Pembroke, regent of England from 1216-1219, which was found and subsequently edited by Paul Meyer (Société de l'histoire de France, 3 vols., 1891-1901). This masterpiece of historiography was composed in 1225 or 1226 by a professional poet of talent at the request of William, son of the marshal. It was compiled from the notes of the marshal's squire, John d'Early († 1230 or 1231), who shared all the vicissitudes of his master's life and was one of the executors of his will. This work is of great value for the history of the period 1186-1219, as the information furnished by John d'Early is either personal or obtained at first hand. In the part which deals with the period before 1186, it is true, there are various mistakes, due to the author's ignorance of contemporary history, but these slight blemishes are amply atoned for by the literary value of the work. The style is concise, the anecdotes are well told, the descriptions short and picturesque; the whole constitutes one of the most living pictures of medieval society. Very pale by the side of this work appear the Chronique of Peter of Langtoft, written between 1311 and 1320, and mainly of interest for the period 1294-1307 (ed. by T. Wright, London, 1866-1868); the Chronique of Nicholas Trevet, dedicated to Princess Mary, daughter of Edward I. (Duffus Hardy, Descr. Catal. III., 349-350); the Scala Chronica compiled by Thomas Gray of Heaton, which carries us to the year 1362-1363 (ed. by J. Stevenson, Maitland Club, Edinburgh, 1836); the Black Prince, a poem by the poet Chandos Herald, composed about 1386, and relating the life of the Black Prince from 1346-1376 (re-edited by Francisque Michel, London and Paris, 1883); and, lastly, the different versions of the Brutes, the form and historical importance of which have been indicated by Paul Meyer (Bulletin de la Société des Anciens Textes, 1878, pp. 104-145), and by F. W. D. Brie (Geschichte und Quellen der mittelenglischen Prosachronik, The Brute of England or The Chronicles of England, Marburg, 1905).

Finally we may mention, as ancient history, the translation of Eutropius and Dares, by Geoffrey of Waterford (13th century), who gave also the Secret des Secrets, a translation from a work wrongly attributed to Aristotle, which belongs to the next division (Rom. xxiii. 314).

6

Modern English Literature

WALTER BAGEHOT (1826-1877)

Bagehot was a critic, essayist and writer on political and economic affairs best known for The English constitution published in 1867. In 1860 he became editor of The Economist, which had been founded by his father-in-law, James Wilson, in 1843.

The collection consists of Bagehot's correspondence with Eliza Wilson prior to their marriage in 1858, and with her father. This was edited by E.I. Barrington and published under the title The love letters of Walter Bagehot and Eliza Wilson in 1933.

DOUGLAS EAGLESHAM DUNN (1942-)

After qualifying as a librarian at the Scottish School of Librarianship, Douglas Dunn worked in a number of libraries in Britain and America before becoming a student at the University of Hull, where he graduated in English in 1969. His first collection of poetry, Terry Street, based on his observations while living in this now redeveloped street in central Hull, was published in 1969. Dunn then worked as an assistant librarian in the Brynmor Jones Library for two years before leaving to work full-time as a writer. He was Fellow in Creative Writing in the University in 1974/75 and continued to live in Hull until the death of his wife Lesley in 1981. He then returned to his native Scotland, where he now lives near Dundee with his second wife, also Lesley, and family. Since 1991 he has been a Professor of English at the University of St. Andrews. He has published several collections of poetry and works of literary criticism. Among the many awards he has received are the Whitbread Poetry prize in 1985 and Whitbread Book of the Year 1986 for Elegies (1985), a moving commemoration of the death of his first wife. He became a Fellow of the Royal Society of Literature in 1981 and is a member of the Scottish Arts Council.

The Dunn collection includes notebooks and drafts of poems, the typescript of Terry Street, letters from Philip Larkin, and the annotated typescript of the speech made by Dunn at the opening of the Philip Larkin Suite in the Brynmor Jones Library in December 1987. There are letters from Dunn to Ted Tarling, publisher of the poetry magazine Wave, and to Harry Chambers, editor of Phoenix, along with typescripts of poems published in these magazines. Letters from Dunn to the poets Tony Griffin, Peter Didsbury and Tony Flynn are also available all three feature in the first Bloodaxe anthology, A rumoured city: new poets from Hull (1982), edited by Dunn.

SIR WILLIAM EMPSON (1906-1984)

William Empson, the university teacher, poet, literary analyst and critic, read maths and then English at Magdalene College, Cambridge, studying under IA Richards. His first book, Seven types of ambiguity (1930), was written largely whilst an undergraduate and is regarded as one of the most influential critical works of the century. He also quickly established himself as a poet-much of the content of Poems (1935) was written at Cambridge. By the time of his appointment in 1931 as professor of English Literature at Tokyo University of Literature and Science he had already published numerous poems and review articles. He was offered the professorship in English at Peking National University in 1937, but after the outbreak of war in Europe he returned to England. He was editor of the BBC Monitoring Department between 1940 and 1941, and from then until 1946 Chinese editor in the Far Eastern Section. This work brought him into contact with a wide literary and artistic circle, including George Orwell and Dylan Thomas. He also met and married Hetta Crouse, who was then also working for the BBC. In 1947, William returned to China to his pre-war professorship; his wife and two young sons Mogador and Jacob accompanied him. The family lived through the Chinese Civil War and the Communist Revolution and by 1952 were the only Europeans left in Peking. The Empsons decided to return to England at this point. William Empson was almost immediately offered a chair in English at Sheffield University, where he remained until his 'retirement' in 1971. Empson's career went from strength to strength, and he was in much demand as a teacher, writer and speaker both in Britain and the United States. He published major works on Milton, Shakespeare and Faustus, and received a knighthood in 1979.

The majority of William Empson's papers are held at the University of Harvard. This photocopied collection comprises mainly his wife's correspondence, including William's letters to Hetta and hers in reply, over the period 1948 to 1975. There is also a set of correspondence between William Empson and David Jones, with whom he collaborated on his study of Faustus, between 1976 and 1982. The original papers were transferred to Sheffield University Library Department of Special Collections in 2005.

GAVIN BUCHANAN EWART (1916-1995)

Ewart first published poems at the age of 17 in Geoffrey Grigson's New verse of 1933. After graduating at Christ's College, Cambridge, he served in the Royal Artillery from 1940 to 1946, and worked for the British Council from 1946 to 1952, and then as a copywriter in advertising until 1971, when he became a full-time freelance writer. He became a Fellow of the Royal Society of Literature in 1981. The Ewart archive contains worksheets of over 500 poems, including those published in Be my guest (1975), Or Where a young penguin lies screaming (1978), and All my little ones (1978); typescripts of poems published in The first eleven (1977) and No fool like an old fool (1976); prose pieces, photographs and correspondence. Correspondents include Kingsley Amis, John Betjeman, Robert Conquest, Roy Fuller, Christopher Logue, Philip Larkin, Douglas Dunn, Anthony Thwaite and Fleur Adcock. [DP/163]

MAJOR OA FORSYTH-MAJOR (1886-1970)

Major Forsyth-Major was a prolific but unsuccessful writer who wrote under many different noms de plume including John Beverley, Don Beverley, Guy Beverley, Barry Macdonald, Ian

Mac. Ivor McIvor, Randolph Major, and Maxim Major. The only work by him to achieve publication was a collection of lectures entitled Elements of tactics (1916).

The collection contains typescripts of plays and other literary works (1910-1969) and a large correspondence with authors such as JM Barrie, Arnold Bennett, John Buchan, John Galsworthy, Thomas Hardy, John Masefield, William Somerset Maugham and George Bernard Shaw (1914-1944).

WILLIAM (WILLIE) GALLACHER (1881-1965)

Willie Gallacher was a founder of the Communist Party of Great Britain, its president from 1956 to 1963, and a Communist Member of Parliament for the constituency of West Fife between 1935 and 1950. He was an able journalist, pamphleteer and polemicist, and his published memoirs are well known, but he also wrote novels and poetry. A number of his manuscripts are found amongst the papers of Robin Page Arnot (1890-1986), a fellow leading member of the Party. They include undated parts of a murder story, a western and a detective novel, the full manuscript of a western novel, The big feller (c.1950), written under the pen name of Random Scott, and several typescripts and manuscript poems, together with correspondence and other items of political interest.

JEAN HARTLEY (1933-)

Jean Hartley was born and continues to live in Hull and has always been involved in the literary life of the city. With her husband, George Hartley, Jean founded The Marvell Press, which published Philip Larkin's first mature poetry collection, The less deceived in 1955. Later publications included work of other poets and recordings of poetry by Larkin. The Hartleys also established Listen, which George Hartley edited from 1954 to 1962.

Jean Hartley's personal archive reflects her 30 year friendship with Larkin and includes letters from him, papers relating to her biography Philip Larkin, the Marvell Press and me, published in 1989 and correspondence with contributors to the Larkin Society magazine About Larkin. There are also numerous letters from literary figures such as Ted Tarling, Tony Harrison and Maurice Rutherford. In addition to her interest in literary life,

Jean Hartley also wrote a Radio 4 programme The wayward girls (1992) on the experience of single motherhood in Hull during the 1950s and the archive includes interesting material gathered in the course of her research.

WINIFRED HORRABIN (1887-1971)

Winifred Batho was born in 1887 and attended Sheffield School of Art where she met her future husband Frank Horrabin (1884-1962). He was a political cartoonist and journalist, and the couple shared socialist convictions, working together in the labour college movement. Winifred Horrabin became a feminist and socialist writer, and the Archives hold the only significant surviving collection of her manuscripts, comprising diaries, journals, notebooks and correspondence with, amongst others, HG Wells, Vera Brittain and Brigid Brophy. Her journals cover 1926-1953 and contain accounts of events or journeys (including to Russia and Poland), interspersed with comment, literary notes, observations and self-analytical notes. Several of her notebooks document her research into Olive Schreiner, the South African author of Women and labour (1911). Amongst her literary manuscripts is her unpublished collection of autobiographical essays, 'The summer of a dormouse: a collage', compiled c.1965 and there are also notes for her unpublished autobiographical novel, 'Death of a woman'.

THOMAS ERNEST HULME (1883-1917)

Thomas Ernest Hulme, the poet, philosopher and critic, was born in Staffordshire and studied at St. John's College, Cambridge, but failed to take a degree there. He became a leading exponent of the poetic movement known as Imagism, a reaction against romanticism and symbolism and a champion of modern abstract art and anti-liberalism. He was killed in action in France in 1917. Very little of his work was published in his lifetime, but he became popular after his death. Speculations: essays on humanism and the philosophy of art was published in 1924 and Notes on language and style in 1929, both edited by HE Read. The collection consists of miscellaneous letters, photographs and notes, 1908-1938, collected by AR Jones in connection with his book The life and opinions of TE Hulme, published by Gollancz in 1960.

PHILIP ARTHUR LARKIN (1922-1985)

Born in Coventry and educated at King Henry VIII School there, Philip Larkin first showed his literary talent in regular contributions to the school magazine, The Coventrian. He gained a first class honours degree in English at St John's College, Oxford, in 1943. He then became a librarian, working successively in the public library at Wellington, and the libraries of Leicester University College and, from 1950, Queen's University, Belfast. In 1955 he was appointed Librarian of the University of Hull, where he remained until his death at the age of 63 in 1985. His first poem to achieve a national circulation was 'Ultimatum' in The Listener in 1940. Other poems were published in anthologies of Oxford poetry before his first personal collection, The north ship, appeared in 1945. This was followed by two novels, Jill (1946) and A girl in winter (1947). A lean period followed after the rejection by publishers of In the Grip of Light (1948), but he continued to write, and his next collection, The less deceived (1955) established him as a major poet. The Whitsun weddings (1964) won him the Queen's Gold Medal for Poetry. He edited The Oxford book of twentieth-century English verse (1973), and the last collection of his poems, High windows, appeared in 1974. The posthumous publication of his Collected poems (1988) and Selected letters (1989) revealed a much more prolific writer than had previously been imagined. He received many honours, including the CBE in 1975 and the Order of the Companion of Honour just before his death in 1985.

The Archives hold a number of research collections, the most important being the manuscripts deposited by the trustees of the Larkin Estate [DPL]. Highlights include poetry workbooks 2-8, as well as notebooks, typescripts and worksheets featuring early and variant drafts of poems and plays, drafts of the novels written under the pseudonym Brunette Coleman, photocopies of correspondence with Kingsley Amis during the 1940s and tape recordings of Larkin with Monica Jones and with his mother Eva. Larkin's correspondence with fellow poets, such as Douglas Dunn, Gavin Ewart, Anthony Thwaite, and Andrew Motion, and friends such as James Sutton and Colin Gunner, is also available. Other material includes correspondence with his bibliographer Barry Bloomfield, publishers such as Ted Tarling, colleagues such as

Brenda Moon and his professional correspondence as Librarian of the Brynmor Jones Library from 1955 to 1985 [LIB]. The Philip Larkin collection of published works by and about Larkin is described under RARE AND SPECIAL BOOK COLLECTIONS. There is also a more detailed subject guide on Philip Larkin in this series.

ROGER MCGOUGH (1937-)

Roger McGough was educated at Hull University before becoming well known as one of the Liverpool poets along with Adrian Henri and Brian Patten, producing The Mersey sound (1967), The Liverpool scene (1967) and New volume (1983). He was also a member of the pop group, Scaffold. He has subsequently published several personal volumes of poetry, including Selected poems 1967-1987 (1989) and children's books. He won a BAFTA award for Kurt, Mungo, BP and me (1984), and wrote the lyrics for Wind in the willows, performed on Broadway in 1985-86. The collection comprises four writing pads containing notes for and drafts of poems (1974-1976), and copies of two letters to and one from Philip Larkin.

E ARCHIE MARKHAM (1939-)

Archie Markham, the Anglo-Caribbean writer and poet, was born in Montserrat in 1939, and has lived mainly in Britain since the 1950s. He directed the Caribbean Theatre Workshop for a couple of years and, from 1972-74, was a member of the Cooperative Ouvriere du Batiment, restoring houses in the South of France. Markham has held residencies in various universities and colleges, including Creative Writing Fellow of Hull College of Higher Education, 1978/79. He has edited several literary magazines, including Sheffield Thursday and organises the annual, international Sheffield Thursday poetry and short story competitions. He is currently Professor of Creative Writing at Sheffield Hallam University.

Markham's work as a playwright has included Tim, I'm in danger of losing my respect for you (with others, Theatre 69); The masterpiece and, with the Caribbean Theatre Workshop (1970-71), The private life of the public man and Dropping out is violence. He has published several volumes of poetry, notably

Human rites (1984); Living in disguise (1986); Towards the end of a century (1989); Letter from Ulster & The Hugo poems (1993), and Misapprehensions (1995). In 1989 he edited Hinterland, the Bloodaxe book of Caribbean Poetry, and in 1996, The Penguin Book of Caribbean short stories. He has also written a travel book about Papua-New Guinea, and several collections of short stories. Markham's papers were purchased in several instalments and cover the full range of his literary work. The collection is not yet catalogued.

ANDREW MARVELL (1621-1678)

Andrew Marvell was born in Winestead, Holderness, and educated at Hull Grammar School and Trinity College, Cambridge. He was a tutor to Mary, daughter of the Parliamentary general Sir Thomas Fairfax, from 1650 to 1652, and wrote many of his best poems during these years, spent at Nun Appleton in Yorkshire. He acted as unofficial laureate to Cromwell from 1654 and succeeded Milton as Latin Secretary to the Council of State in 1657. He was elected MP for Hull in 1659 and continued to represent the city for the rest of his life. He was influential in releasing Milton from imprisonment in 1660. In his later years he was best known for his satires, such as Last instructions to a painter (1667), attacking corruption in court and government. Many of his poems were not published until after his death.

There are very few surviving letters by Marvell. The archives contain four original letters and one photocopy from the period 1673-1677-these form part of his correspondence with Sir Henry Thompson and his brother Edward, both wine merchants in York. With the exception of the photocopy letter, these have been published in the 3rd edition of H M Margoliouth's, The poems and letters of Andrew Marvell (1971). There are also holograph drafts of and notes for a book, The art of Marvell's poetry (1966), and lectures on Marvell by JB Leishman, 1955.

EDWARD HARRY WILLIAM MEYERSTEIN (1889-1952)

Meyerstein was a poet, scholar and man of letters. Born in London, he was educated at Harrow and Magdalen College, Cambridge. He joined the Department of Manuscripts in the British Museum in 1913 before serving in the 1914-1918 War.

Thereafter he became a full-time writer. His first publication was a slim volume of poetry, The door (1911). He subsequently produced many lyrical and narrative poems, translations, short stories, novels, plays and biographies. He died at his London home in September 1952. The Meyerstein collection contains about 300 items, including manuscripts of plays and poems. There are also about 200 letters and postcards to Donald Mitchell between 1944 and 1949. The Library also holds first editions of a number of his works, including The door.

ANDREW PETER MOTION (1952-)

After graduating from University College, Oxford in 1974, Motion became a lecturer in English at Hull between 1977 and 1981. His first collection of poems, The pleasure steamers was well received on its publication in 1978. He returned to Oxford as editor of Poetry Review (1981-1983), and worked as poetry editor at Chatto & Windus from 1983 to 1989 and subsequently with Faber & Faber. He was co-editor with Blake Morrison of the controversial Penguin book of contemporary English poetry (1982). He has published collections of poems, novels and criticisms and received a number of awards. In 1982 he became a Fellow of the Royal Society of Literature and he was appointed Poet Laureate in 1999. His first work on Philip Larkin appeared in the Contemporary Writers series in 1982. He is now a literary executor of the Larkin Estate and wrote the authorised biography, Philip Larkin: a writer's life (1993).

The Archives hold a working notebook containing nine poems dated 1976, as well as his correspondence with Philip Larkin over the period 1978 to 1984.

HUBERT NICHOLSON (1908-1996)

The journalist, poet and novelist Hubert Nicholson was born in Hull and worked on several provincial newspapers, including the Hull-based Eastern Morning News, before moving to London to work in Fleet Street. He joined Reuters after the war as a senior sub-editor, retiring in 1968. His first collection of poems to appear in print was Date (1935) and he continued to write poetry until late in life, publishing his Selected poems 1930-1980 in 1981. He also began writing novels in the 1930s, beginning with Face your lover (1935). His last novel, Late light, appeared in 1987. He founded the Epsom Poetry Group in 1950 and was literary executor to the poet ASJ Tessimond. His autobiography of life in artistic and literary circles in London in the 1920s and 1930s, Half my days and nights (1941), was reprinted in 1983 to favourable reviews. His literary output included over 30 books, including poetry, novels, criticism and plays.

His literary manuscripts and personal papers were acquired after his death in 1996 and span circa 1950 to 1979 [DNI]. The collection is not yet catalogued. A small set of typescript poems, letters to Barbara Elsdale and obituaries are also held.

PETER PINDAR (1738-1819)

John Wolcot was a physician and clergyman who wrote satirical verses under the name of Peter Pindar, caricaturing George III, Pitt, Boswell and others in works such as The Lousiad. He became blind late in life. The Archives hold about 120 manuscript sheets reputedly by Wolcot, comprising 19 poems (c. 1794-1819). There are also a number of his publications in the Library.

ALAN FREDERICK PLATER (1935-)

Alan Plater was brought up in Hull and educated at King's College, Newcastle. He trained and worked as an architect before becoming a freelance writer in 1960. He has written extensively for radio, television, the theatre, films and the press. He has won many awards, including a BAFTA award, and is a FRSL and FRSA. His stage works include Close the coalhouse door and Sweet sorrow, a play about Philip Larkin; and his film scripts The virgin and the gypsy. Amongst his television scripts there are individual plays, situation comedies, documentaries, series such as Z Cars and The Beiderbecke affair, and dramatisations such as The Barchester chronicles and the award winning Fortunes of war, based on the novels by Olivia Manning. His publications include books based on the Beiderbecke series and a number of plays.

Plater deposited the first instalment of his archive in 1992. This contains numerous scripts, drafts, plot schedules, letters and press cuttings, and his architectural thesis, with good coverage of all of the works highlighted above. Some of the works are still unpublished and unperformed. Two further deposits have been received, the most recent in 2004. This material remains uncatalogued, but includes a large amount of correspondence and audiotapes of programmes, radio plays and interviews, as well as further files on his works for stage and television.

HOWARD SERGEANT (1914-1987)

Herbert ('Howard') Sergeant was born in Hull and qualified as an accountant. He served in the RAF and the Air Ministry during the Second World War and with the assistance of his friend Lionel Monteith, edited and published the first issue of his poetry magazine Outposts in February 1944. Outposts is the longest running independent poetry magazine in Britain and over the decades, has specialised in publishing unrecognised poets alongside the well established. Sergeant had been writing poetry since childhood and his first poem to be published was 'Thistledown magic', in Chambers Journal in 1943. Sergeant's own poetry was included in the first issue of Outposts (but rarely thereafter) and his first published collection, The leavening air, appeared in 1946. He was involved in setting up the Dulwich Group (a branch of the British Poetry Association) in 1949, and again, when it re-formed in 1960.

In 1956, Sergeant published the first of the Outposts Modern Poets Series of booklets and hardbacks devoted to individual poets. During his lifetime he served on the Executive Councils of the PEN, the English Association, the National Book League and the Poetry Society, as well as on the panel of judges for the EC Gregory Awards. As a poetry editor he specialised particularly in anthologies of Commonwealth poetry and children's poetry. Alongside his literary work, he had a career first as a company accountant, and then from 1963, as a lecturer. He retired as head of the School of Management at Brooklands Technical College in Weybridge in 1978 and received an MBE in the same year. After a gap of many years, he began to write poetry again and several of his poetry collections date from the 1980s, including his Selected poems. After his death in 1987, the editorship of Outposts was taken over by Roland John.

The Sergeant archive was purchased from his widow, Jean Sergeant, in 1998 and provides extensive coverage of the full range of his literary work. The collection is catalogued in draft and includes correspondence with fellow poets, poetry and fiction by Sergeant, files relating to Outposts, files relating to anthologies edited by Sergeant, reviews, articles and lectures by and about him, and files relating to poetry competitions and awards.

STEVIE SMITH (1902-1971)

Florence Margaret ['Stevie'] Smith was born in Hull but lived in north London from the age of three. She worked as secretary to the publisher Sir Neville Pearson and later to Sir Frank Newnes. She won instant success with her first work, Novel on yellow paper (1936). Her poetry was at first less successful, but became known through her readings and broadcasts in the 1950s and 1960s, when she also achieved fame in America.

The Archives hold the typescript of Novel on yellow paper, with manuscript corrections and 32 pages of an earlier version, and seven letters to her friend Ladislav Horvat dating from 1957. A large roller blind on which she wrote a well-known stanza by Emperor Hadrian, beginning 'Animula vagula blandula', was purchased in 1980. The blind originally hung at the home of her friend Ronald Orr Ewing and Smith is said to have written the poem for him at a party in 1969. The Stevie Smith collection of published works is described under RARE AND SPECIAL BOOK COLLECTIONS.

ANTHONY SIMON THWAITE (1930-)

Anthony Thwaite studied at Christ Church, Oxford, and has lectured in a number of universities in Britain and overseas. His first collection of poetry was Home truths (1957). The stones of emptiness (1967) was awarded the Richard Hillary Prize in 1968. He received the Cholmondely Award for Poetry in 1983, became a Fellow of the Royal Society of Literature in 1978 and was awarded the OBE in 1990. In addition to poetry, he has written a number of volumes of criticism and travel, and has been literary editor of The Listener and New Statesman, co-editor of Encounter and Director of Andre Deutsch Ltd. He is a literary executor of the estate of Philip Larkin, for whom he produced

Larkin at sixty (1982), later editing The Collected poems (1988) and Selected letters (1992).

The collection includes manuscript drafts, typescripts and notebooks, chiefly relating to his poetry collections The owl in the tree (1963), The stones of emptiness (1967) and A portion for foxes (1977); and The deserts of Hesperides (1969), a travel book on Libya. There are typescripts of poems published in Wave and letters to pubiisher Harry Chambers. Also available are Thwaite's correspondence with Philip La over the period 1958 to 1985, his correspondence and other papers relating to Larkin at sixty and photocopies of several hundred letters assembled during his work on Larkin's Selected letters, including many not included in the published wor Henry Treece (1911-1966)

Born in Wednesbury, Staffordshire, Henry Treece won a scholarship to read English at Birmingham University, from which he graduated 1933. Apart from wartime service in the RAF, he spent the next 25 years as an English teacher in various places including Tynemouth and, from September 1938, at the Grammar School in Barton-on-Humber in Lincolnshire. He started to produce poetry in the late 1930s, and was joint leader (with JF Hendry) of a movement called the New Apocalypse, associated principally with Dylan Thomas.

Apart from his own poetry (published by Fortune Press and then Faber & Faber) he also edited anthologies such as The white horseman (1944). In the early 0s Treece moved to prose writing, including plays and novels, but principally stories for children, beginning with Legions of the Eagle (1954). A heart condition forced him to retire from teaching in 1959 to concentrate on his writing. He regularly gave public lectures, the last being on the topic of 'Perception and vision' at Hull's Regional College of Arts and Crafts on 1 June 1966.

He died of a heart attack on 10 June having just completed his last work The dream-time (published posthumously in 1967). His numerous publications included seven volumes of poetry and 35 books for children. The Treece collection includes the original manuscripts of The dream-tim otes for and script of his last lecture entitled 'Perception and Vision', and 54 letters from Treece to Antony Kamm, his editor at the Brockhampton Press.

VICKY (ALIAS OF VICTOR WEISZ) (1913-1966)

The celebrated c onist Vicky was born in Germany of Hungarian Jewish parents and was educated at Berlin Art School. His loathing of injustice and inhumanity led him to become a committed socialist without joining any political party. After publishing ant tler cartoons, he escaped to Britain in 1935. He became a cartoonist at the News Chronicle in 1941 and subsequently at the Daily Mirror, Evening Standard and New Statesman. Few public figures escaped his visual lampoons, but perhaps his most famous creation was 'Supermac'-Sir Harold Macmillan, the Prime Minister. He committed suicide in 1966. The Vicky archive covers 1937-1966 and includes nine scrap books of cartoons, 152 illustrated letters to his second wife, Lucielle Gray (November 1945-May 1946) and 269 letters to his fourth wife, Inge Lew (c. July 1962-February 1966)

Small Collections and Individual Items: Literature

There are 65 letters to the art and social critic John Ruskin (1819-1900) dated between 1863 and 1889, copies of 46 letters from him to a Mr Fletcher dated 1882-1887 [DP/8] and an undated letter from him to a Mrs Baines. There is a wide variety of material relating to the journalist, playwright and socialist George Bernard Shaw (1856-1950), mainly linked to his political interests. The papers of Robin Page Arnot include a file of letters and postcards from Shaw, 1941-1948, the annotated typescript of his article 'The Lysenko muddle', and papers of the Shaw Society, 1958-1972. The Forsyth-Major papers [q.v.] include eleven letters from Shaw between 1914 and 1944. There is also a letter by Shaw about evidence to be given to the Select Committee on Stage Plays in July 1919, and a letter to J Henry Lloyd dated July 1944. The papers of Professor TE Jessop include manuscripts and typescripts by his wife Dora Jessop, a lecturer in English literature in the Department of Adult Education at Hull-there are poems, articles, two novels The fortress and the bridge and Fantasia in C minor and a book, The pleasures of travel, written between 1918 and c.1960. Amongst the correspondence of Irene Forbes-Adam, there are four letters from Victoria ['Vita'] Sackville-West (1892-1962) from the 1920s and some 250 letters from Iris Origo (Marchesa Val D'Orcia) (1902-88) over the period 1916-1949

Small Collections and Individual Items: Poetry

There is a short untitled poem by John Adams from 1976 and the annotated typescript of 'Miss Very Rich has scrubbed a floor today' by Christopher Logue from 1960, also an undated typescript autobiographical note by Robert Conquest and an undated letter from C Day Lewis to Richard Church. There is correspondence, 1919-1945, from Hull poet J Redwood Anderson (1883-1964) to Frank Noble Wood and J Bertram Wood, with press cuttings relating to Anderson, and correspondence from Clifford Dyment (1914-1971) to J Bertram Wood. A small amount of original and photocopied material relating to Roden Noel (1834-1894), including manuscripts of several poems is in the collection of his son, Conrad Noel. There is correspondence from German poet Fritz Usinger (1895-1982) to Rex Last, Christine Barker and other members of the University of Hull between 1969 and 1973, and a transcript of a ta ecording of Usinger speaking about his poetry. There is a collection of autograph letters from poets WH Auden, TS Eliot, Ald Huxley and others addressed to Professor WS Vines in reply to his request to be allowed to include their work in an Anthology of English verse satire, 1914-1931. There are 269, largely unpublished, poems by the socialist Myfanwy Westrope. Letters and other items found on John Masefield's desk after his death in August 1967, regarding the Queen's Gold Medal for Poetry 1967 [the year it was awarded to Philip Larkin] are accompanied by one of his poems, `Des englischen Dichters Gruss an die andern Deutschen' ('Some verses to some Germans'). The corrected galley proofs of The Lady with the unicorn (1948), by the Welsh poet Vernon Watkins (1906-1967), were donated by Philip Larkin

Small Collections and Individual Items: Theatre

There is a manuscript volume entitled 'The dangers of a lea shore; or, An Impartial view of the Bath Theatre in the year 1759' by J Brownsmith in the hand of Myrton Hamilton. The papers of Reginald Bridgeman contain correspondence, rules, programmes and other papers of the Pioneer Theatre Society Limited, 1946-1952. There is a scrap album of press cuttings relating to Ellen Terry, Edith Craig and the Pioneer Players, 1913-18, with related photographs and other items. A small collection of playbills of the

Theatre Royal, Hull for 1833-34 is complemented by letters to John Brook of Messrs Brook & Bulmer, Solicitors, of York, secretary to the trustees of the Theatres Royal of York, Leeds, Hull, Doncaster and Wakefield (the York Circuit) between 1813 and 1833. The papers of the Trotskyist Jock Haston include the annotated typescript of the only play written by the West Indian author, CLR James (1901-1989), Toussaint l'Ouverture: the story of the only successful slave revolt in history, first staged in 1936 with Paul Robeson and James himself in the cast. There are scripts of several plays on the theme of anti-vivisection contained within the archives of the British Union for the Abolition of Vivisection, and of two plays on the theme of war and pacifism from the First World War period amongst the papers of P Smith. The Theatre Playbill Collection is described under RARE AND SPECIAL BOOK COLLECTIONS.

Small Collections and Individual Items: Miscellaneous

The papers of Jock Haston (1913-1986), Secretary of the Revolutionary Communist Party between 1944 and 1949, include correspondence with literary figures such as George Orwell and HG Wells. The papers of the trade union leader Julia Varley (1871-1952) include some of her prose writings and poems. A portfolio of items in the collection of ethical reformer and trade unionist J Henry Lloyd relating to brothers Karel Capek (1890-1938), a leading Czech dramatist of the inter-War years, and Josef Capek (1887-1945), principally an artist but collaborator with his brother in such works as The insect play, includes letters from them and notes on their work [DHL]. The papers of Sir Mark Sykes (1879-1919), Conservative MP for Central Hull and architect of the Sykes-Picot Agreement of 1916, include plays, poems and short stories by him, 1900-1918 [DDSY(2)/6/1-28]. There are poems and five plays by local writer Charles Hamilton Simms, c. 1825-1827 [DP/157/6-17] and an undated typescript of a play 'Gefahr der Klugheit' by Felix Sternheim [DP/154]. There are three letters from Anthony Powell to E Gillett in 1970 [DX/85/1] and a letter from Samuel Beckett to Professor WE Styler in 1963 [DX/81/2]. A collection of letters (1803-1912) thought to have been assembled by Elizabeth Lawton Thomassen contains letters from Leigh Hunt, Thomas Carlyle, Benjamin Disraeli and Ellen Terry [DX/163]. The archives of the National

Council for Civil Liberties (Liberty) include letters from many literary figures, including EM Forster and HG Wells [DCL]. The papers of Audrey Jupp-Thomas (1914-1994) include the typescripts of novels and a short story which she wrote in the late 1980s and early 1990s

THE EARLY TWENTIETH CENTURY

Irish drama flowered in the early 20th cent., largely under the aegis of the Abbey Theatre in Dublin. John Millington Synge, William Butler Yeats, and Sean O'Casey all wrote on Irish themes-mythical in Yeats's poetic drama, political in O'Casey's realistic plays. Also Irish, George Bernard Shaw wrote biting dramas that reflect all aspects of British society. In fact, many of the towering figures of 20th-century English literature were not English; Shaw, Yeats, Joyce, O'Casey, and Beckett were Irish, Dylan Thomas was Welsh, T. S. Eliot was born an American, and Conrad was Polish.

Poetry in the early 20th cent. was typified by the conventional romanticism of such poets as John Masefield, Alfred Noyes, and Walter de la Mare and by the experiments of the imagists, notably Hilda Doolittle (H. D.), Richard Aldington, Herbert Read, and D. H. Lawrence. The finest poet of the period was Yeats, whose poetry fused romantic vision with contemporary political and aesthetic concerns. Though the 19th-century tradition of the novel lived on in the work of Arnold Bennett, William Henry Hudson, and John Galsworthy, new writers like Henry James, H. G. Wells, and Joseph Conrad expressed the skepticism and alienation that were to become features of post-Victorian sensibility.

World War I shook England to the core. As social mores were shaken, so too were artistic conventions. The work of war poets like Siegfried Sassoon and Wilfred Owen, the latter killed in the war (as were Rupert Brooke and Isaac Rosenberg), was particularly influential. Ford Madox Ford's landmark tetralogy, Parade's End, is perhaps the finest depiction of the war and its effects. The new era called for new forms, typified by the work of Gerard Manley Hopkins, first published in 1918, and of T. S. Eliot, whose long poem The Waste Land (1922) was a watershed in both American and English literary history. Its difficulty, formal invention, and bleak antiromanticism were to influence poets for decades. Equally important was the novel Ulysses, also published in 1922, by the expatriate Irishman James Joyce. Although his books were controversial because of their freedom of language and content, Joyce's revolutions in narrative form, the treatment of time, and nearly all other techniques of the novel made him a master to be studied, but only intermittently copied. Though more conventional in form, the novels of D. H. Lawrence were equally challenging to convention; he was the first to champion both the primitive and the supercivilized urges of men and women.

Sensitivity and psychological subtlety mark the superb novels of Virginia Woolf, who, like Dorothy Richardson, experimented with the interior forms of narration. Woolf was the center of the brilliant Bloomsbury group, which included the novelist E. M. Forster, the biographer Lytton Strachey, and many important English intellectuals of the early 20th cent. Aldous Huxley and Evelyn Waugh satirized the group and the period, while Katharine Mansfield and Elizabeth Bowen captured their flavor in fiction.

Moved by the Great Depression, the rise of fascism, and English policies of appeasement, many writers and intellectuals sought solutions in the politics of the left-or the right. Wyndham Lewis satirized what he thought was the total dissolution of culture in Apes of Gods (1930). George Orwell fought with the Republicans in the Spanish Civil War. The experience left him profoundly disillusioned with Communism, a feeling he eloquently expressed in such works as Animal Farm (1946) and Nineteen Eighty-four (1949). The poets W. H. Auden, Christopher Isherwood, Stephen Spender, and C. Day Lewis all proclaimed their leftist respective political commitments, but the pressing demands of World War II superseded these long-term ideals.

7

The Journey of English Literature

English literature, literature written in English since c.1450 by the inhabitants of the British Isles; it was during the 15th cent. that the English language acquired much of its modern form. For the literature of previous linguistic periods, see the articles on Anglo-Saxon literature and Middle English literature.

For literature written by English speakers elsewhere, see American literature; Australian literature; Canadian literature, English; New Zealand literature; and South African literature.

THE TUDORS AND THE ELIZABETHAN AGE

The beginning of the Tudor dynasty coincided with the first dissemination of printed matter. William Caxton's press was established in 1476, only nine years before the beginning of Henry VII's reign. Caxton's achievement encouraged writing of all kinds and also influenced the standardization of the English language. The early Tudor period, particularly the reign of Henry VIII, was marked by a break with the Roman Catholic Church and a weakening of feudal ties, which brought about a vast increase in the power of the monarchy.

Stronger political relationships with the Continent were also developed, increasing England's exposure to Renaissance culture. Humanism became the most important force in English literary and intellectual life, both in its narrow sense-the study and imitation of the Latin classics-and in its broad sense-the affirmation of the secular, in addition to the otherworldly, concerns of people. These forces produced during the reign (1558-1603) of Elizabeth I one of the most fruitful eras in literary history.

The energy of England's writers matched that of its mariners and merchants. Accounts by men such as Richard Hakluyt, Samuel Purchas, and Sir Walter Raleigh were eagerly read. The activities and literature of the Elizabethans reflected a new nationalism, which expressed itself also in the works of chroniclers (John Stow, Raphael Holinshed, and others), historians, and translators and even in political and religious tracts. A myriad of new genres, themes, and ideas were incorporated into English literature. Italian poetic forms, especially the sonnet, became models for English poets.

Sir Thomas Wyatt was the most successful sonneteer among early Tudor poets, and was, with Henry Howard, earl of Surrey, a seminal influence. Tottel's Miscellany (1557) was the first and most popular of many collections of experimental poetry by different, often anonymous, hands. A common goal of these poets was to make English as flexible a poetic instrument as Italian. Among the more prominent of this group were Thomas Churchyard, George Gascoigne, and Edward de Vere, earl of Oxford. An ambitious and influential work was A Mirror for Magistrates (1559), a historical verse narrative by several poets that updated the medieval view of history and the morals to be drawn from it.

The poet who best synthesized the ideas and tendencies of the English Renaissance was Edmund Spenser. His unfinished epic poem The Faerie Queen (1596) is a treasure house of romance, allegory, adventure, Neoplatonic ideas, patriotism, and Protestant morality, all presented in a variety of literary styles. The ideal English Renaissance man was Sir Philip Sidney-scholar, poet, critic, courtier, diplomat, and soldier-who died in battle at the age of 32. His best poetry is contained in the sonnet sequence Astrophel and Stella (1591) and his Defence of Poesie is among the most important works of literary criticism in the tradition.

Many others in a historical era when poetic talents were highly valued, were skilled poets. Important late Tudor sonneteers include Spenser and Shakespeare, Michael Drayton, Samuel Daniel, and Fulke Greville. More versatile even than Sidney was Sir Walter Raleigh-poet, historian, courtier, explorer, and soldier-who wrote strong, spare poetry.

Early Tudor drama owed much to both medieval morality plays and classical models. Ralph Roister Doister (c.1545) by Nicholas Udall and Gammer Gurton's Needle (c.1552) are considered the first English comedies, combining elements of classical Roman comedy with native burlesque. During the late 16th and early 17th cent., drama flourished in England as never before or since. It came of age with the work of the University Wits, whose sophisticated plays set the course of Renaissance drama and paved the way for Shakespeare.

The Wits included John Lyly, famed for the highly artificial and much imitated prose work Euphues (1578); Robert Greene, the first to write romantic comedy; the versatile Thomas Lodge and Thomas Nashe; Thomas Kyd, who popularized neo-Senecan tragedy; and Christopher Marlowe, the greatest dramatist of the group. Focusing on heroes whose very greatness leads to their downfall, Marlowe wrote in blank verse with a rhetorical brilliance and eloquence superbly equal to the demands of high drama. William Shakespeare, of course, fulfilled the promise of the Elizabethan age. His history plays, comedies, and tragedies set a standard never again equaled, and he is universally regarded as the greatest dramatist and one of the greatest poets of all time.

THE JACOBEAN ERA, CROMWELL, AND THE RESTORATION

Elizabethan literature generally reflects the exuberant self-confidence of a nation expanding its powers, increasing its wealth, and thus keeping at bay its serious social and religious problems. Disillusion and pessimism followed, however, during the unstable reign of James I (1603-25). The 17th cent. was to be a time of great upheaval-revolution and regicide, restoration of the monarchy, and, finally, the victory of Parliament, landed Protestantism, and the moneyed interests.

Jacobean literature begins with the drama, including some of Shakespeare's greatest, and darkest, plays. The dominant literary figure of James's reign was Ben Jonson, whose varied and dramatic works followed classical models and were enriched by his worldly, peculiarly English wit. His satiric dramas, notably the great Volpone (1606), all take a cynical view of human nature. Also cynical were the horrific revenge tragedies of John Ford,

Thomas Middleton, Cyril Tourneur, and John Webster (the best poet of this grim genre). Novelty was in great demand, and the possibilities of plot and genre were exploited almost to exhaustion. Still, many excellent plays were written by men such as George Chapman, the masters of comedy Thomas Dekker and Philip Massinger, and the team of Francis Beaumont and John Fletcher. Drama continued to flourish until the closing of the theaters at the onset of the English Revolution in 1642.

The foremost poets of the Jacobean era, Ben Jonson and John Donne, are regarded as the originators of two diverse poetic traditions-the Cavalier and the metaphysical. Jonson and Donne shared not only a common fund of literary resources, but also a dryness of wit and precision of expression. Donne's poetry is distinctive for its passionate intellection, Jonson's for its classicism and urbane guidance of passion.

Although George Herbert and Donne were the principal metaphysical poets, the meditative religious poets Henry Vaughan and Thomas Traherne were also influenced by Donne, as were Abraham Cowley and Richard Crashaw. The greatest of the Cavalier poets was the sensuously lyrical Robert Herrick. Such other Cavaliers as Thomas Carew, Sir John Suckling, and Richard Lovelace were lyricists in the elegant Jonsonian tradition, though their lyricism turned political during the English Revolution. Although ranked with the metaphysical poets, the highly individual Andrew Marvell partook of the traditions of both Donne and Jonson.

Among the leading prose writers of the Jacobean period were the translators who produced the classic King James Version of the Bible (1611) and the divines Lancelot Andrewes, Jeremy Taylor, and John Donne. The work of Francis Bacon helped shape philosophical and scientific method. Robert Burton's Anatomy of Melancholy (1621) offers a varied, virtually encyclopedic view of the moral and intellectual preoccupations of the 17th cent. Like Burton, Sir Thomas Browne sought to reconcile the mysteries of religion with the newer mysteries of science. Izaak Walton, author of The Compleat Angler (1653), produced a number of graceful biographies of prominent writers. Thomas Hobbes wrote the most influential political treatise of the age, Leviathan (1651).

The Jacobean era's most fiery and eloquent author of political tracts (many in defense of Cromwell's government, of which he was a member) was also one of the greatest of all English poets, John Milton. His Paradise Lost (1667) is a Christian epic of encompassing scope. In Milton the literary and philosophical heritage of the Renaissance merged with Protestant political and moral conviction.

With the restoration of the English monarchy in the person of Charles II, literary tastes widened. The lifting of Puritan restrictions and the reassembling of the court led to a relaxation of restraints, both moral and stylistic, embodied in such figures as the Earl of Rochester. Restoration comedy reveals both the influence of French farce (the English court spent its exile in France) and of Jacobean comedy. It generously fed the public's appetite for broad satire, high style, and a licentiousness that justified the worst Puritan imaginings. Such dramatists as Sir George Etherege, William Wycherley, and William Congreve created superbly polished high comedy. Sparkling but not quite so brilliant were the plays of George Farquhar, Thomas Shadwell, and Sir John Vanbrugh.

John Dryden began as a playwright but became the foremost poet and critic of his time. His greatest works are satirical narrative poems, notably Absalom and Achitophel (1681), in which prominent contemporary figures are unmistakably and devastatingly portrayed. Another satiric poet of the period was Samuel Butler, whose Hudibras (1663) satirizes Puritanism together with all the intellectual pretensions of the time. During the Restoration Puritanism or, more generally, the Dissenting tradition, remained vital. The most important Dissenting literary work was John Bunyan's Pilgrim's Progress (1675), an allegorical prose narrative that is considered a forerunner of the novel. Lively and illuminating glimpses of Restoration manners and mores are provided by the diaries of Samuel Pepys and John Evelyn.

THE EIGHTEENTH CENTURY

The Glorious Revolution of 1688 firmly established a Protestant monarchy together with effective rule by Parliament. The new science of the time, Newtonian physics, reinforced the belief that everything, including human conduct, is guided by a rational order. Moderation and common sense became intellectual values as well as standards of behavior.

These values achieved their highest literary expression in the poetry of Alexander Pope. Pope-neoclassicist, wit, and master of the heroic couplet-was critical of human foibles but generally confident that order and happiness in human affairs were attainable if excesses were eschewed and rational dictates heeded. The brilliant prose satirist Jonathan Swift was not so sanguine. His "savage indignation" resulted in devastating attacks on his age in A Tale of a Tub (1704), Gulliver's Travels (1726), and A Modest Proposal (1729).

Middle-class tastes were reflected in the growth of periodicals and newspapers, the best of which were the Tatler and the Spectator produced by Joseph Addison and Sir Richard Steele. The novels of Daniel Defoe, the first modern novels in English, owe much to the techniques of journalism. They also illustrate the virtues of merchant adventure vital to the rising middle class. Indeed, the novel was to become the literary form most responsive to middle-class needs and interests.

The 18th cent. was the age of town life with its coffeehouses and clubs. One of the most famous of the latter was the Scriblerus Club, whose members included Pope, Swift, and John Gay (author of The Beggar's Opera). Its purpose was to defend and uphold high literary standards against the rising tide of middle-class values and tastes. Letters were a popular form of polite literature. Pope, Swift, Horace Walpole, and Thomas Gray were masters of the form, and letters make up the chief literary output of Lady Mary Wortley Montagu and Lord Chesterfield. The novels of Samuel Richardson, including the influential Clarissa (1747), were written in epistolary form. With the work of Richardson, Fanny Burney, Henry Fielding, Tobias Smollett, and Laurence Sterne the English novel flourished.

Probably the most celebrated literary circle in history was the one dominated by Samuel Johnson. It included Joshua Reynolds, David Garrick, Edmund Burke, Oliver Goldsmith, and James Boswell, whose biography of Johnson is a classic of the genre. Other great master prose writers of the period were the historian Edward Gibbon and the philosopher David Hume. Dr.

Johnson, who carried the arts of criticism and conversation to new heights, both typified and helped to form mid-18th-century views of life, literature, and conduct. The drama of the 18th cent, failed to match that of the Restoration. But Oliver Goldsmith and Richard Brinsley Sheridan rose above the prevalent "weeping comedy"-whose sentimentalism infected every literary genre of the period-to achieve polished comedy in the Restoration tradition.

Among the prominent poets of the 18th cent. were James Thomson, who wrote in The Seasons (1726) of nature as it reflected the Newtonian concept of order and beauty, and Edward Young, whose Night Thoughts (1742) combined melancholy and Christian apologetics. Anticipations of romanticism can be seen in the odes of William Collins, the poems of Thomas Gray, and the Scots lyrics of Robert Burns. The work of William Blake, the first great romantic poet, began late in the 18th cent. Blake is unique: poet, artist, artisan, revolutionist, and visionary prophet.

In prose fiction, departures from social realism are evident in the Gothic romances of Horace Walpole, Anne Radcliffe, "Monk" Lewis, Charles Maturin, and others. These works catered to a growing interest in medievalism, northern antiquities, ballads, folklore, chivalry, and romance, also exploited in two masterpieces of forgery-the Ossian poems of James Macpherson and the "medieval" Rowley poems of Thomas Chatterton.

THE ROMANTIC PERIOD

At the turn of the century, fired by ideas of personal and political liberty and of the energy and sublimity of the natural world, artists and intellectuals sought to break the bonds of 18th-century convention. Although the works of Jean Jacques Rousseau and William Godwin had great influence, the French Revolution and its aftermath had the strongest impact of all. In England initial support for the Revolution was primarily utopian and idealist, and when the French failed to live up to expectations, most English intellectuals renounced the Revolution. However, the romantic vision had taken forms other than political, and these developed apace.

In Lyrical Ballads (1798 and 1800), a watershed in literary history, William Wordsworth and Samuel Taylor Coleridge presented and illustrated a liberating aesthetic: poetry should express, in genuine language, experience as filtered through personal emotion and imagination; the truest experience was to be found in nature. The concept of the Sublime strengthened this turn to nature, because in wild countrysides the power of the sublime could be felt most immediately. Wordsworth's romanticism is probably most fully realized in his great autobiographical poem, "The Prelude" (1805-50). In search of sublime moments, romantic poets wrote about the marvelous and supernatural, the exotic, and the medieval. But they also found beauty in the lives of simple rural people and aspects of the everyday world.

The second generation of romantic poets included John Keats, Percy Bysshe Shelley, and George Gordon, Lord Byron. In Keats's great odes, intellectual and emotional sensibility merge in language of great power and beauty. Shelley, who combined soaring lyricism with an apocalyptic political vision, sought more extreme effects and occasionally achieved them, as in his great drama Prometheus Unbound (1820). His wife, Mary Wollstonecraft Shelley, wrote the greatest of the Gothic romances, Frankenstein (1818).

Lord Byron was the prototypical romantic hero, the envy and scandal of the age. He has been continually identified with his own characters, particularly the rebellious, irreverent, erotically inclined Don Juan. Byron invested the romantic lyric with a rationalist irony. Minor romantic poets include Robert Southey-best-remembered today for his story "Goldilocks and the Three Bears"-Leigh Hunt, Thomas Moore, and Walter Savage Landor.

The romantic era was also rich in literary criticism and other nonfictional prose. Coleridge proposed an influential theory of literature in his Biographia Literaria (1817). William Godwin and his wife, Mary Wollstonecraft, wrote ground-breaking books on human, and women's, rights. William Hazlitt, who never forsook political radicalism, wrote brilliant and astute literary criticism. The master of the personal essay was Charles Lamb, whereas Thomas De Quincey was master of the personal confession. The periodicals Edinburgh Review and Blackwood's Magazine, in which leading writers were published throughout the century, were major forums of controversy, political as well as literary.

Although the great novelist Jane Austen wrote during the romantic era, her work defies classification. With insight, grace, and irony she delineated human relationships within the context of English country life. Sir Walter Scott, Scottish nationalist and romantic, made the genre of the historical novel widely popular. Other novelists of the period were Maria Edgeworth, Edward Bulwer-Lytton, and Thomas Love Peacock, the latter noted for his eccentric novels satirizing the romantics.

THE VICTORIAN AGE

The Reform Bill of 1832 gave the middle class the political power it needed to consolidate-and to hold-the economic position it had already achieved. Industry and commerce burgeoned. While the affluence of the middle class increased, the lower classes, thrown off their land and into the cities to form the great urban working class, lived ever more wretchedly. The social changes were so swift and brutal that Godwinian utopianism rapidly gave way to attempts either to justify the new economic and urban conditions, or to change them. The intellectuals and artists of the age had to deal in some way with the upheavals in society, the obvious inequities of abundance for a few and squalor for many, and, emanating from the throne of Queen Victoria (1837-1901), an emphasis on public rectitude and moral propriety.

THE NOVEL

The Victorian era was the great age of the English novel-realistic, thickly plotted, crowded with characters, and long. It was the ideal form to describe contemporary life and to entertain the middle class. The novels of Charles Dickens, full to overflowing with drama, humor, and an endless variety of vivid characters and plot complications, nonetheless spare nothing in their portrayal of what urban life was like for all classes. William Makepeace Thackeray is best known for Vanity Fair (1848), which wickedly satirizes hypocrisy and greed.

Emily Brontë's single novel, Wuthering Heights (1847), is a unique masterpiece propelled by a vision of elemental passions but controlled by an uncompromising artistic sense. The fine novels of Emily's sister Charlotte Brontë, especially Jane Eyre (1847) and Villette (1853), are more rooted in convention, but daring in their own ways. The novels of George Eliot (Mary Ann

Evans) appeared during the 1860s and 70s. A woman of great erudition and moral fervor, Eliot was concerned with ethical conflicts and social problems. George Meredith produced comic novels noted for their psychological perception. Another novelist of the late 19th cent. was the prolific Anthony Trollope, famous for sequences of related novels that explore social, ecclesiastical, and political life in England.

Thomas Hardy's profoundly pessimistic novels are all set in the harsh, punishing midland county he called Wessex. Samuel Butler produced novels satirizing the Victorian ethos, and Robert Louis Stevenson, a master of his craft, wrote arresting adventure fiction and children's verse. The mathematician Charles Lutwidge Dodgson, writing under the name Lewis Carroll, produced the complex and sophisticated children's classics Alice's Adventures in Wonderland (1865) and Through the Looking Glass (1871). Lesser novelists of considerable merit include Benjamin Disraeli, George Gissing, Elizabeth Gaskell, and Wilkie Collins. By the end of the period, the novel was considered not only the premier form of entertainment but also a primary means of analyzing and offering solutions to social and political problems.

NONFICTION

Among the Victorian masters of nonfiction were the great Whig historian Thomas Macaulay and Thomas Carlyle, the historian, social critic, and prophet whose rhetoric thundered through the age. Influential thinkers included John Stuart Mill, the great liberal scholar and philosopher; Thomas Henry Huxley, a scientist and popularizer of Darwinian theory; and John Henry, Cardinal Newman, who wrote earnestly of religion, philosophy, and education. The founders of Communism, Karl Marx and Friedrich Engels, researched and wrote their books in the free environment of England. The great art historian and critic John Ruskin also concerned himself with social and economic problems. Matthew Arnold's theories of literature and culture laid the foundations for modern literary criticism, and his poetry is also notable.

POETRY

The preeminent poet of the Victorian age was Alfred, Lord Tennyson. Although romantic in subject matter, his poetry was tempered by personal melancholy; in its mixture of social certitude and religious doubt it reflected the age. The poetry of Robert Browning and his wife, Elizabeth Barrett Browning, was immensely popular, though Elizabeth's was more venerated during their lifetimes. Browning is best remembered for his superb dramatic monologues. Rudyard Kipling, the poet of the empire triumphant, captured the quality of the life of the soldiers of British expansion. Some fine religious poetry was produced by Francis Thompson, Alice Meynell, Christina Rossetti, and Lionel Johnson.

In the middle of the 19th cent. the so-called Pre-Raphaelites, led by the painter-poet Dante Gabriel Rossetti, sought to revive what they judged to be the simple, natural values and techniques of medieval life and art. Their quest for a rich symbolic art led them away, however, from the mainstream. William Morris-designer, inventor, printer, poet, and social philosopher-was the most versatile of the group, which included the poets Christina Rossetti and Coventry Patmore.

Algernon Charles Swinburne began as a Pre-Raphaelite but soon developed his own classically influenced, sometimes florid style. A. E. Housman and Thomas Hardy, Victorian figures who lived on into the 20th cent., share a pessimistic view in their poetry, but Housman's well-constructed verse is rather more superficial. The great innovator among the late Victorian poets was the Jesuit priest Gerard Manley Hopkins. The concentration and originality of his imagery, as well as his jolting meter ("sprung rhythm"), had a profound effect on 20th-century poetry.

During the 1890s the most conspicuous figures on the English literary scene were the decadents. The principal figures in the group were Arthur Symons, Ernest Dowson, and, first among them in both notoriety and talent, Oscar Wilde. The Decadents' disgust with bourgeois complacency led them to extremes of behavior and expression. However limited their accomplishments, they pointed out the hypocrisies in Victorian values and institutions. The sparkling, witty comedies of Oscar Wilde and the comic operettas of W. S. Gilbert and Sir Arthur Sullivan were perhaps the brightest achievements of 19th-century British drama.

THE POSTWAR ERA TO THE PRESENT

After the war most English writers chose to focus on aesthetic or social rather than political problems; C. P. Snow was perhaps the notable exception.

The novelists Henry Green, Ivy Compton-Burnett, Joyce Cary, and Lawrence Durrell, and the poets Robert Graves, Edwin Muir, Louis MacNeice, and Edith Sitwell tended to cultivate their own distinctive voices. Other novelists and playwrights of the 1950s, often called the angry young men, expressed a deep dissatisfaction with British society, combined with despair that anything could be done about it.

While the postwar era was not a great period of English literature, it produced a variety of excellent critics, including William Empson, Frank Kermode, and F. R. Leavis. The period was also marked by a number of highly individual novelists, including Kingsley Amis, Anthony Burgess, William Golding, Doris Lessing, Iris Murdoch, and Muriel Spark. Anthony Powell and Richard Hughes continued to work in the expansive 19th-century tradition, producing a series of realistic novels chronicling life in England during the 20th cent.

Some of the most exciting work of the period came in the theater, notably the plays of John Osborne, Harold Pinter, Tom Stoppard, David Storey, and Arnold Wesker. Among the best postwar British authors were the Welsh poet Dylan Thomas and the Irish expatriate novelist and playwright Samuel Beckett.

Thomas's lyricism and rich imagery reaffirmed the romantic spirit, and he was eventually appreciated for his technical mastery as well. Beckett, who wrote many of his works in French and translated them into English, is considered the greatest exponent of the theater of the absurd. His uncompromisingly bleak, difficult plays (and novels) depict the lonely, alienated human condition with compassion and humor.

Other outstanding contemporary poets include Hugh MacDiarmid, the leading figure of the Scottish literary renaissance; Ted Hughes, whose harsh, postapocalyptic poetry celebrates simple survival, and Seamus Heaney, an Irish poet who is hailed for his exquisite style. Novelists generally have found as little in the Thatcher and Major eras as in the previous period to inspire them, but the work of Margaret Drabble, John Fowles, David Lodge stands out, and the Scottish writer James Kelman stands out.

EPIC POETRY-

The epic is a broadly defined genre of poetry, and one of the major forms of narrative literature. It retells in a continuous narrative the life and works of a heroic or mythological person or group of persons. In the West, the Iliad, Odyssey and Nibelungenlied; and in the East, the Epic of Gilgamesh, Mahabharata, Ramayana, Shahnama and Epic of King Gesar are often cited as examples of the epic genre. The composition of epic poetry, or of long poems in general, has become uncommon in the Western world since the early 20th century. The meaning of the term epic, however, has evolved to refer to prose works, films, and similar works which are characterized by great length, multiple settings, large numbers of characters, or long span of time involved. As a result of this change in the use of the word, many prose works of the past may be called "epics" which were not composed or originally understood as such.

Oral Epics or World Folk Epics

The first epics are associated strongly with preliterate societies and oral poetic traditions. In these traditions, poetry is transmitted to the audience and from performer to performer by purely oral means. Studies of living oral epic traditions in the Balkans by Milman Parry and Albert Lord demonstrated the paratactic model used for composing these poems. What they demonstrated was that oral epics tend to be constructed in short episodes, each of equal status, interest and importance. This facilitates memorisation, as the poet is recalling each episode and using them to recreate the entire epic as they perform it.

Parry and Lord also showed that the most likely source for written texts of the epics of Homer was dictation from an oral performance.

Epics in Literate Societies

Literate societies have often copied the epic format; the earliest European examples of which the text survives are the Argonautica of Apollonius of Rhodes and Virgil's Aeneid, which follow both the style and subject matter of Homer. Other obvious examples are Nonnus' Dionysiaca, Tulsidas' Sri Ramacharit Manas, which follows the style and subject matter of Valmiki's Ramayana, and the Persian epic Shahnama by Ferdowsi.

Classical epic conventions include:

Invocation (prayer to the inspiring muse [of the epic]), praepositio (introduction of the epic's theme), enumeratio (counting the fighting heroes and their armies), the principles termed "in medias res" (starting from the middle of an event), Deus ex machina (divine intervention), anticipatio (prediction), and Epithet (permanent attributes of a heroic figure).

Notable Epic Poems

This list can be compared with two others, National epic and List of world folk-epics.

Ancient Epics (to 500)

- 20th century BC:
  - o Epic of Gilgamesh (Mesopotamian mythology)
- 18th century BC:
  - o Atrahasis (Mesopotamian mythology)
- 8th to 6th century BC:
  - o Enuma Elish (Babylonian mythology)
  - o Iliad, ascribed to Homer (Greek mythology)
  - o Odyssey, ascribed to Homer (Greek mythology)
  - o Jaya, ascribed to Vyasa (Hindu mythology)
  - o Lost Greek epics ascribed to the Cyclic poets:
- Epic Cycle including Cypria, Aethiopis, Little Iliad, Sack of Troy, Return from Troy, Telegony
- Theban Cycle including Oedipodea, Thebaid, Epigoni (epic), Alcmeonis
- Others: Titanomachy, Heracleia, Capture of Oechalia, Naupactia, Phocais, Minyas, Danais
- 7th to 5th century BC:
  - o Bharata, ascribed to Vaisampayana (Hindu mythology)

- 6th to 4th century BC:
  - o Mahabharata, ascribed to Ugrasravas (Hindu mythology)
  - o Ramayana, ascribed to Valmiki (Hindu mythology)
  - o Lost Greek epics: poems by Aristeas (Arimaspeia), Asius of Samos, Chersias of Orchomenus
  - o The Book of Job
- 3rd century BC:
  - o Argonautica by Apollonius of Rhodes
- 2nd century BC:
  - o Annales by Ennius
- 1st century BC:
  - o De Rerum Natura (On the Nature of Things) by Lucretius
  - o Aeneid by Virgil
  - o Kumaarasambhavam by Kalidasa (Indian epic poetry)
- 1st century AD:
  - o Metamorphoses by Ovid
  - o Pharsalia (Bellum Civile or Civil War) by Lucan
  - o Punica (Bellum Punicum or Punic War) by Silius Italicus
  - o Argonautica by Gaius Valerius Flaccus
  - o Thebaid by Statius
- 2nd century:
  - o Buddhacarita by Asvaghona (Indian epic poetry)
- 2nd to 5th century:
  - o The Five Great Epics of Tamil Literature:
- Cilappatikaram by Prince Ilango Adigal
- Manimekalai by Seethalai Saathanar
- Civaka Cintamani by Tirutakakatevar
- Valayapati by a Jaina poet

- Kundalakesi by a Buddhist poet
- 3rd century:
    - o Posthomerica by Quintus of Smyrna
- 4th century:
    - o Evangeliorum libri by Juvencus
- 5th century:
    - o Dionysiaca by Nonnus

Medieval Epics (500-1500)

- 8th to 10th century:
    - o Beowulf (retelling of Anglo-Saxon legends)
    - o Waldere, Old English version of the story told in Waltharius, known only as a brief fragment
- 9th century:
    - o The Book of One Thousand and One Nights (Arabian Nights) compiled by Abu abd-Allah Muhammed el-Gahshigar from earlier sources
    - o Bhagavata Purana (Sanskrit "Stories of the Lord") written from earlier sources
- 10th century:
    - o Shahnama by Firdowsi (Persian mythology)
    - o Waltharius by Ekkehard of St Gall, Latin version of the story of Walter of Aquitaine
    - o The Battle of Maldon, brief Old English epic describing a recent battle
- 11th century:
    - o Poetic Edda (Norse mythology) (collection of poems of Norse mythology from various sources; dates of composition vary within the collection, but the majority of poems existed before the 12th century based on the excerpts in the Prose Edda)
    - o Ruodlieb, Latin epic by a German author
    - o Digenis Akritas (Byzantine epic poem)
    - o La Chanson de Roland (The Song of Roland)

  - Epic of King Gesar (Tibetan epic; compiled from earlier sources)
  - Epic of Manas (possibly later)
- 12th century:
  - The Knight in the Panther Skin by Shota Rustaveli
  - Alexandreis, Latin epic by Walter of Châtillon
  - De bello Troiano and the lost Antiocheis by Joseph of Exeter
  - Carmen de Prodicione Guenonis (Latin version of the story of the Song of Roland)
  - Architrenius, satirical Latin epic by John of Hauville
  - Liber ad honorem Augusti by Peter of Eboli, Latin narrative of the conquest of Sicily by Henry VI, Holy Roman Emperor
- 13th century:
  - Nibelungenlied (Germanic mythology)
  - Brut by Layamon
  - Chanson de la Croisade Albigeoise ("Song of the Albigensian Crusade"; Occitan)
  - Epic of Sundiata
  - El Cantar de Mio Cid, Spanish epic of the Reconquista
  - De triumphis ecclesiae, Latin literary epic by Johannes de Garlandia
- 14th century:
  - Cursor Mundi by an anonymous cleric (c. 1300)
  - Divina Commedia (The Divine Comedy) by Dante Alighieri
  - Africa, Latin literary epic by Petrarch
  - The Canterbury Tales by Geoffrey Chaucer
  - The Tale of the Heike (Japanese epic war tale)
- 15th century:
  - Alliterative Morte Arthure
  - Orlando innamorato by Matteo Maria Boiardo (1495)

Modern Epics (from 1500)

- 16th century:
  - Orlando furioso by Ludovico Ariosto (1516)
  - Os Lusíadas by Luís de Camões (c.1555)
  - La Gerusalemme liberata by Torquato Tasso (1575)
  - Ramacharitamanasa (based on the Ramayana) by Goswami Tulsidas (1577)
  - Lepanto by King James VI of Scotland (1591)
  - Matilda by Michael Drayton (1594)
  - The Faerie Queene by Edmund Spenser (1596)
- 17th century:
  - The Barons' Wars by Michael Drayton (1603; early version 1596 entitled Mortimeriados)
  - Szigeti veszedelem, also known under the Latin title Carmen Obsidionis Szigetianae, a Hungarian epic by Miklós Zrínyi (1651)
  - Paradise Lost by John Milton (1667)
  - Paradise Regained by John Milton (1671)
  - Prince Arthur by Richard Blackmore (1695)
  - King Arthur by Richard Blackmore (1697)
- 18th century:
  - Eliza by Richard Blackmore (1705)
  - Redemption by Richard Blackmore (1722)
  - Henriade by Voltaire (1723)
  - Alfred by Richard Blackmore (1723)
  - Utendi wa Tambuka by Bwana Mwengo (1728)
  - Leonidas by Richard Glover (1737)
  - Epigoniad by William Wilkie (1757)
  - The Works of Ossian by James MacPherson (1765)
  - Caoineadh Airt Uí Laoghaire** by Eibhlín Dubh Ní Chonaill (1773)
  - Der Messias by Friedrich Gottlieb Klopstock (1773)

- Rossiada by Mikhail Matveyevich Kheraskov (1771-1779)
- Vladimir by Mikhail Matveyevich Kheraskov (1785)
- Athenaid by Richard Glover (1787)

- 19th century:
  - Columbiad by Joel Barlow (1807)
  - Milton: a Poem by William Blake (1804-1810)
  - Hyperion by John Keats (1818)
  - L'Orléanide, Poème national en vingt-huit chants, by Philippe-Alexandre Le Brun de Charmettes (1821)
  - Don Juan by George Gordon Byron, 6th Baron Byron (1824)
  - Pan Tadeusz by Adam Mickiewicz (1834)
  - Smrt Smail-age Cengica by Ivan Ma□uranic (1846)
  - Kalevala by Elias Lönnrot (1849 Finnish mythology)
  - The Prelude by William Wordsworth
  - The Song of Hiawatha by Henry Wadsworth Longfellow (1855)
  - La Fin de Satan by Victor Hugo (written between 1855 and 1860, published in 1886)
  - La Légende des Siècles (The Legend of the Centuries) by Victor Hugo (1859-1877)
  - Clarel by Herman Melville (1876)
  - Canigó by Jacint Verdaguer (1886)
- 20th century:
  - Lahuta e Malcís by Gjergj Fishta (composed 1902-1937)
  - The Ballad of the White Horse by G K Chesterton (1911)
  - Mensagem by Fernando Pessoa
  - The Hashish-Eater; Or, The Apocalypse of Evil by Clark Ashton Smith (1920)

- o Savitri by Aurobindo Ghose (1950)
- o Astronautilía-Hvezdoplavba by Jan Kresadlo
- o The Odyssey: A Modern Sequel by Nikos Kazantzakis (Greek verse, composed 1924-1938)
- o The Cantos by Ezra Pound (composed 1915-1969)
- o A Cycle of the West by John Neihardt (composed 1921-1949)
- o "A" by Louis Zukofsky (composed 1928-1968)
- o Paterson by William Carlos Williams (composed c.1940-1961)
- o The Maximus Poems by Charles Olson (composed 1950-1970)
- o Aniara by Harry Martinson (composed 1956)
- o Libretto for the Republic of Liberia by Melvin B. Tolson (1953)
- o Mountains and Rivers Without End by Gary Snyder (composed 1965-1996)
- o The Changing Light at Sandover by James Merrill (composed 1976-1982)
- o Omeros by Derek Walcott (1990)
- o Cheikh Anta Diop: Poem for the Living by Mwatabu S. Okantah (1997)

Prose "Epics"

Mythological:

- Shahnameh (Persian mythology) (prose and verse)
- Alpamysh (Central Asian) (prose and verse)
- Táin Bó Cúailnge (Irish mythology) (prose and verse)
- Hervarar saga (Norse mythology) (prose)
- Völsunga saga (Norse mythology) (prose)

14th century:

- Romance of the Three Kingdoms by Chinese author Luo Guanzhong (1330-1400)

16th to 18th Century:

- Journey to the West by Chinese author Wu Cheng'en (1590)
- Don Quixote Parts I & II by Miguel de Cervantes (prose 1605/1615)
- The History of Tom Jones, a Foundling by Henry Fielding (prose 1749)

19th Century:

- The Count of Monte Cristo by Alexandre Dumas, père (prose 1844)
- Moby-Dick by Herman Melville (prose 1851)
- Les Miserables by Victor Hugo (prose 1862)
- War and Peace by Leo Tolstoy (prose 1869)
- Venezuela Heroica, by Eduardo Blanco (history 1881)

20th Century:

- The Making of Americans by Gertrude Stein (prose composed 1906-1908, published 1925)
- À la recherche du temps perdu by Marcel Proust (prose composed 1913-1922, published 1914-1927)
- Ulysses and Finnegans Wake by James Joyce (prose 1922 and 1939)
- The Lord of the Rings and The Silmarillion by J.R.R. Tolkien (prose 1954 and 1977)
- The Recognitions and J R by William Gaddis (prose 1955 and 1975)
- Gravity's Rainbow, Mason & Dixon and Against the Day by Thomas Pynchon (prose 1973, 1997 and 2006)
- Infinite Jest by David Foster Wallace (prose 1996)

Other "Epics"

- The Anathemata by David Jones (1952)
- The Waste Land and The Four Quartets by T. S. Eliot
- Der Ring des Nibelungen by Richard Wagner (opera)

ROMANCE (GENRE)

As a literary genre, romance or chivalric romance refers to a style of heroic prose and verse narrative current in Europe from the Middle Ages to the Renaissance.

Characteristics of the Romance

The term was coined to distinguish popular material in the vernacular (at first the Romance languages French, Portuguese and Spanish, later German, English and others) from scholarly and ecclesiastical literature in Latin.

The boundaries between the romance and the chansons de geste of the troubadours were somewhat fluid. In general, the ballads were the property of professional performers, while the romance was associated more with amateurs and private readers. Nevertheless, a professional poet-performer like Chrétien de Troyes could turn his hand to composing romances. The distinction between an early verse romance and a chanson de geste is often difficult, and perhaps unnecessary, to make.

Unlike the novel (nouvelle romaine or "new romance") and like the chansons de geste, the romance dealt with traditional themes, above all three thematic cycles of tales, assembled in imagination at a late date as the Matter of Rome (actually centered on the life and deeds of Alexander the Great), the Matter of France (Charlemagne and Roland, his principal paladin) and the Matter of Britain (the lives and deeds of King Arthur and the Knights of the Round Table, within which was incorporated the quest for Holy Grail). The Acritic songs (dealing with Digenis Acritas and his fellow frontiersmen) resemble much the chanson de geste, though they developed simultaneously but separately.

A related tradition existed in Northern Europe, and comes down to us in the form of epics, such as Beowulf and the Nibelungenlied. However, the richest set of Germanic Romantic literature comes from Scandinavia in the form of the Fornaldarsagas. The setting is Scandinavia, but occasionally it moves temporarily to more distant and exotic locations. There are also very often mythological elements, such as gods, dwarves, elves, dragons, giants and magic swords. The heroes often embark on dangerous quests where they fight the forces of evil, dragons, witchkings, barrow-wights, and rescue fair maidens.

Many or most of the sagas are based on distant historic events and this is evident in cases where there are corroborating sources, such as Göngu-Hrólfs saga, Ragnars saga loðbrókar, Yngvars saga víðförla and Völsunga saga. In the case of Hervarar saga the names in the Gothic setting indicate a historic basis, and the latter parts of the saga are still used as a historic source for Swedish history. They often contain very old Germanic matter, such as the Hervarar saga and the Völsunga saga which contains poetry about Sigurd that did not find its way into the Poetic Edda and which would otherwise have been lost. Other sagas deal with heroes such as Ragnar Lodbrok, Starkad, Orvar-Odd, Hagbard and Signy.

In the later medieval and Renaissance period, the important European literary trend was to fantastic fiction. Exemplary work, such as the English Le Morte d'Arthur by Sir Thomas Malory (c.1408-1471), and the Spanish/Portuguese Amadis de Gaula (1508), spawned many imitators, and the genre was popularly well-received, producing such masterpiece of renaissance poetry as Ludovico Ariosto's Orlando furioso and Torquato Tasso's Gerusalemme Liberata and other 16th century literary works in the romance genre. But in the judgement of many learned readers of the time, the romance was poor literature, inspiring only broken-down ageing and provincial persons such as Don Quixote, knight of isolated province La Mancha. Hudibras also lampoons the faded conventions of chivalrous romance. Romances had been deemed harmful distractions from more substantive or moral works from the high Middle Ages, in works of piety, but by 1600 most readers would agree.

Many medieval romances recount the marvellous adventures of a chivalrous, heroic knight, often of super-human ability, who, abiding chivalry's strict codes of honour and demeanour, goes on a quest, and fights and defeats monsters and giants, thereby winning favour with a lady. The story of the medieval romance focuses not upon love and sentiment, but upon adventure; some would call contemporary comic books and science fiction the genre's successors.

The first romances heavily drew on the legends and fairy tales to supply their characters with marvelous powers. The tale of Sir Launfal features a fairy bride from folklore, and Sir Orfeo's wife is kidnapped by the fairy king, and Sir Orfeo frees her from there. These marvelous abilities subside with the development of the genre; fairy women such as Morgan le Fay become enchantresses, and knights lose magical abilities.

Romancers wrote many of their stories in three, thematic cycles: (i) the Arthurian (the lives and deeds of King Arthur and the Knights of the Round Table); (ii) the Carlovingian (the lives and deeds of Charlemagne, and Roland, his principal paladin); and, (iii) the Alexandrian (the life and deeds of Alexander the Great). In the later medieval and Renaissance period, the important European literary trend was to fantastic fiction. Exemplary work, such as the English Le Morte d'Arthur (c.1469), by Sir Thomas Malory (c.1408-1471), and the Spanish Amadís of Gaul (1508), spawned many imitators, and the genre was popularly well-received.

Originally, this literature was written in Old English and Provençal, later, in French and German-the notable works being King Horn, Havelok the Dane; and Amis and Amiloun; later romances were written as prose, e.g. Le Morte d'Arthur.

Don Quixote (1605, 1615), by Miguel de Cervantes Saavedra (1547-1616), is a satirical story of an elderly country gentleman, living in La Mancha province, crazed by reading chivalric romances.

Relationship to Modern 'Romantic Fiction'

In later romances, particularly those of French origin, there is a marked tendency to emphasize themes of courtly love, such as faithfulness in adversity. From ca. 1800 the connotations of "romance" moved from fantastic and eerie, somewhat Gothic adventure narratives of novelists like Anne Radcliffe's The Sicilian Romance (1790) or The Romance of the Forest (1791) with erotic content to novels centered on the episodic development of a courtship that ends in marriage. With a female protagonist, during the rise of Romanticism the depiction of the course of such a courtship within contemporary conventions of realism, the female equivalent of the "novel of education", informs much Romantic fiction.

The starting point of the fornaldarsagas' influence on the creation of the Fantasy genre is the publication, in 1825, of the most famous Swedish literary work Frithjof's saga, which was based on the Friðþjófs saga ins frœkna, and it became an instant success in England and Germany. It is said to have been translated twenty-two times into English, twenty times into German, and once at least into every European language, including modern Icelandic in 1866. Their influence on authors, such as J. R. R. Tolkien, William Morris and Poul Anderson and on the subsequent modern fantasy genre is considerable, and can perhaps not be overstated.

Modern usage of Romance novel denotes a particular erotic style in a highly conventionalized modern genre, and its sub-genres in historical settings, the well-named "Bodice rippers" produced by teams of authors often writing under joint pseudonyms.

Despite the popularity of this meaning of Romance, other works are still, occasionally, referred to as romances because of their uses of other elements descended from the medieval romance, or from the Romantic movement: larger-than-life heroes and heroines, drama and adventure, marvels that may become fantastic, themes of honor and loyalty, or fairy-tale-like stories and story settings. Shakespeare's later comedies, such as The Tempest or The Winter's Tale are sometimes called his romances. Modern works may differentiate from love-story as romance into different genres, such as planetary romance or Ruritanian romance.

Northrop Frye's Definition

In one, he separated some essentials of romance from the Medieval historical vehicles, to distinguish Romance as a mode that may be detected as a theme or atmosphere in other fictions, one that falls between the mode of "myth" and that of "high mimetic". Expanding Aristotle's Poetics, Frye classified fictions by the power of the hero's actions, which may be greater than ours, or less, or roughly of the same degree. Thus if the hero is superior in kind to men, the action is a myth. If the hero is superior in degree to others and to his environment, the mode is that of Romance, where the actions are marvellous, but the hero is human.

The hero of romance moves in a world in which the ordinary laws of nature are slightly suspended: prodigies of courage and endurance, unnatural to us, are natural to him, and enchanted weapons, talking animals, terrifying ogres and witches, and talismans of miraculous power violate no rule of probability... Romance divides into two main forms: a-secular form dealing with chivalry and knight-errantry, and a religious form devoted to legends of saints. Both lean heavily on miraculous violations of natural law for their interest as stories" (Frye pp 33-34).

If, on the other hand, the hero is superior to other men but not to his environment, the tale falls into the mode of high mimetic.

He also divided fictions into the fields of comedy, romance, tragedy, and irony. In this division, the essential component of romance is adventure, and the central theme is the hero's resuce of a princess from a dragon.

NOVEL

A novel (from French nouvelle Italian "novella", "new") is an extended, generally fictional narrative, typically in prose. Until the eighteenth century, the word referred specifically to short fictions of love and intrigue as opposed to romances, which were epic-length works about love and adventure. Novels are characterized by 60,000-200,000 words in length, or 300-1,300 pages, in length. During the 18th century the novel adopted features of the old romance and became one of the major literary genres. It is today defined mostly by its ability to become the object of literary criticism demanding artistic merit and a specific 'literary' style-or specific literary styles.

Nomenclature

One meaning of the English word novel has remained stable: "novel" can still signify what is new owing to its "novelty". When it comes to fiction, however, the meaning of the term has changed over time:

- The period 1200-1750 saw a rise of the novel (originally a short piece of fiction) rivaling the romance (the epic-length performanee). This development, which one could describe as the first rise of the novel, occurred across Europe, though only the Spanish and the English went one step further and allowed the word novel (Spanish: novela) to become their regular term for fictional narratives.

- The period 1700-1800 saw the rise of a "new romance" in reaction to the production of potentially scandalous novels. The movement encountered a complex situation in the English market, where the term "new romance" could hardly be ventured, after the novel had done so much to transform taste. The new genre also adopted the name novel: this new novel was a work of new epic proportions, with the effect that the English (and Spanish) eventually needed a new word for the original short "novel": The term novella was created to fill the gap in English; "short story" brought a further refinement.

The meaning of the term "romance" changed within the same complex process, becoming the word for a love story whether in life or fiction. Other meanings include the musicologist's genre "Romance" of a short and amiable piece, or Romance languages for the languages derived from Latin (French, Spanish, Italian, Romanian, and so forth).

History

Ancient World

As Pierre Daniel Huet noted in 1670, the tradition of epic works went back as far as Virgil and Homer. The regular format was verse, suiting the purpose of tradition in a culture of oral performances. Today, we see this tradition as going back even further, to the Sumerian Epic of Gilgamesh, and in Indian epics such as the Ramayana and Mahabharata.

It is more difficult to speak of the influence of the shorter performances of regular storytelling on the medieval traditions which led to the development of the novel/novella.

There was a third tradition of prose fictions, both in a satirical mode (with Petronius' Satyricon, the incredible stories of Lucian of Samosata, and Lucius Apuleius' proto-picaresque The Golden Ass) and a heroic strain (with the romances of Heliodorus and Longus et al.). The ancient Greek romance was revived by Byzantine novelists of the twelfth century. All these traditions were rediscovered in the seventeenth and eighteentl centuries, ultimately influencing the modern book market.

Romance, 1000-1500

The word romance seems to have become the label of romanti fictions because of the "Romance" language in which early (11tl and twelfth century) works of this genre were composed. Th most fashionable genres developed in southern France in the lat twelfth century and spread east-and northwards with translation and individual national performances. Subject matter such a Arthurian knighthood had already at that time traveled in th opposite direction, reaching southern France from Britain an French Brittany. As a consequence, it is particularly difficult t determine how much the early "romance" owed to ancient Greel models and how much to northern folkloric verse epics such a Beowulf and the Nibelungenlied.

The standard plot of the early romance was a series o adventures. Following a plot framework as old as Heliodorus, and so durable as to be still alive in Hollywood movies, a hero would undergo a first set of adventures before he met his lady. A separation would follow, with a second set of adventures leading to a final reunion. Variations kept the genre alive. Unexpected and peculiar adventures surprised the audience in romances like Sir Gawain and the Green Knight. Classics of the romance developed such as the Roman de la Rose, written first in French, and famous today in English thanks to the translation by Geoffrey Chaucer.

These original "romances" were verse works, adopting a "high language" thought suitable for heroic deeds and to inspire the emulation of virtues; prose was considered "low", more suitable for satire). Verse allowed the culture of oral traditions to live on, yet it became the language of authors who carefully composed their texts-texts to be spread in writing, thus to preserve the careful artistic composition. The subjects were aristocratic. The textual tradition of ornamented and illustrated handwritten books afforded patronage by the aristocracy or by the monied urban class developing in the thirteenth and fourteenth centuries, for whom knight errantry most clearly was a world of fiction and fantasy.

The fourteenth and fifteenth centuries saw the emergence of the first prose romances along with a new book market. This market had developed even before the first printing facilities were introduced: prose authors could speak a new language, a language avoiding the repetition inherent in rhymes. Prose could risk a new rhythm and longer thoughts. Yet it needed the written book to preserve the coincidental formulations the author had chosen. While the printing press was yet to arrive, the commercial book production trade had already begun. Legends, lives of saints and mystical visions in prose were the main object of the new market of prose productions. The urban elite and female readers in upper class households and monasteries read religious prose. Prose romances appeared as a new and expensive fashion in this market. They could only truly flourish with the invention of the printing press and with paper becoming a cheaper medium. Both of these achievements arrived in the late fifteenth century, when the old romance was already facing fierce competition from a number of shorter genres; most salient among these genres was the novel, a form that arose in the course of the fourteenth century.

Early Novel, 1000-1600

It is difficult to give a full catalog of the genres that finally culminated-with the The Tale of Genji in the 11th century, followed by the works of Boccaccio, Geoffrey Chaucer, Niccolò Machiave and Miguel de Cervantes-in the original "novel", the production today generally categorized under the term "novella".

The early novel was basically any story told for its spectacular or revealing incidents. The original environment-living on with the typical frame settings-was the entertaining conversation. Stories of grave incidents could just as well augment sermons. Collections of examples facilitated the work of preachers in need of such illustrations. A fable could illu te a moral conclusion; a short historical reflection could do the same. A competition of genres developed. Tastes and social status were decisive, if believes the medieval collections. The working classes loved their own brand of drastic stories: stories of clever cheating, wit and ridicule levelled agai hated social groups (or competitors among the storytellers). Much of the original genre is still alive with the short joke told in everyday life to make a certain humorous point in a conversation.

Artistic performances included the story within a story: situations i ich a series of storieo was allegedly told. They rejoiced in a broad pattern of tastes and genres. The Canterbury Tales constitute a classic example, with their noble storytellers fond of "romantic" stories and their lower na ors preferring stories of everyday life. The genre did not have its own generic term. "Novel" would simply denote the novelty of the accident narrated. The inclusion of frame stories, however, brought an awareness of the fact that genres were developing in this field.

The main advantage of the background story was the justification it put into the hands of the actual authors such as Chaucer and Boccaccio. Romances afforded lofty language and relied on an accepted notion of what deserved to be read as high style. Yet what if the taste in moral teachings and poetry changed? Romances quickly became outdated.

Stories of cheats and pranks, illicit love affairs, and clever intrigues in which certain respectable professions or the citizens of another town were made fun of were, on the other hand, neither morally nor poetically justifiable. They carried their justification outside. The storyteller would offer a few words explaining why he thought this story was worth telling. Again, Chaucer's Canterbury Tales afford the best examples: the real author could tell stories without any other justification than that this story gave a good portrait of the person who told it and of his or her taste, and that justification would remain stable throughout history.

If lofty performances grew tedi-as they did in the fourteenth and fifteenth centuries with the old plots never leading to newer ones-the collections of tales or novels made it easy to criticise the lofty performances and to reduce their status: one of the group of narrators (created by the actual author) could start with the romantic story only to be interrupted by the other narrators listening within the story. They might silence him or order him to speak a language they liked, or they might ask him to speed up and to make his point. The result was a rise of the short genre. The steps of this development can be traced with the short story gaining in appreciation and value to rival romances in new versified collections at the end of the fourteenth century.

Conflict between Novels and Romances, 1600-1700

The invention of printing subjected both novels and romances to a first wave of trivialization and commercialization. Printed books were expensive, yet something people would buy, just as people still buy expensive things they can barely afford. Alphabetization, or the rise of literacy, was a slow process when it came to writing skills, but was faster as far as reading skills were concerned. The Protestant Reformation created new readers of religious pamphlets, newspapers and broadsheets.

The urban population learned to read, but did not aspire to participation in the world of letters. The market of chapbooks developing with the printing press comprised both romances and short histories, tales and fables. Woodcuts were the regular ornament and they were offered without much care. A romance in which the heroic knight had to fight more than ten duels within a few pages could get the same illustration of such a fight again and again if the printer's stock of standard illustrations was small. As their stocks grew, printers repeated the same illustrations in other books with similar plots, mixing these illustrations without respect to style. One can open eighteenth century chapbooks and find illustrations from the early years of printing next to much more modern ones.

Romances were reduced to cheap and abrupt plots resembling modern comic books; neither were the first collections of novels necessarily prestigious projects. They appeared with an enormous variety from folk tales over jests to stories told by Boccaccio and Chaucer, now venerable authors.

A more prestigious market of romances developed in the sixteenth century, with multi-volume works aiming at an audience which would subscribe to this production. The criticism levelled against romances by Chaucer's pilgrims grew in response to both trivialization and the extended multi-volume "romances". Romances like the Amadis de Gaula led their readers into dream worlds of knighthood and fed them with ideals of a past no one could revitalize, or so the critics complained.

Italian authors like Machiavelli were among those who brought the novel into a new format: while it remained a story of intrigue, ending in a surprising point, the observations were now much finer: how did the protagonists manage their intrigue? How did they keep their secrets, what did they do when others threatened to discover them?

The whole question of novels and romances became critical when Cervantes added his Novelas Exemplares (1613) to the two volumes of his Don Quixote (1605/15). The famous satirical romance was levelled against the Amadis which had made Don Quixote lose his mind. Advocates of the lofty romance, however, would claim that the satirical counterpart of the old heroic romance could hardly teach anything: Don Quixote neither offered a hero to be emulated nor did it satisfy with beautiful speeches; all it could do was to make fun of lofty ideals.

The Novelas Exemplares offered an alternative to the heroic and the satiric modes, yet critics were even less sure what to make of this production. Cervantes told stories of adultery, jealousy and crime. If these stories were to give examples, they gave examples of immoral actions. The advocates of the "novel" responded that their stories taught with both good and bad examples. The reader could still feel compassion and sympathy with the victims of crimes and intrigues, if evil examples were to be told.

The alternative to dubious novels and satirical romances were better, lofty romances: a production of romances modeled after Heliodorus arrived as a possible answer with excursions into the bucolic world. Honoré d'Urfé's L'Astrée (1607-27) became the most famous work of this type. The criticism that these romances had nothing to do with real life was answered through the device of the roman à clef (literally "novel with a key")-one that, properly understood, alludes to characters in the real world.

John Barclay's Argenis (1625-26) appeared as a political roman à clef. The romances of Madeleine de Scudéry gained greater influence with plots set in the ancient world and content taken from life. The famous author told stories of her friends in the literary circles of Paris and developed their fates from volume to volume of her serialized production. Readers of taste bought her books, as they offered the finest observation of human motives, characters taken from life, and excellent morals regarding how one should and should not behave if one wanted to succeed in public life and in the intimate circles she portrayed.

The novel went its own way: Paul Scarron (himself a hero in the romances of Madeleine de Scudéry) published the first volume of his Roman Comique in 1651 (successive volumes appeared in 1657 and, by another hand, in 1663) with a plea for the development Cervantes had introduced in Spain. France should (as he wrote in the famous twenty first chapter of the Roman Comique) imitate the Spanish with little stories like those they called "novels". Scarron himself added numerous of such stories to his own work.

Twenty years later Madame de La Fayette took the next decisive steps with her two novels. The first, her Zayde (published in 1670 together with Pierre Daniel Huet's famous Treatise on the Origin of Romances), was a "Spanish history". Her second and more important novel appeared in 1678: La Princesse de Clèves proved that France could actually produce novels of a particularly French taste. The Spanish enjoyed stories of proud Spaniards who fought duels to avenge their reputations. The French had a more refined taste with minute observation of human motives and behavior. The story was firmly a "novel" and not a "romance": a story of unparalleled female virtue, with a heroine who had had the chance to risk an illicit amour and not only withstood the temptation but made herself more unhappy by confessing her feelings to her husband. The gloom her story created was entirely new and sensational.

The regular novel took another turn. The late seventeenth century saw the emergence of a European market for scandal, with French books now appearing mostly in the Netherlands (where censorship was liberal) to be clandestinely imported back into France. The same production reached the neighboring markets of Germany and Britain, where it was welcomed both for its French style and its predominantly anti-French politics. The novel flourished in this market as the best genre to purport scandalous news.

The authors claimed the stories they had to tell were true, told not for the sake of scandal but only for the moral lessons they gave. To prove this, they fictionalized the names of their characters and told these stories as if they were novels. (The audience played its own game in identifying who was who). Journals of little stories appeared-the Mercure Gallant became the most important. Collections of letters added to the market; these included more of these little stories and led to the development of the epistolary novel in the late seventeenth century.

The novel had interested the English audience ever since Chaucer's days, it had been read in translations of Spanish and French novels throughout the 17th century. In the late 1680s English authors decided to create a modern English equivalent. Aphra Behn and William Congreve adopted the old term and wrote new "novels".

Market Around 1700

Early eighteenth century novels and romances were still not considered part of the world of learning, hence not part of "literature"; instead they were market goods. If one opened the term catalogues it was mostly situated in the predominantly political field of "History and Politicks" with some romances like Cervantes' Don Quixote translated into verse becoming poetical.

The centre of the market was held by fictions which claimed to be fictions and which were read as such. They comprised a high production of romances and, at the bottom end, an opposing production of satirical romances. In the centre, the novel had grown, with stories that were neither heroic nor predominantly satirical, yet mostly realistic, short and stimulating with their examples of human actions to be discussed.

Outside the centre, the market had two wings: On the left hand, one had books which claimed to be romances, but which threatened to be anything but fictitious. Delarivier Manley wrote the most famous of them, her New Atalantis, full of stories the author claimed to have invented. The censors were helpless: Manley had hawked stories discrediting the ruling Whigs, yet should they ask the Whigs to prove that all these stories actually happened on British soil rather than on the fairytale island Atalantis? This was what they had to do if they wanted to sue the author. Delarivier Manley escaped the interrogations unscathed and continued her libellous work with three more volumes of the same ilk. Private stories appeared on the same market, creating a different genre of personal love and public battles over lost reputations.

On the other hand, one had a market of titles which claimed to be strictly non-fictional-Daniel Defoe's Robinson Crusoe became the most important of them. The genre-identification: "Sold as true private history, risking to be read as romantic invention" opened the preface: IF ever the Story of any private Man's Adventures in the World were worth making Pvblick, and were acceptable when Publish'd, the Editor of this Account thinks this will be so. The Wonders of this Man's Life exceed all that (he thinks) is to be found extant; the Life of one Man being scarce capable of a greater Variety. The Story is told with Modesty, with Seriousness, and with a religious Application of Events to the Uses to which wise Men always apply them (viz.) to the Instruction of others by this Example, and to justify and honor the Wisdom of Providence in all the Variety of our Circumstances, let them happen how they will.

The Editor believes the thing to be a just History of Fact; neither is there any Appearance of Fiction in it: And however thinks, because all such things are dispatch'd [later editions: disputed], that the Improvement of it, as well as the Diversion, as to the Instruction of the Reader, will be the same; and as such he thinks, without farther Compliment to the World, he does them a great Service in the Publication.

A production of histories of similar verisimilitude dove into the overtly political. Gatien de Courtilz de Sandras (1644-1712) became the most important author in this field with his first version of d'Artagnan's story, told again more than a century later by Alexandre Dumas the elder. Witty, and a distant precursor of Ian Fleming's fictional James Bond, is another book allegedly by his hand: La Guerre d'Espagne (1707), the story of a disillusioned French spy, who gave insight into French politics, and into his own love affairs, with little intrigues he managed wherever he had to do his jobs. Fact and fiction were mixed in all these titles, to the point that one could no longer tell where the author had invented and where he had simply betrayed secrets.

NEW ROMANCE, 1700-1800

The early eighteenth century-with the novel diving into private and public scandal-had reached a state of affairs where a new reform seemed desirable. The old Amadis could be said to have driven its readers into dream worlds, and the new novels, devoid of lofty speeches and incredible acts of heroism, had done much to refine taste. Yet they had created entirely new risks, with stories of love in which children cheated their parents, and with which private and public gossip were published on the open market.

Jane Barker was among the eighteenth century voices who demanded a return to the old antiquated romance. Her "new romance" Exilius (1715) opened with the sketch of a new tradition: the romance had, so Jane Barker claimed, developed from Geoffrey Chaucer to François Fénelon; the latter was the author who had just become famous with his epochal romance Telemachus (1699/1700).

Fénelon's English publishers had carefully avoided the term "romance" and rather published a "new epic in prose"-so the prefaces. Jane Barker insisted, however, on publishing Exilius as "New Romance [...] after the manner of Telemachus", and failed on the market. In 1719 her publisher, Edmund Curll, finally removed the old title pages and offered her works as a collection of novels.

The big market success of the next decade, Daniel Defoe's Robinson Crusoe, appeared that very year and William Taylor, the publisher, avoided these traps with a title page claiming neither the realm of novels nor that of romances, but that of histories, yet with a page design tasting all too much of the "new romance" with which Fénelon had just become famous.

Defoe's Robinson Crusoe was everything but a novel, as the term was understood at the time. It wasn't short, it didn't focus on an intrigue, and it wasn't told for the sake of a clear cut-point. Nor was Crusoe an anti-hero of a satirical romance, though he spoke in the first person singular and had stumbled into all kinds of miseries. He did not really invite laughter (though readers of taste would read, of cours ll his proclamations about being a real man as made in good humour). The feigned author was serious: against his will his life had brought him into this series of most romantic adventures. He had fallen into the hands of pirates and survived years on an uninhabited island. He had survived all this-a mere sailor York-with exemplary heroism. If readers read his work as a romance, full of sheer invention, he could not blame them. He and his publisher knew that all he had to tell was strictly unbelievable, and yet they would claim it was true (and if not, still readable as good allegory)-this is the complex game which puts this work into the fourth column of the pattern above.

Reformation, 1700-1800

The publication of Robinson Crusoe did not directly lead to the mid-18th century market reform. Crusoe's books were published as dubious histories; they played the game of the scand s early eighteenth century market, with the novel fully integrated into the realm of histories. They even appeared reprinted by one of the London newspapers as a possibly true relation of facts. Philosophers like Jean-Jacques Rousseau turned Robinson Crusoe into a classic decades later, and it took another century before one could see Defoe's book as the first English "novel"-published, as Ian Watt saw it in 1957-as an answer to the market of French romances.

The reform of the early eighteenth century market of novels came with the production of classics: 1720 saw the decisive edition of classics of the European novel published in London with titles from Machiavelli to Marie de Lafayette. Aphra Behn's "novels" had over the last decades appeared in collections of her works. The author of the 1680s had become a classic by now. Fénelon had become a classic years ago, as had Heliodorus. The works of Petronius and Longos appeared, equipped with prefaces which put them into the tradition of prose fiction Huet had defined. Prose fi n itself, according to the critics, had a history of ups and downs: having run into a crisis with the Amadis, it found its remedy with the novel. It now needed continuous care. Yet, all in all, it could claim to be the most elegant part of the belles lettres, the new market segment within the bigger market of literature, embracing the new classics.

Huet's Traitté de l'origine des romans, first published in 1670 and now circulating in a number of translations editions, won a central position among those writings which dealt with prose fiction. The Treatise had created the first corpus of texts to be discussed and it had been the first title that demonstrated how one could "interpret" worldly fictions, just as a theologian would interpret parts of the gospel in a theological debate. The interpretation needed its aims, of course, and Huet had offered a number of questions one could ask: What did the fictional work of a foreign culture or distant period tell us about those who constructed the fiction? What were the cultural needs such stories answered? Are there fundamental anthropological premises which make us create fictional worlds? Did these fictions entertain, divert and instruct? Did they-as one could assume when reading ancient and medieval myths-just provide a substitute for better, more scientific knowledge, or did they add to the luxuries of life a particular culture enjoyed? The ancient Mediterranean erotic stories could afford such an interpretation.

The interpretation and analysis of classics placed readers of fictions in a tirely new and improved position: it made a vast difference whether you read a romance and got lost in a dream world or whether you read the same romance with a preface telling you more about the Greeks, Romans, or Arabs who produced titles like the Aethopica or The Book of One Thousand and One Nights (first published in Europe from 1704 to 1715 in French, and translated immediately from this edition into English and German).

Novels as Literature, 1740-1800

The early eighteenth century market for classics of prose fiction inspired living authors. Aphra Behn, writing in relative anonymity, became a celebrated author posthumously. Fénelon achieved the same fame during his lifetime. Delarivier Manley, Jane Barker and Eliza Haywood followed their famous French models who had dared to claim fame with their real names: the Madame d'Aulnoy and Anne Marguerite Petit du Noyer. Most novels had previously been pseu mous; now they became the productions of famous authors.

The discourse necessary to appreciate such a move towards responsibility was yet underdeveloped. Journals discussing literature focussed on "learning", literature in the strict sense of the word. So far, most discussion of novels and romances had taken place within the field itself. Literary criticism, a critical, external discourse about poetry and fiction, arose only in the second half of the eighteenth century. It opened an interaction between separate participants in which novelists would write in order to be criticised and in which the public would observe the interaction between critics and authors. new criticism of the late eighteenth century offered a reform by establishing a market of works worthy to be discussed (whilst the rest of the market would thus continue but lose most of its public appeal). The result was a market division into a low field of popular fictions and a critical literary production. The latter, privileged works-those which rivalled ancient verse epics to be discussed as art, which played with the traditions of prose fiction (they opened an internal discou about the history of literature), and which were of a clearly defined fictional status-these alone could be discussed as works created by an artist who wanted this and no other story to be discussed by the audience.

Design of title pages changed: new novels no longer pretended to sell fictions whilst threatening to betray real sec. Nor did they appear as false "true histories". The new title pages pronounced their works to be fictions, and indicated how the public might discuss them. Samuel Richardson's Pamela, or Vir Rewarded (1740) was one of the titles which brought the novel-title, with its [...], or [...] formula offering an example, into the new format: "Pamela, or Virtue Rewarded-Now first published in order to cultivate the Principles of Virtue Religion in the Minds of the Youth of Both Sexes, A Narrative which has the Foundation in Truth and Nature; and at the same time that it agreeably entertains..." So the title page read, and made it clear that the work was crafted by an artist aiming at a certain effect, yet to be discussed by the critical audience. A decade later novels needed no status other than that of being novels: fiction.

Present-day editions of novels simply state "Fiction" on the cover. It had become prestigious to be sold under the label, asking for discussion and thoug Scandal as published by DuNoyer or Delarivier Manley vanished from the market of prose fiction-whether high or low culture. It could not attract serious critics and was lost if it remained undiscussed. It ultimately needed its own brand of scandalous journalism, which developed into the yellow press. The low market of prose fiction went on to focus on immediate satisfaction of an audience enjoying its stay in the fictional world. The high market grew complex, with works playing new games.

In the high market, one could eventually see two traditions developing: one of works playing with the art of fiction-Laurence Sterne's Tristram Shandy among them-the other closer to the prevailing discussions and moods-of its audience. The great conflict of the nineteenth century, as to whether artists should write to satisfy the public or whether to produce art for art's sake, was yet to come.

Sentimentalism, Psychology, and the New Individual, 1750-1850

The mid-and late eighteenth century "novel of sentimentalism" produced an entirely new individual, one with a different attitude towards privacy and the public. Whereas the early eighteenth century heroine had been bold and ready to protect her reputation if necessary in a press war, her mid-18th century descendant was far too modest and shy to do the same. Early eighteenth century heroines had their secrets, they loved effective intrigues, they tried whatever they felt necessary to get what they wanted. Mid-18th century heroines developed a feeling of modesty. They suffered if they had to keep secrets and felt an urge to confess. They searched for friends and intimacy, for situations in which they could freely open their hearts and speak of their deepest wishes.

The eighteenth century audience saw these new heroes and heroines with amazement. When it came to their most secret wishes they dared to confide in their parents and friends-a trust which would have made them easy victims in the early eighteenth century world of fiction, libel, intrigue and scandal. Now, however, these weak heroines met an environment of compassion. Instead of making their affairs a public entertainment, the new heroes and heroines developed an intimacy into which the novel alone could take a careful look.

Special genres flourished with these protagonists who would not wash their dirty linen in public. Their letters or diaries were found and published only after their deaths. A wave of sentimentalism was the first result, leading to heroes like Henry Mackenzie's Man of Feeling (1771). A second wave followed with more radical heroes who could no longer dream of an environment understanding them. Johann Wolfgang von Goethe's The Sorrows of Young Werther (1774) was at the forefront of the new movement, and yielded a wave of compassion and understanding with readers ready to follow Werther into his suicide.

Critics embraced the new heroes as the best sign of a new literature which aimed at discussions. The understanding these heroes craved for afforded a secondary discussion-a discussion of the nature of the human psyche so much better observed by these new novels.

The novel, with these developments, had turned advocacy of individual and societal moral reform into a genre. With the romantic movement beginning in the 1770s, the development went one step further: the novel became the medium of an avant garde, the genre where emotions found their test cases. German authors developed the Bildungsroman, a novel focussing on the development of the individual, their education and their way into individuality and society. New sciences like sociology to psychology developed along with the new individual and influenced the discussions surrounding the novel in the nineteenth century.

19th Century

At the beginning of the seventeenth century the novel had been a genre of realism fighting the romance with its wild fantasies. The novel had turned first to scandal before undergoing reform over the last decades of the eighteenth century. Fiction eventually became the most honourable field of literature. This development culminated in a wave of novels of fantasy at the turn of the nineteenth century. Sensibility was heightened in these novels. Women, overwrought and prone to imagining worlds beyond their appointed one, became the heroines of the new world of "romances" and "gothic novels" creating stories in distant times and places. Renaissance Italy was a favorite setting of the gothic novel.

The classic gothic novel is Ann Radcliffe's The Mysteries of Udolpho (1794). As in other gothic novels, the notion of the sublime is central. Eighteenth-century aesthetic theory held that the sublime and the beautiful were juxtaposed. The sublime was awful (literally, "awe-inspiring") and terrifying while the beautiful was calm and reassuring. Gothic characters and landscapes rest almost entirely within the sublime, with the heroine the great exception. The "beautiful" heroine's susceptibility to supernatural elements, integral to these novels, both celebrates and problematizes what came to be seen as hypersensibility.

At the beginning of the nineteenth century, the overwrought emotions of sensibility, as expressed through the gothic sublime, had run their course. Jane Austen with Northanger Abbey (1803) parodied the gothic novel, reflecting its death. Moreover, while sensibility did not disappear, it was less valued. Austen introduced a different style of writing, the "comedy of manners". Her novels often are not only funny, but also scathingly critical of the restrictive, rural culture of the early nineteenth century. Her best known novel, Pride and Prejudice (1811), is her happiest, and has been a blueprint for much subsequent romantic fiction. Austen's novels still retain a wide following, despite the distance between their heroines' dilemmas and those of the reader today.

Separation of High and Low Production

The market for novels in the nineteenth century was clearly separated into "high" and "low" production. The new high production can best be viewed in terms of national traditions. The low production was organized rather by genres in a pattern deriving from the spectrum of seventeenth-and eighteenth-century genres.

The position of authors attained its modern form with the establishment of this pattern. The modern author can either aim at a broad market or write with an eye to serious critical discussion. The borders between the realms have developed differently in different nations. While this modern market divide came relatively late to the English-speaking world, Germany and France had an earlier and much stronger interest in creating national literatures-France in the wake of the French Revolution, Germany during its mid-19th-century unification. Both of these nations experienced a division between high literature-discussed in schools and newspapers, and celebrated in public life-and a low production-not worthy to be mentioned in such circles-while the vast commercial market of the English-speaking world still resisted this artificial divide.

The novel proved to be a medium for a communication both intimate (novels can be read privately whereas plays are always a public event) and public (novels are published and thus become a matter touching the public, if not the nation, and its vital interests), a medium of a personal point of view which can get the world into its view. New modes of interaction between authors and the public reflected these developments: authors giving public readings, receiving prestigious prizes, giving interviews in the media and acting as their nations' consciences. This concept of the novelist as public figure arose in the course of the nineteenth century.

20th Century

Important Novels

These are the earliest extant Western precursors to the novel:

- Xenophon, The Education of Cyrus (Greek, 4th century BC), a largely fictional account of the education of Emperor Cyrus the Great of Persia; considered a precursor to the novel
- Petronius, Satyricon (Latin, 1st century AD)
- Apuleius, The Golden Ass (Latin, 2nd century)
- Chariton, The Loves of Chaereas and Callirhoe (Greek, 1st-2nd century)
- Achilles Tatius, Leucippe and Clitophon (Greek, 2nd century)
- Longus, Daphnis and Chloe (Greek, 2nd century)
- Xenophon of Ephesus, Ephesian Tale (Greek, 2nd-3rd century)
- Heliodorus, Ethiopian Tale (Greek, 3rd-4th century)
- Acts of Xanthippe, Polyxena, and Rebecca (Greek, 3rd-4th century)
- Joseph and Aseneth (Greek, 1st-5th century)
- The Story of Apollonius, King of Tyre (Latin adaptation of lost Greek original, 5th-6th century)

Asian Precursors

Early important Asian precursors to the novel include:

- Vishnu Sarma, Panchatantra (Sanskrit, 3rd century BC)

- Vikram and the Vampire (Sanskrit, 1st century BC)
- Hitopadesha (Sanskrit, 1st-2nd century AD)
- Şri Dandin, The Adventures of the Ten Princes (Sanskrit, 6th-7th century)
- Banabhatta, Kadambari (Sanskrit, 7th century)
- Ferdowsi, Shahnameh (Persian, 10th century)
- The Tale of the Bamboo Cutter (Japanese, 10th century)

11th Century

- Murasaki Shikibu, The Tale of Genji (Japanese, 11th century), arguably the first true novel, in the sense of a continued fictional narrative written by one author

13th Century

- Ramon Llull, Blanquerna (Catalan, 1283)

14th Century

- Luo Guanzhong, Romance of the Three Kingdoms (Chinese, 1330)
- Giovanni Boccaccio, Decameron (Italian, 1353)
- Geoffrey Chaucer, Canterbury Tales (English, 1386-1400)

15th Century

- Antoine de la Sale, Petit Jehan de Saintré (French, 1456)
- Thomas Malory, Le Morte d'Arthur (English, 1485)
- Joanot Martorell, Tirant lo Blanc (Catalan, 1490), a chivalric romance
- Shi Nai'an and Luo Guanzhong, Water Margin (Chinese, 15th century)

16th Century

- Jacopo Sannazaro, La Arcadia (Italian, 1504), a pastoral novel
- Garci Rodríguez de Montalvo, Amadis de Gaula (Spanish adaptation of lost 13th century original, 1508)

- Thomas More, Utopia (Latin, 1516)
- François Rabelais, Gargantua and Pantagruel (French, 1532)
- Jorge de Montemayor, La Diana (Spanish, 1559), a pastoral novel
- Lazarillo de Tormes (Spanish, 1554)
- Wu Cheng'en, Journey to the West (Chinese, 1590)
- Mateo Alemán, Guzmán de Alfarache (Spanish, 1599)

17th Century

- Miguel de Cervantes, Don Quixote de la Mancha (Spanish, 1605)
- Honoré d'Urfé, Astrée (French, 1607)
- Francisco de Quevedo, El Buscón (Spanish, 1626), the masterpiece of the picaresque sub-genre
- Hans Jakob Christoffel von Grimmelshausen, Simplicissimus (German, 1668-1669), the Thirty Years' War put into satirical autobiography
- Madame de La Fayette, La Princesse de Clèves (French, 1678)
- Aphra Behn, Love-Letters Between a Noble-Man and his Sister (1684) (English, 1684-1687), the first full-blown epistolary novel
- Aphra Behn, Oroonoko (English, 1688)
- Cao Xueqin, Dream of the Red Chamber (Chinese, 18th century)

18th Century

- Eliza Haywood, Love in Excess (English, 1719)
- Daniel Defoe, Robinson Crusoe (English, 1719)
- Jonathan Swift, Gulliver's Travels (Irish, 1726, amended 1735)
- Antoine François Prévost, Manon Lescaut (French, 1732)
- Samuel Richardson, Clarissa (English, 1740)

- Henry Fielding, Tom Jones (English, 1749)
- John Cleland, Fanny Hill, Memoirs of a Woman of Pleasure (English, 1749)
- Voltaire, Candide (French, 1759)
- Laurence Sterne, Tristram Shandy (Irish, 1759-1767)
- Tobias Smollett, The Expedition of Humphry Clinker (Scottish, 1771)
- Ignacy Krasicki, The Adventures of Nicholas Experience (the first Polish novel, 1776)
- Frances Burney, Evelina (English, 1778)
- Pierre Choderlos de Laclos, Les Liaisons Dangereuses (French, 1782)
- Ann Radcliffe, The Mysteries of Udolpho (English, 1794)

GENRE NOVELS

From the late Victorian period to the present, several types of "genre" novels and romances have been popular. While often slighted by critics and academics, these have been as popular as the more critically and academically acclaimed novels; in recent times, the best of them have been recognized as serious literature. Some categories of genre fiction are:

- Science fiction
- Fantasy
- Crime fiction
- Westerns
- Romance novels
- Spy novels and thrillers

CRITICISM

The word critic comes from the Greek word, kritikós-one who discerns, which itself arises from the Ancient Greek word, krités, meaning a person who offers reasoned judgement or analysis, value judgement, interpretation, or observation. The term can be used to describe an adherent of a position disagreeing with or opposing the object of criticism.

Modern critics include professionals or amateurs who regularly judge or interpret performances or other works (such as that of artists, scientists, musicians or actors) and, typically, publish their observations, often in periodicals. Critics are numerous in certain fields, including art critics, music critics, film critics, theatre or drama, restaurant and scientific publication critics.

Criticism in general terms means democratic judgement over the suitability of a subject for the intended purposes, as opposed to the authoritarian command, which is meant as an absolute realization of the authority's will, thus not open for debate.

Criticism is the activity of judgement or informed interpretation. In literary and academic contexts, the term most frequently refers to literary criticism, art criticism, or other such fields, and to scholars' attempts to understand the aesthetic object in depth. In these contexts the term "critic", used without qualification, most frequently refers to a scholar of literature or another art form. In other contexts, the term describes hostility or disagreement with the object of criticism. Sometimes context, and the contentiousness of the subject, are the only differentiating factors between these two approaches. In politics, for instance (as in the phrase "criticism of U.S. foreign policy"), criticism almost exclusively refers to disagreement-while in an academic, artistic, or literary context (as in "criticism of Romantic poetry") it usually refers to the activity of subtle interpretation or analysis.

Criticism can also be a tool of an anti-social behavior, such as a passive-aggressive attack. Constructive criticism is a form of communication, in which a person tries to correct the behavior of another in a non-authoritarian way, and is generally, a diplomatic approach about what another person is doing socially incorrect. It is 'constructive' as opposed to a command or an insult and is meant as a peaceful and benevolent approach. Participatory Learning in Pedagogy in based on these principles of constructive criticism.

Constructive criticism is the process of offering valid and well-reasoned opinions about the work of others with the intention of helping the reader or the artist, rather than creating an oppositional attitude. An art critic can also be a champion of a new artistic movement in the face of a hostile public (e.g. John Ruskin), using scholarship and insight to show the value and depth of a new style. Critics might even champion a wholly new art medium; for instance the century-long critical struggle to have photography recognised as a valid art form.

There can be a tension between constructive and useful criticism; for instance, a critic might us ly help an individual artist to recognise what is poor or slapdash in their body of work-but the critic may have to appear harsh and judgemental in order to achieve this.

The Critique

Critique, especially in philosophical contexts (where it is used to translate the German word Kritik), has a more clearly defined meaning than criticism. (Confusingly, the adjectival form of both critique and criticism is critical, making some uses ambiguous, e.g. "critical theory"). In this broadly political context, a critique is a systematic inquiry into the conditions and consequences of a concept or set of concepts, and an attempt to understand its limitations. A critical perspective, in this sense, is the opposite of a dogmatic one. In philosophy this sense of the word was defined by Immanuel Kant, who wrote:

We deal with a concept dogmatically...if we consider it as contained under another concept of the object which constitutes a principle of reason and determine it in conformity with this. But we deal with it merely critically if we consider it only in reference to our cognitive faculties and consequently to the subjective conditions of thinking it, without undertaking to decide anything about its object. (Critique of Judgment sec. 74)

Later thinkers used the word critique, in a broader version of Kant's sense of the word, to mean the systematic inquiry into the limits of a doctrine or set of concepts (for instance, much of Karl Marx's work was in the critique of political economy).

The cultural studies approach to criticism arises out of critical theory. It treats cultural products and their reception as sociological evidence, which may be sceptically examined to divine wider social ills such as racism or gender bias.

8

Playwright

A playwright, also known as a dramatist, is one that writes dramatic literature or drama. These works may be written specifically to be performed by actors or they may be closet dramas or literary works written using dramatic forms but not meant for performance.

The term is not a variant spelling of playwrite, but something quite distinct: the word wright is an archaic English term for a craftsman or builder (as in a wheelwr rtwright). Hence the prefix and the suffix combine to indicate someone who crafts s. The homophone with write is in this case coincidental.

The term 'playwright' appears to have been coined by Ben Jonson as an insult, to imply an inferior hack-writer for the theatre. He always described himself as a poet. It later lost this negative connotation.

EARLY HISTORY

The earliest playwrights in Western literature with surviving works are Ancient Greeks with some of the earliest plays being written around the 5th century BC. These playwrights are notable as they established forms that are still relied on by modern playwrights. Notable among them are Aeschylus, Sophocles, Euripides, and Aristophanes.

The most famous playwright is probably Shakespeare. He wrote classical tragedies and comedies which a lot of other work is based on. For example, Kiss Me, Kate is based on The Taming of the Shrew, and Romeo and Juliet has been remade more times than can be counted. Tom Stoppard created the play Rosencrantz and Guildenstern Are Dead in 1966 which is a modern transformation of Hamlet.

Playwrights often do not reach the same level of fame or cultural importance that they have in the past. This may have to do with the current state of professional theatre, in which fewer new works are produced by theatres. Instead, theaters have tended towards remounting past successes. For example, Playwrights Horizons produced only six plays in the 2002-03 seasons, compared with thirty-one in 1973-74. As revivals and large-scale production musicals become the de rigeur Broadway and Off-Broadway productions, it has become much more difficult for playwrights to make a living in the business, let alone become major successes.

However, the most successful playwrights-in stark contrast to the lot of the screenwriter-are often high-status figures in their industry. This is a corollary of the more literary approach that has characterised the theatre since its roots in poetry. The form often has a greater reverence for the text and arguably is less oriented around the work of a director. The playwright's vision often takes precedence.

In recent years this attitude has started change. A less rigidly formal approach to text for performance is more common, informed by practitioners like Joan Littlewood and her protégé Mike Leigh.

Documentary plays are also a common feature of the theatrical landscape since the middle of the Twentieth Century when they were employed, often tendentiously, in agit-prop or general political protest. These plays demand something different of a playwright, often the editing and reproduction of the other people's words within a narrative structure. A recent example is Stuff Happens, David Hare's 2004 play about the Iraq War, in which many of the speeches were taken verbatim from George W. Bush, Tony Blair et al.

POET

A poet is a person who writes poetry. This is usually influenced by a cultural and intellectual tradition, and written in a specific language. Some consider the best poetry to be, to some extent, timeless, and to address issues common to all humanity; others are more absorbed by its particular and ephemeral qualities.

In the English language, poets generally considered to be of the most influential and profound include Chaucer, William Shakespeare, John Milton, Wordsworth, John Keats, W. B. Yeats, T. S. Eliot and Ezra Pound. American poet Walt Whitman was one of the first poets to write a kind of poetry now called free verse, though French poet Jules Laforgue was also writing in free verse around the same time as Whitman. Free verse differed from traditional verse because it was not bound by rhyme or meter. In the Western tradition, Homer, Virgil, Dante, Fernando Pessoa and Goethe round out a basic list. In Chinese, Li Bai, Du Fu and other Tang dynasty poets produced some of the oldest poetry in the world, which is still read today. Basho and Omar Khayyám complete one defensible canon. As the very definition of a canon is political and personal, and the notion of poetry itself is fluid and subject to change, complete objectivity is impossible. Relying on numerous inclusionist lists is a possible, partial solution.

Poets and Society

Perhaps no other occupation demands so much thought for so little output. In the Japanese haiku tradition involves production of seventeen syllable poems. Even in other traditions including thousand-line poems, a poet's total lifetime output might fill only two or three volumes. For this reason, poets occupy a peculiar position in society, even when compared to other artists, tending to reside on the fringes of their culture. Even poets who have achieved prominence within their tradition can remain completely unknown in the world at large.

In the past, bards of remarkable skill might be maintained by a lord or by royalty as part of the artistic coterie at court. Away from the refinement of court, wandering troubadours would have brought their romantic, bawdy chansons from town to town, supporting themselves by passing the hat.

In the east, poets were similarly maintained by royal patronage, and those of high birth were expected to develop this skill alongside many others. Within the tradition of Japanese chivalry, bushido, Japanese knights, known as samurai, were expected to become poets only once: right before death. Thus, the tradition of love poems does not exist in Japan, but the quantity and quality of death poems is renowned.

Poets and Death

Poets' Graves are often the focus of literary pilgrimages. The most famous resting place of dead poets is Poets' Corner in Westminster Abbey, London, England-although Mount Auburn Cemetery in Massachusetts, USA and Pere Lachaise Cemetery in Paris also contain many poets' graves.

PROSE

Prose is writing distinguished from poetry by its greater variety of rhythm and its closer resemblance to the patterns of everyday speech. The word prose comes from the Latin prosa, meaning straightforward. This describes the type of writing that prose embodies, unadorned with obvious stylistic devices. Prose writing is usually adopted for the description of facts or the discussion of whatever one's thoughts are, incorporated in free flowing speech.

Thus, it may be used for newspapers, capers, magazines, encyclopedias, broadcast media, films, letters, debtor's notes, famous quotes, murder mystery, history, philosophy, biography, linguistic geography and many other forms of media along with rants on thoughts. It just depends on the school in which one was taught.

Prose generally lacks the formal structure of meter or rhyme that is often found in poetry. Although some works of prose may happen to contain traces of metrical structure or versification, a conscious blend of the two forms of literature is known as a prose poem. Similarly, poetry with less of the common rules and limitations of verse is known as free verse.

Poetry is considered to be artificially developed ("The best words in the best order"), whereas prose is thought to be less constructed and more reflective of ordinary speech. Pierre de Ronsard, the French poet, said that his training as a poet had proved to him that prose and poetry were mortal enemies. In Molière's play Le Bourgeois Gentilhomme, Monsieur Jourdain asks something to be written in neither verse nor prose. A philosophy master says to him, "Sir, there is no other way to express oneself than with prose or verse". Jourdain replies, "By my faith! For more than forty years I have been speaking prose without knowing anything about it, and I am much obliged to you for having taught me that."

History

The status of prose has changed throughout its history. The early literature of many societies consists mostly of poetry. Early prose was often restricted to mundane and everyday uses, such as legal documents and yearly records. Academic subjects such as philosophy and history were generally written in prose, but fiction does not often appear in prose until much later. Poetry is still often regarded as a higher form of literature than prose, but the relatively recent development of the novel has challenged that view.

Prose was at one time synonymous with dull, unimaginative or laboured writing, and the meaning of the word "prosaic" has developed "containing or characteristic of prose" to "lacking in imagination or spirit; dull." Prose that is too ornate and overblown for its context is called purple prose.

Styles

Prose varies considerably depending on the purpose of the writing. As prose is often considered to be representative of the patterns of normal speech, many rhetorical devices are used in prose to emphasize points and enliven the writing. Prose which aims to be informative and accurate, such as history or journalism, usually strives to use the simplest language possible to express its points. Facts are often repeated and reiterated in various ways so that they are understood by a reader, but excessive use of this technique can make a serious piece of writing seem pedantic.

In fiction, prose can take on many forms. Skilled authors can alter how they use prose throughout a book to suggest different moods and ideas. A thriller often consists of short, "punchy" sentences made up of equally short words, suggesting very rapid actions to heighten the effect of a very fast-moving plot. Conversely, longer sentences can be used to slow down the action of a novel.

When a poem is translated from one language into another (particularly an epic poem) the poem is often converted into prose. Not only does this allow the reader to understand the plot more easily, but it allows the translator to exercise less unwelcome creative input. A translation should be an unchanged representation of the sense of the original; to impose the rhyme and meter structures of a different language is likely to significantly alter the poem.

Speech/Debate

The event 'Prose' in Speech/Debate is in which one person reads a selection from a published book, play, etc., and interprets the piece for the judging audience. The time limit is 8 minutes with a thirty-second grace period.

9

History of Literature

The history of literature is the historical development of writings in prose or poetry which attempt to provide entertainment, enlightenment, or instruction to the reader/hearer/observer, as well as the development of the literary techniques used in the communication of these pieces. Not all writings constitute literature. Some recorded materials, such as compilations of data (e.g., a check register) are not considered literature, and this article relates only to the evolution of the works defined in the first sentence above.

THE BEGINNING OF LITERATURE

Literature and writing, though obviously connected, are not synonymous. The very first writings from ancient Sumer by any reasonable definition do not constitute literature-the same is true of some of the early Egyptian hieroglyphics or the thousands of logs from ancient Chinese regimes. Scholars always have and always will disagree concerning when the earliest records-keeping in writing becomes more like "literature" than anything else: the definition is largely subjective.

Moreover, it must be borne in mind that, given the significance of distance as a cultural isolator in earlier centuries, the historical development of literature did not occur at an even pace across the world. The problems of creating a uniform global history of literature are compounded by the fact that many texts have been lost over the millennia, either deliberately, by accident, or by the total disappearance of the originating culture. Much has been written, for example, about the destruction of the Library of Alexandria in the 3rd century BCE, and the innumerable key texts which are believed to have been lost forever to the flames. The deliberate suppression of texts (and often their authors) by organisations of either a spiritual or a temporal nature further shrouds the subject.

Certain primary texts, however, may be isolated which have a qualifying role as literature's first stirrings. Very early examples are Epic of Gilgamesh, in its Sumerian version predating 2000 BCE, and the Egyptian Book of the Dead written down in the Papyrus of Ani in approximately 250 BCE but probably dates from about the 18th century BCE. Ancient Egyptian literature was not included in early studies of the history of literature because the writings of Ancient Egypt were not translated into European languages until the 19th century when the Rosetta stone was deciphered.

Many texts handed down by oral tradition over several centuries before they were fixed in written form are difficult or impossible to date. The core of the Rigveda may date to the mid 2nd millennium BCE. The Pentateuch is traditionally dated to the 15th century, although modern scholarship estimates its oldest part to date to the 10th century BCE at the earliest.

Homer's The Iliad and The Odyssey date to the 8th century BCE and mark the beginning of Classical Antiquity. They also stand in an oral tradition that stretches back to the late Bronze Age. Indian sruti texts post-dating the Rigveda (such as the Yajurveda, the Atharvaveda and the Brahmanas), as well as the Hebrew Tanakh and the a mystical collection of poems attributed to Lao Tze, the Tao te Ching, date to the Iron Age, but their dating is difficult and controversial. The great Hindu epics were also transmitted orally, likely predating the Maurya period.

Other oral traditions were fixed in writing much later, such as the Elder Edda, written down in the 12th or 13th century.

There are various different possible answers to the question "Which was the first novel ever written?"

EARLY INDIAN LITERATURE

Indian epics such as Ramayana and Mahabharata, have influenced countless other works, including Balinese Kecak and other performances such as shadow puppetry (wayang), and many European influenced works. Pali literature has an important position in the rise of Buddhism.

EARLY CHINESE LITERATURE

The first great author on military tactics and strategy was Sun Tzu, whose The Art of War remains on the shelves of many modern military officers (and its advice has been applied to the corporate world as well). Philosophy developed far differently in China than in Greece-rather than presenting extended dialogues, the Analects of Confucius and Lao Zi's Tao Te Ching presented sayings and proverbs more directly and didactically.

THE GREEKS AND THE ROMANS

The Greeks

Ancient Greek society placed considerable emphasis upon literature. Many authors consider the western literary tradition to have begun with the epic poems The Iliad and The Odyssey, which remain giants in the literary canon for their skillful and vivid depictions of war and peace, honor and disgrace, love and hatred. Notable among later Greek poets was Sappho, who defined, in many ways, lyric poetry as a genre.

A playwright named Aeschylus changed Western literature forever when he introduced the ideas of dialogue and interacting characters to playwriting. In doing so, he essentially invented "drama": his Oresteia trilogy of plays is seen as his crowning achievement. Other refiners of playwriting were Sophocles and Euripides. Sophocles is credited with skillfully developing irony as a literary technique, most famously in his play Oedipus the King. Euripedes, conversely, used plays to challenge societal norms and mores-a hallmark of much of Western literature for the next 2,300 years and beyond-and his works such as Medea, The Bacchae and The Trojan Women are still notable for their ability to challenge our perceptions of propriety, gender, and war. Aristophanes, a comic playwright, defines and shapes the idea of comedy almost as Aeschylus had shaped tragedy as an art form-Aristophanes' most famous plays include the Lysistrata and The Frogs.

Philosophy entered literature in the dialogues of Plato, who converted the give and take of Socratic questioning into written form. Aristotle, Plato's student, wrote dozens of works on many scientific disciplines, but his greatest contribution to literature was likely his Poetics, which lays out his understanding of drama, and thereby establishes the first criteria for literary criticism.

The Romans

In many respects, the writers of the Roman Republic and the Roman Empire chose to avoid innovation in favor of imitating the great Greek authors. Virgil's Aeneid, in many respects, emulated Homer's Iliad; Plautus, a comic playwright, followed in the footsteps of Aristophanes; Tacitus' Annals and Germania follow essentially the same historical approaches that Thucydides devised (the Christian historian Eusebius does also, although far more influenced by his religion than either Tacitus or Thucydides had been by Greek and Roman polytheism); Ovid and his Metamorphoses explore the same Greek myths again in new ways. It can be argued, and has been, that the Roman authors, far from being mindless copycats, improved on the genres already established by their Greek predecessors. For example Ovid's Metamorphoses creates a form which is a clear predecessor of the stream of consciousness genre. What is undeniable is that the Romans, in comparison with the Greeks, innovate relatively few literary styles of their own.

Satire is one of the few Roman additions to literature-Horace was the first to use satire extensively as a tool for argument, and Juvenal made it into a weapon. The New Testament is an unusual collection of texts--Paul's epistles are the first collection of personal letters to be treated as literature, the Gospels arguably present the first realistic biographies in Western literature, and John's Book of Revelation, though not the first of its kind, essentially defines apocalypse as a literary genre. Augustine of Hippo and his The City of God do for religious literature essentially what Plato had done for philosophy, but Augustine's approach was far less conversational and more didactive. His Confessions is perhaps the first true autobiography, and certainly it gives rise to the genre of confessional literature which is now more popular than ever.

TURKISH LITERATURE

The history of Turkish literature spans a period of nearly 1,500 years. The oldest extant records of written Turkish are the Orhon inscriptions, found in the Orhon River valley in central Mongolia and dating to the 8th century. Subsequent to this period, between the 9th and 11th centuries, there arose among the nomadic Turkic peoples of Central Asia/Turkistan a tradition of oral epics, such as the Book of Dede Korkut of the Oghuz Turks-ancestors of the modern Turkish people-and the Manas epic of the Kyrgyz Turks.

Among the early written prose Yusuf Has Hajib's "Kutat-Ku Bilik" (Blessings and Wisdom) a book on Turkic philosophy, the "Divan-i Lugat-it Turk" an encyclopedic dictionary written by Mahmut Kasgari and Mir Ali Shir Nava'i the Chaucer of the Turks are early epic masterpieces.

PERSIAN LITERATURE

The Medieval Period

After the fall of Rome (in roughly 476), many of the literary approaches and styles invented by the Greeks and Romans fell out of favor in Europe. In the millennium or so that intervened between Rome's fall and the Florentine Renaissance, medieval literature focused more and more on faith and faith-related matters, in part because the works written by the Greeks had not been preserved in Europe, and therefore there were few models of classical literature to learn from and move beyond. What little there was became changed and distorted, with new forms beginning to develop from the distortions. Some of these distorted beginnings of new styles can be seen in the literature generally described as Matter of Rome, Matter of France and Matter of Britain.

Following Rome's fall, Islam's spread across Asia and Africa brought with it a desire to preserve and build upon the work of the Greeks, especially in literature. Although much had been lost to the ravages of time (and to catastrophe, as in the burning of the Library of Alexandria), many Greek works remained extant: they were preserved and copied carefully by Muslim scribes.

Among the innovations of Arabic literature was Ibn Khaldun's perspective on chronicling past events-by fully rejecting supernatural explanations, Khaldun essentially invented the scientific or sociological approach to history.

In Europe Hagiographies, or "lives of the saints", are frequent among early medieval texts. The writings of Bede-Historia ecclesiastica gentis Anglorum-and others continue the faith-based historical tradition begun by Eusebius in the early 300s. Playwriting essentially ceased, except for the mystery plays and the passion plays that focused heavily on conveying Christian belief to the common people. Around 400 AD the Prudenti Psychomachia began the tradition of allegorical tales. Poetry flourished, however, in the hands of the troubadours, whose courtly romances and chanson de geste amused and entertained the upper classes who were their patrons. Geoffrey of Monmouth wrote works which he claimed were histories of Britain. These were highly fanciful and included stories of Merlin the magician and King Arthur. Epic poetry continued to develop with the addition of the mythologies of Northern Europe: Beowulf and the Norse sagas have much in common with Homer and Virgil's approaches to war and honor, while poems such as Dante's Divine Comedy and Geoffrey Chaucer's The Canterbury Tales take much different stylistic directions.

From Persian culture the book which would, eventually, become the most famous in the west is the Rubaiyat of Omar Khayyam. The Rubáiyát is a collection of poems by the Persian mathematician and astronomer Omar Khayyám (1048-1122). "Rubaiyat" means "quatrains": verses of four lines.

In November 1095-Pope Urban II preached the First Crusade at the Council of Clermont. The crusades would affect everything in Europe and the Middle East for many years to come and literature would, along with everything else, be transformed by the wars between these two cultures. For instance the image of the knight would take on a different significance. Also the Islamic emphasis on scientific investigation and the presevation of the Greek philosophical writings would eventually affect European literature.

Between Augustine and The Bible, religious authors had numerous aspects of Christianity that needed further explication and interpretation. Thomas Aquinas, more than any other single person, was able to turn theology into a kind of science, in part because he was heavily influenced by Aristotle, whose works were returning to Europe in the 1200s.

LATER CHINESE LITERATURE

Lyric poetry advanced far more in China than in Europe prior to 1000, as multiple new forms developed in the Han, Tang, and Song dynasties: perhaps the greatest poets of this era in Chinese literature were Li Bai and Du Fu.

Printing began in China. A copy of the Diamond Sutra, a key Buddhist text, found sealed in a cave in China in the early 20th century, is the oldest known dated printed book, with a printed date of 868. The method used was block printing.

Some authors feel that China originated the novel form with the Romance of the Three Kingdoms by Luo Guanzhong (in the 14th century), although others feel that this epic is distinct from the novel in key ways.

EUROPEAN RENAISSANCE LITERATURE

Had nothing occurred to change literature in the 1400s but the Renaissance, the break with medieval approaches would have been clear enough. The 1400s, however, also brought Johann Gutenberg and his invention of the printing press, an innovation (for Europe, at least) that would change literature forever. Texts were no longer precious and expensive to produce-they could be cheaply and rapidly put into the marketplace. Literacy went from the prized possession of the select few to a much broader section of the population (though by no means universal). As a result, much about literature in Europe was radically altered in the two centuries following Gutenberg's unveiling of the printing press in 1455.

William Caxton was the first English printer and published English language texts including Le Morte d'Arthur (a collection of oral tales of the Arthurian Knights which is a forerunner of the novel) and Geoffrey Chaucer's Canterbury Tales. These are an indication of future directions in literature. With the arrival of the printing press a process begins in which folk yarns and legends are collected within a frame story and then mass published.

In the Renaissance, the focus on learning for learning's sake causes an outpouring of literature. Petrarch popularized the sonnet as a poetic form; Giovanni Boccaccio's Decameron made romance acceptable in prose as well as poetry; François Rabelais rejuvenates satire with Gargantua and Pantagruel; Michel de Montaigne single-handedly invented the essay and used it to catalog his life and ideas. Perhaps the most controversial and important work of the time period was a treatise printed in Nuremberg, entitled De Revolutionibus Orbium Coelestium: in it, the astronomer Nicolaus Copernicus removed the Earth from its privileged position in the universe, which had far-reaching effects, not only in science, but in literature and its approach to humanity, hierarchy, and truth.

THE EARLY MODERN PERIOD IN WESTERN EUROPE

A new spirit of science and investigation in Europe was part of a general upheaval in human understanding which began with the discovery of the New world in 1492 and continues through the subsequent centuries, even up to the present day.

The form of writing now commonplace across the world-the novel-originated from the early modern period and grew in popularity in the next century. Before the modern novel became established as a form there first had to be a transitional stage when "novelty" began to appear in the style of the epic poem.

Plays for entertainment (as opposed to religious enlightenment) returned to Europe's stages in the early modern period. William Shakespeare is the most notable of the early modern playwrights, but numerous others made important contributions, including Christopher Marlowe, Molière, and Ben Jonson. From the 16th to the 18th century Commedia dell'arte performers improvised in the streets of Italy and France. Some Commedia dell'arte plays were written down. Both the written plays and the improvisation were influential upon literature of the time, particularly upon the work of Molière. Shakespeare, and his associate Robert Armin, drew upon the arts of jesters and strolling players in creating new style comedies. All the parts, even the female ones, were played by men (en travesti) but that would change, first in France and then in England too, by the end of the 17th century.

The epic Elizabethan poem The Faerie Queene by Edmund Spenser was published, in its first part, in 1590 and then in completed form in 1597. The Fairie Queen marks the transitional period in which "novelty" begins to enter in to the narative in the sense of overturning and playing with the flow of events. Theatrical forms known in Spenser's time such as The Masque and the Mummers' Play are incorporated into the poem in ways which twist tradition and turn it to political propaganda in the service of Queen Elizabeth I.

The earliest work considered an opera in the sense the work is usually understood dates from around 1597. It is Dafne, (now lost) written by Jacopo Peri for an elite circle of literate Florentine humanists who gathered as the "Camerata".

Miguel de Cervantes's Don Quixote de la Mancha has been called "the first novel" by many literary scholars (or the first of the modern European novels). It was published in two parts. The first part was published in 1605 and the second in 1615. It might be viewed as a parody of Le Morte d'Arthur (and other examples of the chivalric romance), in which case the novel form would be the direct result of poking fun at a collection of heroic folk legends. This is fully in keeping with the spirit of the age of enlightenment which began from about this time and delighted in giving a satirical twist to the stories and ideas of the past. It's worth noting that this trend toward satirising previous writings was only made possible by the printing press. Without the invention of mass produced copies of a book it would not be possible to assume the reader will have seen the earlier work and will thus understand the references within the text.

The new style in English poetry during the 17th century was that of the metaphysical movement. The metaphysical poets were John Donne, George Herbert, Andrew Marvell, Thomas Traherne, Henry Vaughan and others. Metaphysical poetry is characterised by a spirit of intellectual investigation of the spiritual, rather than the mystical reverence of many earlier English poems. The metaphysical poets were clearly trying to understand the world around them and the spirit behind it, instead of accepting dogma on the basis of faith.

In the middle of the century the king of England was overthrown and a republic declared. In the new regime (which lasted from 1649 to 1653) the arts suffered. In England and the rest of the British Isles Oliver Cromwell's rule temporarily banned all theatre, festivals, jesters, mummers plays and frivolities. The ban was lifted when the monarchy was restored with Charles II. Thomas Killigrew and the Drury Lane theatre were favorites of King Charles.

In contrast to the metaphysical poets was John Milton's Paradise Lost, an epic religious poem in blank verse. Milton had been Oliver Cromwell's chief propagandist and suffered when the Restoration came. Paradise Lost is one of the highest developments of the epic form in poetry immediately preceding the era of the modern prose novel.

An allegorical novel, The Pilgrim's Progress from This World to That Which Is to Come was published by John Bunyan in 1678.

Other early novelists include Daniel Defoe (born 1660) and Jonathan Swift (born 1667).

10

Rhetoric

Rhetoric (from Greek word, rhêtôr, orator, teacher) is the art or technique of persuasion through the use of oral or written language. Rhetoric is one of the three original liberal arts or trivium (the other members are dialectic and grammar) in Western culture. In ancient and medieval times, grammar concerned itself with correct, accurate, pleasing, and effective language use through the study and criticism of literary models, dialectic concerned itself with the testing and invention of new knowledge through a process of question and answer, and rhetoric concerned itself with persuasion in public and political settings such as assemblies and courts of law. As such, rhetoric is said to flourish in open and democratic societies with rights of free speech, free assembly, and political enfranchisement for some portion of the population.

The concept of rhetoric has shifted widely during its 2500-year history. Today rhetoric is described more broadly as the art or practice of persuasion through any symbolic system, but especially language. Or, rhetoric can be described as the persuasive or "suasory" function of all human action, including symbolic action like language use. So while rhetoric clearly has a place in such arenas as politics, law, public relations, lobbying, marketing and advertising, many scholars also find elements of rhetoric in such apparently non-rhetorical fields as science, journalism, history, literature and even cartography or architecture.

The terms "rhetoric" and "sophistry" are also used today in a pejorative or dismissive sense, when someone wants to refer to demagogic politicians, distinguish between "empty" words and action, or between true or accurate information and misinformation, propaganda, or "spin." Another current use of the word rhetoric is to denigrate specific forms of verbal reasoning as irrelevant, fallacious, inflammatory, or spurious. Nonetheless, rhetoric, as the art of persuasion, continues to play an important function in contemporary public life.

HISTORY

Introduction

The scholarly literature on the 2500-year history and theory of rhetoric in Western culture is far too voluminous to be listed at the end of this entry. Useful reference works include George Kennedy's Classical Rhetoric and its Christian and Secular Tradition from Ancient to Modern Times, Thomas O. Sloane, ed., Encyclopedia of Rhetoric (Oxford University Press, 2001); Heinrich Lausberg, Handbook of Literary Rhetoric: A Foundation for Literary Study (1960; 2nd ed. 1973; English trans, Brill, 1998); Richard A. Lanham, A Handlist of Rhetorical Terms (University of California Press, 1968; 2nd ed. 1991). For overview surveys of the scholarly literature, see Winifred Bryan Horner, ed., The Present State of Scholarship in Historical and Contemporary Rhetoric (University of Missouri Press, 1983; rev. ed. 1990); and Theresa Enos and Stuart C. Brown, eds., Defining the New Rhetorics (Sage, 1993).

Ancient Greece

Western thinking about rhetoric grew out of the public and political life of Ancient Greece, much of which revolved around the use of oratory as the medium through which political and judicial decisions were made, and through which philosophical ideas were developed and disseminated. For modern students today, it can be difficult to remember that the wide use and availability of written texts is a phenomenon that was just coming into vogue in Classical Greece. In Classical times, many of the great thinkers and political leaders performed their works before an audience, usually in the context of a competition or contest for fame, political influence, and cultural capital; in fact, many of them are known only through the texts that their students, followers, or detractors wrote down. As has already been noted, rhetor was the Greek term for orator: A rhetor was a citizen who regularly addressed juries and political assemblies and who was thus understood to have gained some knowledge about public speaking in the process, though in general facility with language was often referred to as logôn techne, "skill with arguments" or "verbal artistry." See, Mogens Herman Hansen The Athenian Democracy in the Age of Demosthenes (Blackwell, 1991); Josiah Ober Mass and Elite in Democratic Athens (Princeton UP, 1989); Jeffrey Walker, Rhetoric and Poetic in Antiquity (Oxford UP, 2000).

Rhetoric thus evolved as an important art, one that provided the orator with the forms, means, and strategies of persuading an audience of the correctness of the orator's arguments. Today the term rhetoric can be used at times to refer only to the form of argumentation, often with the pejorative connotation that rhetoric is a means of obscuring the truth. Classical philosophers believed quite the contrary: the skilled use of rhetoric was essential to the discovery of truths, because it provided the means of ordering and clarifying arguments.

THE SOPHISTS

Organized thought about rhetoric began in ancient Greece. Possibly, the first study about the power of language may be attributed to the philosopher Empedocles (d. ca. 444 BC), whose theories on human knowledge would provide a basis for many future rhetoricians. The first written manual is attributed to Corax and his pupil Tisias. Their work, as well as that of many of the early rhetoricians, grew out of the courts of law; Tisias, for example, is believed to have written judicial speeches that others delivered in the courts. Rhetoric was popularized in the 5th century BC by itinerant teachers known as sophists, the best known of whom were Protagoras (c.481-420 BC), Gorgias (c.483-376 BC), and Isocrates (436-338 BC). The Sophists were a disparate group who travelled from city to city making public displays to attract students who were then charged a fee for their education. Their central focus was on logos or what we might broadly refer to as discourse. They defined parts of speech, analyzed poetry, parsed close synonyms, invented argumentation strategies, and debated the nature of reality. They claimed to make their students "better," or, in other words, to teach virtue. They thus claimed that human "excellence" was not an accident of fate or a prerogative of noble birth, but an art or "techne" that could be taught and learned. Several sophists also questioned-received wisdom about the gods and about the inherent supremacy of Greek culture, taken for granted by Greeks of their time. They argued, for example, that cultural practices were a function of convention or nomos rather than blood or birth or phusis, and further that the morality or immorality of any action could not be judged outside of the cultural context within which it occurred. The well-known phrase, "Man is the measure of all things" arises from this belief. One of their most famous, and infamous, doctrines has to do with probability and counter arguments. They taught that every argument could be countered with an opposing argument, that an argument's effectiveness derived from how "likely" it appeared to the audience (its probability of seeming true), and that any probability argument could be countered with an inverted probability argument. Thus, if it seemed likely that a strong, poor man were guilty of robbing a rich, weak man, the strong poor man could argue, on the contrary, that this very likelihood (that he would be a suspect) makes it unlikely that he committed the crime. Aristophanes famously parodies the clever inversions that sophists were known for in his play The Clouds.

The word "sophistry" has negative connotations today, but in ancient Greece sophists were popular and well-paid professionals, widely respected for their abilities but also widely criticized for their excesses.

ISOCRATES

Isocrates (436-338 BC), like the sophists, taught public speaking as a means of human improvement, but he worked to distinguish himself from the Sophists, whom he saw as claiming far more than they could deliver. He suggested that while an art of virtue or excellence did exist, it was only one piece, and the least, in a process of self-improvement that relied much more heavily on native talent and desire, constant practice, and the imitation of good models. Isocrates believed that practice in speaking publicly about noble themes and important questions would function to improve the character of both speaker and audience while also offering the best service to a state. He thus wrote his speeches as "models" for his students to imitate in the same way that poets might imitate Homer or Hesiod. His was the first permanent school in Athens and it is likely that Plato's Academy and Aristotle's Lyceum were founded in part as a response to Isocrates. Though he left no handbooks, his speeches ("Antidosis" and "Against the Sophists" are most relevant to students of rhetoric) became models of oratory (he was one of the canonical "Ten Attic Orators") and he had a marked influence on Cicero and Quintilian, and through them, on the entire educational system of the west.

PLATO

Plato (427-347 BC) has famously outlined the differences between true and false rhetoric in a number of dialogues, but especially the Gorgias and the Phaedrus. Both dialogues are complex and difficult, but in both Plato disputes the Sophistic notion that an art of persuasion, the art of the Sophists which he calls "rhetoric" (after the public speaker or rhêtôr) can exist independent of the art of dialectic. Plato claims that since Sophists appeal only to what seems likely or probable, rather than to what is true, they are not at all making their students and audiences "better," but simply flattering them with what they want to hear. While Plato's condemnation of rhetoric is clear in the Gorgias, in the Phaedrus he seems to suggest the possibility of a true art of rhetoric based upon the knowledge produced by dialectic, and he relies on such a dialectically informed rhetoric to appeal to the main character, Phaedrus, to take up philosophy. Plato's animosity against the Sophists derives not only from their inflated claims to teach virtue and their reliance on appearances, but from the fact that his teacher, Socrates, was accused of being a sophist and ultimately sentenced to death for his teaching. In his dialogues, Plato attempts to distinguish the rhetoric common to Socratic questioning from Sophistry.

ARISTOTLE

Plato's student Aristotle (384-322 BC) famously set forth an extended treatise on rhetoric that still repays careful study today.

In the first sentence of The Art of Rhetoric, Aristotle says that "rhetoric is the counterpart [literally, the antistrophe] of dialectic." As the "antistrophc" of a Greek ode responds to and is patterned after the structure of the "strophe" (they form two sections of the whole and are sung by two parts of the chorus), so the art of rhetoric follows and is structurally patterned after the art of dialectic because both are arts of discourse production. Thus, while dialectical methods are necessary to find truth in theoretical matters, rhetorical methods are required in practical matters such as adjudicating somebody's guilt or innocence when charged in a court of law, or adjudicating a prudent course of action to be taken in a deliberative assembly.

For Plato and Aristotle, dialectic involves persuasion, so when Aristotle says that rhetoric is the antistrophe of dialectic, he means that rhetoric as he uses the term has a domain or scope of application that is parallel to but different from the domain or scope of application of dialectic.

In Nietzsche Humanist (1998: 129), Claude Pavur explains that "the Greek prefix 'anti' does not merely designate opposition, but it can also mean 'in place of.'" When Aristotle characterizes rhetoric as the antistrophe of dialectic, he no doubt means that rhetoric is used in place of dialectic when we are discussing civic issues in a court of law or in a legislative assembly. The domain of rhetoric is civic affairs and practical decision making in civic affairs, not theoretical considerations of operational definitions of terms and clarification of thought--these, for him, are in the domain of dialectic.

Aristotle's treatise on rhetoric is an attempt to systematically describe civic rhetoric as a human art or skill (techne). His definition of rhetoric as a mode of discovery seems to limit the art to the inventional process, and Aristotle heavily emphasizes the logical aspect of this process. But the treatise in fact also discusses not only elements of style and (briefly) delivery, but also emotional appeals (pathos) and characterological appeals (ethos). He thus identifies three steps or "offices" of rhetoric--invention, arrangement, and style--and three different types of rhetorical proof:

- ethos: how the character and credibility of a speaker influence an audience to consider him to be believable.

- This could be any position in which the speaker--from being a college professor of the subject, to being an acquaintance of person who experienced the matter in question--knows about the topic.
- pathos: the use of emotional appeals to alter the audience's judgment.
- This can be done through metaphor, amplification, storytelling, or presenting the topic in a way that evokes strong emotions in the audience.
- logos: the use of reasoning, either inductive or deductive, to construct an argument.

Inductive reasoning uses examples (historical, mythical, or hypothetical) to draw conclusions.

Deductive or "enthymematic" reasoning uses generally accepted propositions to derive specific conclusions. The term logic evolved from logos. Aristotle emphasized enthymematic reasoning as central to the process of rhetorical invention, though later rhetorical theorists placed much less emphasis on it.

Aristotle also identifies three different types or genres of civic rhetoric: forensic (also known as judicial, was concerned with determining truth or falsity of events that took place in the past), deliberative (also known as political, was concerned with determining whether or not particular actions should or should not be taken in the future), and epideictic (also known as ceremonial, was concerned with praise and blame, demonstrating beauty and skill in the present).

One of the most fruitful of Aristotelian doctrines was the idea of topics (also referred to as common topics or commonplaces). Though the term had a wide range of application (as a memory technique or compositional exercise, for example) it most often referred to the "seats of argument"--the list of categories of thought or modes of reasoning--that a speaker could use in order to generate arguments or proofs. The topics were thus a heuristic or inventional tool designed to help speakers categorize and thus better retain and apply frequently used types of argument. For example, since we often see effects as "like" their causes, one way to invent an argument (about a future effect) is by discussing the cause (which it will be "like"). This and other rhetorical topics derive from Aristotle's belief that there are certain predictable ways in which humans (particularly non-specialists) draw conclusions from premises. Based upon and adapted from his dialectical Topics, the rhetorical topics became a central feature of later rhetorical theorizing, most famously in Cicero's work of that name.

ROMAN RHETORICIANS

The Romans, for whom oration also became an important part of public life, saw much value in Greek rhetoric, hiring Greek rhetoricians to teach in their schools and as private tutors, and imitating and adapting Greek rhetorical works in Latin and with Roman examples. Roman rhetoric thus largely extends upon and develops its Greek roots, though it tends to prefer practical advice to the theoretical speculations of Greek rhetoricians. Cicero (106-43 BC) and Quintilian (35-100 AD) were chief among Roman rhetoricians, and their work is an extension of sophistic, Isocratean, Platonic and Aristotelian rhetorical theory.

Latin rhetoric was developed out of the Rhodian schools of rhetoric. In the second century BC, Rhodes became an important educational center, particularly of rhetoric, and the sons of noble Roman families studied there.

Although not widely read in Roman times, the Rhetorica ad Herennium (sometimes attributed to Cicero, but probably not his work) is a notable early work on Latin rhetoric. Its author was probably a Latin rhetorician in Rhodes, and for the first time we see a systematic treatment of Latin elocutio. The Ad Herennium provides a glimpse into the early development of Latin rhetoric, and in the Middle Ages and Renaissance, it achieved wide publication as one of the basic school texts on rhetoric.

Whether or not he wrote the Rhetorica ad Herennium, Cicero, along with Quintilian (the most influential Roman teacher of rhetoric), is considered one of the most important Roman rhetoricians. His works include the early and very influential De Inventione (On Invention, often read alongside the Ad Herennium as the two basic texts of rhetorical theory throughout the Middle Ages and into the Renaissance), De Oratore (a fuller statement of rhetorical principles in dialague form), Topics (a rhetorical treatment of common topics, highly influential through the

Renaissance), Brutus (a discussion of famous orators)and Orator (a defense of Cicero's style). Cicero also left a large body of speeches and letters which would establish the outlines of Latin eloquence and style for generations to come. It was the rediscovery of Cicero's speeches (such as the defence of Archias) and letters (to Atticus) by Italians like Petrach that, in part, ignited the cultural innovations that we know as the Rennaisance.

Quintilian's career began as a pleader in the courts of law; his reputation grew so great that Vespasian created a chair of rhetoric for him in Rome. The culmination of his life's work was the Institutio oratoria (or Institutes of Oratory), a lengthy treatise on the training of the orator in which he discusses the training of the "perfect" orator from birth to old age and, in the process, reviews the doctrines and opinions of many influential rhetoricians who preceeded him.

In the Institutes, Quintilian organizes rhetorical study through the stages of education that an aspiring orator would undergo, beginning with the selection of a nurse. Aspects of elementary education (training in reading and writing, grammar, and literary criticism) are followed by preliminary rhetorical exercises in composition (the progymnasmata) that include maxims and fables, narratives and comparisons, and finally full legal or political speeches. The delivery of speeches within the context of education or for entertainment purposes became widespread and popular under the term "declamation." Rhetorical training proper was categorized under five canons that would persist for centuries in academic circles:

- Inventio (invention) is the process that leads to the development and refinement of an argument.
- Once arguments are developed, dispositio (disposition, or arrangement) is used to determine how it should be organized for greatest effect, usually beginning with the exordium.
- Once the speech content is known and the structure is determined, the next steps involve elocutio (style) and pronuntiatio (presentation).
- Memoria (memory) comes to play as the speaker recalls each of these elements during the speech.

- Actio (delivery) is the final step as the speech is presented in a gracious and pleasing way to the audience-the Grand Style.

This work was available only in fragments in medieval times, but the discovery of a complete copy at Abbey of St. Gall in 1416 led to its emergence as one of the most influential works on rhetoric during the Renaissance.

Quintilian's work attempts to describe not just the art of rhetoric, but the formation of the perfect orator as a politically active, virtuous, publically minded citizen. His emphasis on the real life application of rhetorical training was in part nostalgia for the days when rhetoric was an important political tool, and in part a reaction against the growing tendency in Roman schools toward standarization of themes and techniques and increasing separation between school exercises and actual legal practice, a tendency equally powerful today in public schools and law schools alike.

At the same time that rhetoric was becoming divorced from political decision making, rhetoric rose as a culturally vibrant and important mode of entertainment and cultural criticism in a movement known as the "second sophistic," a development which gave rise to the charge (made by Quintilian and others) that teachers were emphasizing ornamentation over substance in rhetoric. Quintilian's masterful work was not enough to curb this movement, but his dismayed response cemented the scholarly opinion that 2nd Century C.E. rhetoric fell into decadence and political irrelevance, despite its wide popularity and cultural importance.

Although he is not commonly regarded as a rhetorician, St. Augustine (354-430) was trained in rhetoric and was at one time a teacher of Latin rhetoric. After his conversion to Christianity, he became interested in using these "pagan" arts for spreading his religion. This new use of rhetoric is explored in the Fourth Book of his De Doctrina Christiana, which laid the foundation of what would become homiletics, the rhetoric of the sermon.

A valuable collection of studies can be found in Stanley E. Porter, ed., Handbook of Classical Rhetoric in the Hellenistic Period 330 B.C.-A.D. 400 (Brill, 1997).

RHETORIC FROM THE RENAISSANCE TO THE ENLIGHTENMENT

After the Roman Empire, the study of rhetoric continued to be central to the study of the verbal arts; but the study of the verbal arts went into decline for several centuries, followed eventually by a gradual rise in formal education, culminating in the rise of medieval universities. But rhetoric transmuted during this period in the arts of letter writing (ars dictaminis) and writing sermons (ars praedicandi). As part of the trivium, rhetoric was secondary to the study of logic, and its study was highly scholastic: students were given repetitive exercises in the creation of discourses on historical subjects (suasoriae) or on classic legal questions (controversiae).

In his 1943 Cambridge University doctoral dissertation in English, Marshall McLuhan (1911-1980) surveys the verbal arts from approximately the time of Cicero down to the time of Thomas Nashe (1567-1600). His dissertation is still noteworthy for undertaking to study the history of the verbal arts together as the trivium, even though the developments that he surveys have been studied in greater detail since he undertook his study. As noted below, McLuhan became one of the most widely publicized thinkers in the 20th century, so it is important to note his scholarly roots in the study of the history of rhetoric and dialectic.

Sixteenth Century

Walter J. Ong's encyclopedia article "Humanism" in the 1967 New Catholic Encyclopedia provides a well-informed survey of Renaissance humanism, which defined itself broadly as disfavoring medieval scholastic logic and dialectic and as favoring instead the study of classical Latin style and grammar and philology and rhetoric. (Reprinted in Ong's Faith and Contexts (Scholars Press, 1999; 4: 69-91.)

One influential figure in the rebirth of interest in classical rhetoric was Erasmus (c.1466-1536). His work, De Duplici Copia Verborum et Rerum (1512), was widely published (it went through more than 150 editions throughout Europe) and became one of the basic school texts on the subject. Its treatment of rhetoric is less comprehensive than the classic works of antiquity, but provides a traditional treatment of res-verba (matter and form):

its first book treats the subject of elocutio, showing the student how to use schemes and tropes; the second book covers inventio. Much of the emphasis is on abundance of variation (copia means "plenty" or "abundance", as in copious or cornucopia), so both books focus on ways to introduce the maximum amount of variety into discourse. For instance, in one section of the De Copia, Erasmus presents two hundred variations of the sentence "Semper, dum vivam, tui meminero". Another of his works, the extremely popular The Praise of Folly also had considerable influence on the teaching of rhetoric in the later sixteenth century. Its orations in favour of qualities such as madness spawned a type of exercise popular in Elizabethan grammar schools, later called adoxography, which required pupils to compose passages in praise of useless things.

Juan Luis Vives (1492-1540) also helped shape the study of rhetoric in England. A Spaniard, he was appointed in 1523 to the Lectureship of Rhetoric at Oxford by Cardinal Wolsey, and was entrusted by Henry VIII to be one of the tutors of Mary. Vives fell into disfavor when Henry VIII divorced Catherine of Aragon and left England in 1528. His best-known work was a book on education, De Disciplinis, published in 1531, and his writings on rhetoric included Rhetoricae, sive De Ratione Dicendi, Libri Tres (1533), De Consultatione (1533), and a rhetoric on letter writing, De Conscribendis Epistolas (1536).

It is likely that many well-known English writers would have been exposed to the works of Erasmus and Vives (as well as those of the Classical rhetoricians) in their schooling, which was conducted in Latin (not English) and often included some study of Greek and placed considerable emphasis on rhetoric. See, for example, T.W. Baldwin's William Shakspere's Small Latine and Lesse Greeke, 2 vols. (University of Illinois Press, 1944).

The mid-1500s saw the rise of vernacular rhetorics-those written in English rather than in the Classical languages; adoption of works in English was slow, however, due to the strong orientation toward Latin and Greek. A successful early text was Thomas Wilson's The Arte of Rhetorique (1553), which presents a traditional treatment of rhetoric. For instance, Wilson presents the five canons of rhetoric (Invention, Disposition, Elocutio, Memoria, and Utterance or Actio). Other notable works included Angel

Day's The English Secretorie (1586, 1592), George Puttenham's The Arte of English Poesie (1589), and Richard Rainholde's Foundacion of Rhetorike (1563).

During this same period, a movement began that would change the organization of the school curriculum in Protestant and especially Puritan circles and lead to rhetoric losing its central place. A French scholar, Petrus Ramus (1515-1572), dissatisfied with what he saw as the overly broad and redundant organization of the trivium, proposed a new curriculum.

In his scheme of things, the five components of rhetoric no longer lived under the common heading of rhetoric. Instead, invention and disposition were determined to fall exclusively under the heading of dialectic, while style, delivery, and memory were all that remained for rhetoric. See Walter J. Ong, Ramus, Method, and the Decay of Dialogue: From the Art of Discourse to the Art of Reason (Harvard University Press, 1958; reissued by the University of Chicago Press, 2004, with a new foreword by Adrian Johns).

One of Ramus' followers, Audomarus Talaeus (Omer Talon) published his rhetoric, Institutiones Oratoriae, in 1544. This work provided a simple presentation of rhetoric that emphasized the treatment of style, and became so popular that it was mentioned in John Brinsley's (1612) Ludus literarius; or The Grammar Schoole as being the "most used in the best schooles."

Many other Ramist rhetorics followed in the next half-century, and by the 1600s, their approach became the primary method of teaching rhetoric in Protestant and especially Puritan circles. See Walter J. Ong, Ramus and Talon Inventory (Harvard University Press, 1958); Joseph S. Freedman, Philosophy and the Arts in Central Europe, 1500-1700: Teaching and Texts at Schools and Universities (Ashgate, 1999).

John Milton (1608-1674) wrote a textbook in logic or dialectic in Latin based on Ramus' work, which has now been translated into English by Walter J. Ong and Charles J. Ermatinger in The Complete Prose Works of John Milton (Yale University Press, 1982; 8: 206-407), with a lengthy introduction by Ong (144-205). The introduction is reprinted in Ong's Faith and Contexts (Scholars Press, 1999; 4: 111-41).

But Ramism did not strongly influence the established Catholic schools and universities or the new Catholic schools and universities founded by members of the religious order known as the Society of Jesus, as can be seen in the Jesuit document known as the Ratio Studiorum that Claude Pavur, S.J., has recently translated into English, with the Latin text in the parallel column on each page (St. Louis: Institute of Jesuit Sources, 2005). The influence of Cicero and Quintilian permeates the Ratio Studiorum.

Seventeenth Century

In New England and at Harvard College (founded 1636), Ramus and his followers dominated, as Perry Miller shows in The New England Mind: The Seventeenth Century (Harvard University Press, 1939). However, in England, several writers influenced the course of rhetoric during the seventeenth century, many of them carrying forward the dichotomy that had been set forth by Ramus and his followers during the preceding decades. Of greater importance is that this century saw the development of a modern, vernacular style that looked to English, rather than to Greek, Latin, or French models.

Francis Bacon (1561-1626), although not a rhetorician, contributed to the field in his writings. One of the concerns of the age was to find a suitable style for the discussion of scientific topics, which needed above all a clear exposition of facts and arguments, rather than the ornate style favored at the time. Bacon in his The Advancement of Learning criticized those who are preoccupied with style rather than "the weight of matter, worth of subject, soundness of argument, life of invention, or depth of judgment." On matters of style, he proposed that the style conform to the subject matter and to the audience, that simple words be employed whenever possible, and that the style should be agreeable. See Lisa Jardine, Francis Bacon: Discovery and the Art of Discourse (Camb e University Press, 1975).

Thomas Hobbes (1588-1679) also wrote on rhetoric. Along with a shortened translation of Aristotle's Rhetoric, Hobbes also produced a number of other works on the subject. Sharply contrarian on many subjects, Hobbes, like Bacon, also promoted a simpl nd more natural style that used figures of speech sparingly.

Perhaps the most influential development in English style came out of the work of the Royal Society (founded in 1660), which in 1664 set up a committee to improve the English language. Am ttee's members were John Evelyn (1620-1706), Thomas Sprat (1635-1713), and John Dryden (1631-1700). Sprat regarded "fine speaking" as a disease, and thought that a proper style should "reject all amplifications, digressions, and swellings of style" and instead "return back to a primitive purity and shortness" (History of the Royal Society, 1667).

While the work of this committee never went beyond planning, John Dryden is often credited with creating and exemplifying a new and modern English style. His central tenet was that the style should be proper "to the occasion, the subject, and the persons." As such, he advocated the use of English words whenever possible instead of foreign ones, as well as vernacular, rather than Latinate, syntax. His own prose (and his poetry) became exemplars of this new style.

MODERN DEVELOPMENTS

Walter Jost has examined Rhetorical Thought in John Henry Newman (1989). (John Henry Newman lived from 1801-1890.)

The Canadian Jesuit philosopher and theologian Bernard Lonergan (1904-1984), who was deeply influenced by Newman's An Essay in Aid of a Grammar of Assent (1870), worked out what he styles the generalized empirical method in Insight: A Study of Human Understanding (1957) and elsewhere. In a review article originally published in the Quarterly Journal of Speech (1985: 476-88), John Angus Campbell has characterized Lonergan's generalized empirical method as his rhetoric, an astute observation that has not yet been widely noted. Even so, Lonergan's generalized empirical method holds enormous potential for taking the theory of rhetoric to the next level of significance. (Campbell's essay is reprinted in Communication and Lonergan (Sheed & Ward, 1991: 3-22).

At the turn of the twentieth century, there was a revival of rhetorical study manifested in the establishment of departments of rhetoric and speech at academic institutions, as well as the formation of national and international professional organizations.

Theorists generally agree that a significant reason for the revival of the study of rhetoric was the renewed importance of language and persuasion in the increasingly mediated environment of the twentieth century. The rise of advertising and of mass media such as photography, telegraphy, radio, and film brought rhetoric more prominently into people's lives.

For example, when McLuhan was working on his 1943 Cambridge University doctoral dissertation on the verbal arts and Nashe, mentioned above, he was also preparing the materials that were eventually published as the book The Mechanical Bride: The Folklore of Industrial Man (Vanguard Press, 1951). This book is a compilation of exhibits of ads and other materials from popular culture with short essays about them by McLuhan. The essays involve rhetorical analyses of the ways in which the material in an item aims to persuade, and commentary on the persuasive strategies in each item.

After studying the persuasive strategies involved in such an array of items in popular culture, McLuhan shifted the focus of his rhetorical analysis and began to consider how communication media themselves have an impact on us as persuasive, in a manner of speaking. In other words, the communication media as such embody and carry a persuasive dimension. McLuhan uses hyperbole to express this insight when he says "the medium is the message." This shift in focus from his 1951 book led to his two most widely known books, The Gutenberg Galaxy: The Making of Typographic Man (University of Toronto Press, 1962) and Understanding Media: The Extensions of Man (McGraw-Hill, 1964). These two books led McLuhan to become one of the most publicized thinkers in the 20th century. No other scholar of the history and theory of rhetoric was as widely publicized in the 20th century as McLuhan.

McLuhan read Lonergan's Insight, mentioned above, in 1957 (see Letters of Marshall McLuhan, 1987: 251). Lonergan's book is an elaborate guidebook to cultivate one's inwardness and on attending to and reflecting on one's inward consciousness. McLuhan's 1962 and 1964 books represent an inward turn to attending to one's consciousness that is far more pronounced than anything found in his 1951 book or in his 1943 dissertation. By contrast, many other thinkers in the study of rhetoric are more outward oriented toward sociological considerations and symbolic interaction.

McLuhan's famous dictum "the medium is the message" can be paraphrased with terminology from Lonergan. At the empirical level of consciousness, the medium is the message, whereas at the intelligent and rational levels of consciousness, the content is the message. McLuhan is thus ordering us to pay attention to the empirical level of consciousness.

CURRENT STATE

Rhetorical theory today is as much influenced by the research results and research methods of the behavioral sciences and by theories of literary criticism as by ancient rhetorical theory. Early rhetorical theorists attempted to turn the study of rhetoric into a social science that allowed predictive analyses of human behavior. Interdisciplinary scholars of symbol systems, such as Ernst Cassirer (1874-1945), Hugh Duncan, and most notably Kenneth Burke (1897-1993), influenced a new generation of rhetorical scholars who drew from various disciplines to more fully comprehend the phenomenon of human communication in all its aspects. While ancient rhetorical scholarship had focused primarily on rhetoric as speech, contemporary rhetorical theorists are interested in the panoply of human symbolic behavior-both the spoken and written word as well as music, film, radio, television, etc. Thus Kenneth Burke, who defined the human being as the "symbol-using animal," defined rhetoric as "the use of symbols to induce cooperation in those who by nature respond to symbols." Current rhetorical theory also draws heavily from cultural studies, performance studies, and design studies. Topics of interest to contemporary scholars include the relationships between rhetoric and gender, studies of non-traditional or alternative rhetorics, and rhetorics of science, technology, and new media.

Other notable 20th-century authors in the study of the history and theory of rhetoric include Herbert Wichelns, Edwin Black, Ernest Wrage, Wayne C. Booth, Cleanth Brooks, Karlyn Kohrs Campbell, Barbara Biesecker, Dana L. Cloud, Celeste M. Condit, Edward P.J. Corbett, James Darsey, Paul de Man, Raymie McKerrow, Dilip Parameshwar Gaonkar, G. Thomas Goodnight,

Susan Jarrett, James Kinneavy, Ernesto Laclau, Richard A. Lanham, Michael Leff, Andrea Lunsford, Michael Calvin McGee, Martin Medhurst, Marie Hochmuth Nichols, Lucy Olbrechts-Tyteca, Chaim Perelman, I.A. Richards, Edward Schiappa, Stephen Toulmin, Mark Turner, Victor J. Vitanza, Robert Penn Warren, and Richard M. Weaver.

Contemporary scholars in rhetoric come from diverse academic backgrounds, and are often housed in departments of English, Communication Studies, Rhetoric, Education, or Speech Communication. Rhetorical scholars meet at conferences such as the Conference on College Composition and Communication, the National Communication Association conference, and the Rhetoric Society of America conference. They publish research in journals including the Quarterly Journal of Speech, College Composition and Communication, the Rhetoric Society Quarterly, Rhetoric Review, Rhetoric and Public Affairs, and Philosophy and Rhetoric.

11

Poetry

Poetry (from the Greek, poiesis, "making" or "creating") is a form of art in which language is used for its aesthetic qualities in addition to, or in lieu of, its ostensible meaning. Poetry may be written independently, as discrete poems, or may be used in conjunction with other arts, as in poetic drama, hymns or lyrics.

Poetry has a long history. Early attempts to define it, such as Aristotle's Poetics, focused on the uses of speech in rhetoric, drama, song and comedy. Later attempts focused on features such as repetition and rhyme, and emphasised the aesthetics which distinguish poetry from prose. From the mid-20th century, poetry has sometimes been more loosely defined as a fundamental creative act using language.

Poetry often uses particular forms and conventions to expand the literal meaning of the words, or to invoke emotional or sensual responses. Devices such as assonance, alliteration and rhythm are sometimes used to achieve musical or incantatory effects. Poetry's use of ambiguity, symbolism, irony and other stylistic elements of poetic diction often leaves a poem open to multiple interpretations. Similarly, metaphor and simile create a resonance between otherwise disparate images-a layering of meanings, forming connections previously not perceived. Kindred forms of resonance may exist, between individual verses, in their patterns of rhyme or rhythm.

Some forms of poetry are specific to particular cultures and genres, responding to the characteristics of the language in which the poet writes. While readers accustomed to identifying poetry with Dante, Shakespeare, Goethe and Mickiewicz may think of it as being written in rhyming lines and regular meter, there are other traditions, such as those of Du Fu and Beowulf, that use other approaches to achieve rhythm and euphony.

In today's globalized world, poets often borrow styles, techniques and forms from diverse cultures and languages.

HISTORY

Poetry as an art form may predate literacy. Thus many ancient works, from the Vedas (1800-1500 BC) to the Odyssey (700-500 BC), appear to have been composed in poetic form to aid memorization and oral transmission, in prehistoric and ancient societies. Poetry appears among the earliest records of most literate cultures, with poetic fragments found on early monoliths, rune stones and stelae.

The oldest surviving poem is the Epic of Gilgamesh, from the 3rd millennium BC in Sumer (in Iraq/Mesopotamia), which was written in cuneiform script on clay tablets and, later, papyrus. The Epic of Gilgamesh is based on the historical king Gilgamesh. The oldest love poem, found on a clay tablet now known as Istanbul #2461, was also a Sumerian poem. It was recited by a bride of the Sumerian king Shu-Sin, who ruled 2037-2029 BC. The oldest epic poetry besides the Epic of Gilgamesh are the Greek epics, Iliad and Odyssey, and the Indian epics, Ramayana and Mahabharata. The longest epic poems ever written were the Mahabharata and the Tibetan Epic of King Gesar.

The efforts of ancient thinkers to determine what makes poetry distinctive as a form, and what distinguishes good poetry from bad, resulted in "poetics"-the study of the aesthetics of poetry. Some ancient societies, such as the Chinese through the Shi Jing, one of the Five Classics of Confucianism, developed canons of poetic works that had ritual as well as aesthetic importance. More recently, thinkers have struggled to find a definition that could encompass formal differences as great as those between Chaucer's Canterbury Tales and Matsuo Basho's Oku no Hosomichi, as well as differences in context spanning Tanakh religious poetry, love poetry, and rap.

Context can be critical to poetics and to the development of poetic genres and forms. Poetry that records historic events in epics, such as Gilgamesh or Ferdowsi's Shahnameh, will necessarily be lengthy and narrative, while poetry used for liturgical purposes (hymns, psalms, suras and hadiths) is likely to have an inspirational tone, whereas elegy and tragedy are meant to evoke deep emotional responses. Other contexts include Gregorian chants, formal or diplomatic speech, political rhetoric and invective, light-hearted nursery and nonsense rhymes, and even medical texts.

The Polish historian of aesthetics, Wladyslaw Tatarkiewicz, in a paper on "The Concept of Poetry," traces the evolution of what is in fact two concepts of poetry. Tatarkiewicz points out that the term is applied to two distinct things that, as the poet Paul Valéry observes, "at a certain point find union. Poetry [...] is an art based on language. But poetry also has a more general meaning [...] that is difficult to define because it is less determinate: poetry expresses a certain state of mind."

TWENTIETH-CENTURY DISPUTES

Some 20th-century literary theorists, relying less on the opposition of prose and poetry, focused on the poet as simply one who creates using language, and poetry as what the poet creates. The underlying concept of the poet as creator is not uncommon, and some modernist poets essentially do not distinguish between the creation of a poem with words, and creative acts in other media such as carpentry. Yet other modernists challenge the very attempt to define poetry as misguided, as when Archibald MacLeish concludes his paradoxical poem, "Ars Poetica," with the lines: "A poem should not mean / but be."

Disputes over the definition of poetry, and over poetry's distinction from other genres of literature, have been inextricably intertwined with the debate over the role of poetic form. The rejection of traditional forms and structures for poetry that began in the first half of the twentieth century, coincided with a questioning of the purpose and meaning of traditional definitions of poetry and of distinctions between poetry and prose, particularly given examples of poetic prose and prosaic "poetry." Numerous modernist poets have written in non-traditional forms or in what traditionally would have been considered prose, although their writing was generally infused with poetic diction and often with rhythm and tone established by non-metrical means. While there was a substantial formalist reaction within the modernist schools to the breakdown of structure, this reaction focused as much on the development of new formal structures and syntheses as on the revival of older forms and structures.

More recently, postmodernism has fully embraced MacLeish's concept and come to regard boundaries between prose and poetry, and also among genres of poetry, as having meaning only as cultural artifacts. Postmodernism goes beyond modernism's emphasis on the creative role of the poet, to emphasize the role of the reader of a text, and to highlight the complex cultural web within which a poem is read. Today, throughout the world, poetry often incorporates poetic form and diction from other cultures and from the past, further confounding attempts at definition and classification that were once sensible within a tradition such as the Western canon.

BASIC ELEMENTS

Prosody

Prosody is the study of the meter, rhythm, and intonation of a poem. Rhythm and meter, although closely related, should be distinguished. Meter is the definitive pattern established for a verse (such as iambic pentameter), while rhythm is the actual sound that results from a line of poetry. Thus, the meter of a line may be described as being "iambic", but a full description of the rhythm would require noting where the language causes one to pause or accelerate and how the meter interacts with other elements of the language. Prosody also may be used more specifically to refer to the scanning of poetic lines to show meter.

Rhythm

The methods for creating poetic rhythm vary across languages and between poetic traditions. Languages are often described as having timing set primarily by accents, syllables, or moras, depending on how rhythm is established, though a language can be influenced by multiple approaches. Japanese is a mora-timed language. Syllable-timed languages include Latin, Catalan, French and Spanish. English, Russian and, generally, German are stress-timed languages. Varying intonation also affects how rhythm is perceived. Languages also can rely on either pitch, such as in

Vedic or ancient Greek, or tone. Tonal languages include Chinese, Vietnamese, Lithuanian, and most subsaharan languages.

Metrical rhythm generally involves precise arrangements of stresses or syllables into repeated patterns called feet within a line. In Modern English verse the pattern of stresses primarily differentiate feet, so rhythm based on meter in Modern English is most often founded on the pattern of stressed and unstressed syllables (alone or elided). In the classical languages, on the other hand, while the metrical units are similar, vowel length rather than stresses define the meter. Old English poetry used a metrical pattern involving varied numbers of syllables but a fixed number of strong stresses in each line. The chief device of ancient Hebrew Biblical poetry, including many of the psalms, was parallelism, a rhetorical structure in which successive lines reflected each other in grammatical structure, sound structure, notional content, or all three. Parallelism lent itself to antiphonal or call-and-response performance, which could also be reinforced by intonation. Thus, Biblical poetry relies much less on metrical feet to create rhythm, but instead creates rhythm based on much larger sound units of lines, phrases and sentences. Some classical poetry forms, such as Venpa of the Tamil language, had rigid grammars (to the point that they could be expressed as a context-free grammar) which ensured a rhythm. In Chinese poetry, tones as well as stresses create rhythm. Classical Chinese poetics identifies four tones: the level tone, rising tone, falling tone, and entering tone. Note that other classifications may have as many as eight tones for Chinese and six for Vietnamese.

The formal patterns of meter used developed in Modern English verse to create rhythm no longer dominate contemporary English poetry. In the case of free verse, rhythm is often organized based on looser units of cadence than a regular meter. Robinson Jeffers, Marianne Moore, and William Carlos Williams are three notable poets who reject the idea that regular accentual meter is critical to English poetry. Jeffers experimented with sprung rhythm as an alternative to accentual rhythm.

Meter

In the Western poetic tradition, meters are customarily grouped according to a characteristic metrical foot and the number of feet per line. Thus, "iambic pentameter" is a meter comprising five feet per line, in which the predominant kind of foot is the "iamb." This metric system originated in ancient Greek poetry, and was used by poets such as Homer, Pindar, Hesiod and Sappho, and by the great tragedians of Athens.

Meter is often scanned based on the arrangement of "poetic feet" into lines. In English, each foot usually includes one syllable with a stress and one or two without a stress. In other languages, it may be a combination of the number of syllables and the length of the vowel that determines how the foot is parsed. For example, in Greek, one syllable with a long unstressed vowel may be treated as the equivalent of two syllables with short vowels. In Anglo-Saxon meter, the unit on which lines are built is a half-line containing two stresses rather than a foot. Scanning meter can often show the basic or fundamental pattern underlying a verse, but does not show the v ng re f stress, as well as the differing pitches and lengths of syllables.

As an example of how a line of meter is defined, in English-language iambic pentameter, each line has five metrical feet, and each foot is an iamb, or an unstressed syllable followed by a stressed syllable. When a particular line is scanned, there may be variations upon the basic pattern of the meter; for example, the first foot of English iambic pentameters is quite often inverted, meaning that the stress falls on the first syllable. The generally accepted names for some of the most commonly used kinds of feet include:

- spondee-two stressed syllables together
- iamb-unstressed syllable followed by a stressed syllable
- trochee-one stressed syllable followed by an unstressed syllable
- dactyl-one stressed syllable followed by two unstressed syllables
- anapest-two unstressed syllables followed by one stressed syllable

The number of metrical feet in a line are described in Greek terminology as follows:

- dimeter-two feet

- trimeter-three feet
- tetrameter-four feet
- pentameter-five feet
- hexameter-six feet
- heptameter-seven feet
- octameter-eight feet

There are a wide range of names for other types of feet, right up to a choriamb of four syllable metric foot with a stressed syllable followed by two unstressed syllables and closing with a stressed syllable. The choriamb is derived from some ancient Greek and Latin poetry. Languages which utilize vowel length or intonation rather than or in addition to syllabic accents in determining meter, such as Ottoman Turkish or Vedic, often have concepts similar to the iamb and dactyl to describe common combinations of long and short sounds.

Each of these types of feet has a certain "feel," whether alone or in combination with other feet. The iamb, for example, is the most natural form of rhythm in the English language, and generally produces a subtle but stable verse. The dactyl, on the other hand, almost gallops along. And, as readers of The Night Before Christmas or Dr. Seuss realize, the anapest is perfect for a light-hearted, comic feel.

There is debate over how useful a multiplicity of different "feet" is in describing meter. For example, Robert Pinsky has argued that while dactyls are important in classical verse, English dactylic verse uses dactyls very irregularly and can be better described based on patterns of iambs and anapests, feet which he considers natural to the language.

Actual rhythm is significantly more complex than the basic scanned meter described above, and many scholars have sought to develop systems that would scan such complexity. Vladimir Nabokov noted that overlaid on top of the regular pattern of stressed and unstressed syllables in a line of verse was a separate pattern of accents resulting from the natural pitch of the spoken words, and suggested that the term "scud" be used to distinguish an unaccented stress from an accented stress.

Metrical Patterns

Different traditions and genres of poetry tend to use different meters, ranging from the Shakespearian iambic pentameter and the Homerian dactylic hexameter to the Ánapestic tetrameter used in many nursery rhymes. However, a number of variations to the established meter are common, both to provide emphasis or attention to a given foot or line and to avoid boring repetition. For example, the stress in a foot may be inverted, a caesura (or pause) may be added (sometimes in place of a foot or stress), or the final foot in a line may be given a feminine ending to soften it or be replaced by a spondee to emphasize it and create a hard stop. Some patterns (such as iambic pentameter) tend to be fairly regular, while other patterns, such as dactylic hexameter, tend to be highly irregular. Regularity can vary between language. In addition, different patterns often develop distinctively in different languages, so that, for example, iambic tetrameter in Russian will generally reflect a regularity in the use of accents to reinforce the meter, which does not occur or occurs to a much lesser extent in English.

Some common metrical patterns, with notable examples of poets and poems who use them, include:

- Iambic pentameter (John Milton, Paradise Lost)
- Dactylic hexameter (Homer, Iliad; Ovid, The Metamorphoses)
- Iambic tetrameter (Andrew Marvell, "To His Coy Mistress")
- Iambic tetrameter (Aleksandr Pushkin, Eugene Onegin)
- Trochaic octameter (Edgar Allan Poe, "The Raven")
- Anapestic tetrameter (Lewis Carroll, "The Hunting of the Snark"; Lord Byron, Don Juan)
- Alexandrine, also known as iambic hexameter (Jean Racine, Phèdre)

Rhyme, Alliteration, Assonance

Rhyme, alliteration, assonance and consonance are ways of creating repetitive patterns of sound. They may be used as an independent structural element in a poem, to reinforce rhythmic patterns, or as an ornamental element.

Rhyme consists of identical ("hard-rhyme") or similar ("soft-rhyme") sounds placed at the ends of lines or at predictable locations within lines ("internal rhyme"). Languages vary in the richness of their rhyming structures; Italian, for example, has a rich rhyming structure permitting maintenance of a limited set of rhymes throughout a lengthy poem. The richness results from word endings that follow regular forms. English, with its irregular word endings adopted from other languages, is less rich in rhyme. The degree of richness of a language's rhyming structures plays a substantial role in determining what poetic forms are commonly used in that language.

Alliteration and assonance played a key role in structuring early Germanic, Norse and Old English forms of poetry. The alliterative patterns of early Germanic poetry interweave meter and alliteration as a key part of their structure, so that the metrical pattern determines when the listener expects instances of alliteration to occur. This can be compared to an ornamental use of alliteration in most Modern European poetry, where alliterative patterns are not formal or carried through full stanzas. Alliteration is particularly useful in languages with less rich rhyming structures.

Assonance, where the use of similar vowel sounds within a word rather than similar sounds at the beginning or end of a word, was widely used in skaldic poetry, but goes back to the Homeric epic. Because verbs carry much of the pitch in the English language, assonance can loosely evoke the tonal elements of Chinese poetry and so is useful in translating Chinese poetry. Consonance occurs where a consonant sound is repeated throughout a sentence without putting the sound only at the front of a word. Consonance provokes a more subtle effect than alliteration and so is less useful as a structural element.

Rhyming Schemes

In many languages, including modern European languages and Arabic, poets use rhyme in set patterns as a structural element for specific poet forms, such as ballads, sonnets and rhyming couplets. However, the use of structural rhyme is not universal even within the European tradition. Much modern poetry avoids traditional rhyme schemes. Classical Greek and

Latin poetry did not use rhyme. Rhyme entered European poetry in the High Middle Ages, in part under the influence of the Arabic language in Al Andalus (modern Spain).

Arabic language poets have always used rhyme extensively, most notably in their long, rhyming qasidas. Some rhyming schemes have become associated with a specific language, culture or period, while other rhyming schemes have achieved use across languages, cultures or time periods. Some forms of poetry carry a consistent and well-defined rhyming scheme, such as the chant royal or the rubaiyat, while other poetic forms have variable rhyme schemes.

Most rhyme schemes are described using letters that correspond to sets of rhymes, so if the first, second and fourth lines of a quatrain rhyme with each other and the third line does not rhyme, the quatrain is said to have an "a-a-b-a" rhyme scheme. This rhyme scheme is the one used, for example, in the rubaiyat form. Similarly, an "a-b-b-a" quatrain (what is known as "enclosed rhyme") is used in such forms as the Petrarchan sonnet. Some types of more complicated rhyming schemes have developed names of their own, separate from the "a-b-c" convention, such as the ottava rima and terza rima. The types and use of differing rhyming schemes is discussed further in the main article.

The ottava rima is a poem with a stanza of eight lines with an alternating a-b rhyming scheme for the first six lines followed by a closing couplet first used by Boccaccio. This rhyming scheme was developed for heroic epics but has also been used for mock-heroic poetry.

Dante and Terza Rima

Dante's Divine Comed is written in terza rima, where each stanza has three lines, with the first and third rhyming, and the second line rhyming with the first and third lines of the next stanza (thus, a-b-a / b-c-b / c-d-c, etc.) in a chain rhyme. The terza rima provides a flowing, progressive sense to the poem, and used skillfully it can evoke a sense of motion, both forward and backward. Terza rima is appropriately used in lengthy poems in languages with rich rhyming schemes (such as Italian, with its many common word endings).

POETIC FORM

Poetic form is very much more flexible nowadays than ever before. Many modern poets eschew recognisable structures or forms, and write in 'free verse'. However, major structural elements often used in poetry are the line, the stanza or verse paragraph, and larger combinations of stanzas or lines such as cantos. The broader visual presentation of words and calligraphy can also be utilized. These basic units of poetic form are often combined into larger structures, called poetic forms or poetic modes, such as in the sonnet or haiku.

LINES

Poetry is often separated into lines on a page. These lines may be based on the number of metrical feet, or may emphasize a rhyming pattern at the ends of lines. Lines may serve other functions, particularly where the poem is not written in a formal metrical pattern. Lines can separate, compare or contrast thoughts expressed in different units, or can highlight a change in tone.

Lines may be combined into couplets, a combination of two lines which may or may not relate to each other by rhyme or rhythm. For example, a couplet may be two lines with identical meters which rhyme or two lines held together by a common meter alone. Lines also may be combined into triplets, or sets of three lines. Lines are often grouped into verses or stanzas, which often have related couplets or triplets within them.

STANZAS AND PARAGRAPHS

Related lines of poems are often organized into stanzas, which are denominated by the number of lines included. Thus a collection of two lines is a couplet (or distich), three lines a triplet (or tercet), four lines a quatrain, five lines a quintain (or cinquain), six lines a sestet, and eight lines an octet.

Other poems may be organized into verse paragraphs, in which regular rhymes with established rhythms are not used, but the poetic tone is instead established by a collection of rhythms, alliterations, and rhymes established in paragraph form. Many medieval poems were written in verse paragraphs, even where regular rhymes and rhythms were used.

In many forms of poetry, stanzas are interlocking, so that the rhyming scheme or other structural elements of one stanza determine those of succeeding stanzas. Examples of such interlocking stanzas include, for example, the ghazal and the villanelle, where a refrain (or, in the case of the villanelle, refrains) is established in the first stanza which then repeats in subsequent stanzas. Related to the use of interlocking stanzas is their use to separate thematic parts of a poem. For example, the strophe, antistrophe and epode of the ode form are often separated into one or more stanzas. In such cases, or where structures are meant to be highly formal, a stanza will usually form a complete thought, consisting of full sentences and cohesive thoughts.

In some cases, particularly lengthier formal poetry such as some forms of epic poetry, stanzas themselves are constructed according to strict rules and then combined. In skaldic poetry, the dróttkvætt stanza had eight lines, each having three "lifts" produced with alliteration or assonance. In addition to two or three alliterations, the odd numbered lines had partial rhyme of consonants with dissimilar vowels, not necessarily at the beginning of the word; the even lines contained internal rhyme in set syllables (not necessarily at the end of the word). Each half-line had exactly six syllables, and each line ended in a trochee. The arrangement of dróttkvætts followed far less rigid rules than the construction of the individual dróttkvætts.

VISUAL PRESENTATION

Even before the advent of printing, the appearance of written poetry often added significant meaning or depth. Acrostic poems included clues or meanings in the letters beginning lines or in other specific places in a poem. In Arabic, Hebrew, and Chinese poetry, the presentation of the poems in fine calligraphy has always been an important part of the overall artistic and poetic effect for many poems.

With the advent of printing, poets gained greater control over the mass produced visual presentation of their work. As a result, the use of visual elements became an important part of the poet's toolbox, and many poets have sought to use visual presentation for a wide range of purposes. Some Modernist poetry takes this to an extreme, with the placement of individual lines or groups of lines on the page forming an integral part of the poem's composition, whether to complement the poem's rhythm through various lengthed visual caesuras, to create juxtapositions to accentuate meaning, ambiguity or irony, or simply to create an aesthetically pleasing form. In its most extreme form, this can lead to concrete poetry or asemic writing.

POETIC DICTION

Poetic diction describes the manner in which language is used and refers not only to the sound but also to the underlying meaning and its interaction with sound and form. Many languages and poetic forms have very specific poetic dictions, to the point where separate grammars and dialects are used specifically for poetry. Poetic diction can include rhetorical devices such as simile and metaphor, as well as tones of voice, such as irony. Aristotle wrote in the Poetics that "the greatest thing by far is to be a master of metaphor". Since the rise of Modernism, some poets have opted for a poetic diction that deemphasizes rhetorical devices, attempting the direct presentation of things and experiences and the exploration of tone. On the other hand, Surrealists have pushed rhetorical devices to their limits, making frequent use of catachresis.

Allegorical stories are central to the poetic diction of many cultures, and were prominent in the west during classical times, the late Middle Ages and Renaisance. Rather than being fully allegorical, a poem may contain symbols or allusion that deepens the meaning or impact of its words without constructing a full allegory. Another strong element of poetic diction can be the use of vivid imagery for effect. The juxtaposition of unexpected or impossible images is, for example, a particularly strong element in surrealist poetry and haiku. Vivid images are often endowed with symbolism as well.

Many poetic dictions will use repetitive phrases for effect, either a short phrase (such as Homer's "rosy-fingered dawn") or a longer refrain. Such repetition can add a somber tone to a poem, as in many odes, or can be laced with irony as the contexts of the words change. For example, in Antony's famous eulogy to in Shakespeare's Julius Caesar, Anthony's repetition of the words, "for Brutus is an honorable man," moves from a sincere tone to one that exudes irony.

SPECIFIC POETIC FORMS

Specific poetic forms have been developed by many cultures. In more developed, closed or "received" poetic forms, the rhyming scheme, meter and other elements of a poem are based on sets of rules, ranging from the relatively loose rules that govern the construction of an elegy to the highly formalized structure of the ghazal or villanelle.

Sonnets

Among the most common form of poetry through the ages is the sonnet, which, by the thirteenth century, was a poem of fourteen lines following a set rhyme scheme and logical structure. The conventions associated with the sonnet have changed during its history, and so there are several different sonnet forms. Traditionally, English poets use iambic pentameter when writing sonnets, with the Spenserian and Shakespearean sonnets being especially notable. In the Romance languages, the hendecasyllable and Alexandrines are the most widely used meters, although the Petrarchan sonnet has been used in Italy since the 14th century. Sonnets are particularly associated with love poetry, and often use a poetic diction heavily based on vivid imagery, but the twists and turns associated with the move from octave to sestet and to final couplet make them a useful and dynamic form for many subjects. Shakespeare's sonnets are among the most famous in English poetry, with 20 being included in the Oxford Book of English Verse.

Jintishi

The jintishi is a Chinese poetic form based on a series of set tonal patterns using the four tones of the classical Chinese language in each couplet: the level, rising, falling and entering tones. The basic form of the jintishi has eight lines in four couplets, with parallelism between the lines in the second and third couplets. The couplets with parallel lines contain contrasting content but an identical grammatical relationship between words. Jintishi often have a rich poetic diction, full of allusion, and can have a wide range of subject, including history and politics. One of the masters of the form was Du Fu, who wrote during the Tang Dynasty (8th century). There are several variations on the basic form of the jintishi.

Villanelle

The Villanelle is a nineteen-line poem made up of five triplets with a closing quatrain; the poem is characterized by having two refrains, initially used in the first and third lines of the first stanza, and then alternately used at the close of each subsequent stanza until the final quatrain, which is concluded by the two refrains. The remaining lines of the poem have an a-b alternating rhyme. The villanelle has been used regularly in the English language since the late nineteenth century by such poets as Dylan Thomas, W.H. Auden, and Elizabeth Bishop. It is a form that has gained heavier use at a time when the use of received forms of poetry has generally been declining.

Tanka

The Tanka is a form of Japanese poetry, generally not possessing rhyme, with five lines structured in a 5-7-5 7-7 patterns. The 5-7-5 phrase (the "upper phrase") and the 7-7 phrase (the "lower phrase") generally show a shift in tone and subject matter. Tanka were written as early as the Nara period by such poets as Kakinomoto no Hitomaro, at a time when Japan was emerging from a period where much of its poetry followed Chinese form. Tanka was originally the shorter form of Japanese formal poetry, and was used more heavily to explore personal rather than public themes. It thus had a more informal poetic diction. By the 13th century, Tanka had become the dominant form of Japanese poetry, and it is still widely written today.

Ode

Odes were first developed by poets writing in ancient Greek, such as Pindar, and Latin, such as Horace, and forms of odes appear in many of the cultures influenced by the Greeks and Latins. The ode generally has three parts: a strophe, an antistrophe, and an epode. The antistrophes of the ode possess similar metrical structures and, depending on the tradition, similar rhyme structures. In contrast, the epode is written with a different scheme and structure. Odes have a formal poetic diction, and general dealing with a serious subject. The strophe and antistrophe look at the subject from different, often conflicting, perspectives, with the epode moving to a higher level to either view or resolve the underlying issues. Odes are often intended to be recited or sung by two choruses (or individuals), with the first reciting the strophe, the second the antistrophe, and both together the epode. Over time, differing forms for odes have developed with considerable variations in form and structure, but generally showing the original influence of the Pindaric or Horatian ode. One non-Western form which resembles the ode is the qasida in Persian poetry.

Ghazal

The ghazal is a form of poetry common in Arabic, Persian, Urdu and Bengali poetry. In classic form, the ghazal has from five to fifteen rhyming couplets that share a refrain at the end of the second line (which need be of only a few syllables). Each line has an identical meter, and there is a set pattern of rhymes in the first couplet and among the refrains. Each couplet forms a complete thought and stands alone, and the overall ghazal often reflects on a theme of unattainable love or divinity. The last couplet generally includes the signature of the author.

As with other forms with a long history in many languages, many variations have been developed, including forms with a quasi-musical poetic diction in Urdu. Ghazals have a classical affinity with Sufism, and a number of major Sufi religious works are written in ghazal form. The relatively steady meter and the use of the refrain produce an incantatory effect, which complements Sufi mystical themes well. Among the masters of the form is the Persian poet Rumi.

POETIC GENRES

Narrative Poetry

Narrative poetry is a genre of poetry that tells a story. Broadly it subsumes epic poetry, but the term "narrative poetry" is often reserved for smaller works, generally with more direct appeal than the epic to human interest.

Narrative poetry may be the oldest genre of poetry. Many scholars of Homer have concluded that his Iliad and Odyssey were composed from compilations of shorter narrative poems that related individual episodes and were more suitable for an evening's entertainment. Much narrative poetry-such as Scots and English ballads, and Baltic and Slavic heroic poems-is performance poetry with roots in a preliterate oral tradition. It has been speculated that some features that distinguish poetry from prose, such as meter, alliteration and kennings, once served as memory aids for bards who recited traditional tales. Notable narrative poets have included Ovid, Dante, Chaucer, William Langland, Shakespeare, Alexander Pope, Robert Burns, Adam Mickiewicz, Alexander Pushkin, Tennyson and Poe.

Epic Poetry

Epic poetry is a genre of poetry, and a major form of narrative literature. It recounts, in a continuous narrative, the life and works of a heroic or mythological person or group of persons. Western epic poems include Homer's Iliad and Odyssey, Vergil's Aeneid and the Nibelungenlied. Eastern examples are the Epic of Gilgamesh, the Mahabharata, Valmiki's Ramayana, Ferdowsi's Shahnama, and the Epic of King Gesar. The composition of epic poetry, and of long poems generally, became uncommon in the west after the early 20th century, while the meaning of the term "epic" evolved to refer also to prose writings, films and similar works that are characterized by great length, multiple settings, large numbers of characters, or long span of time involved.

Dramatic Poetry

Dramatic poetry is drama written in verse to be spoken. Verse drama was long the dominant form of drama in Europe, and was also important in non-European cultures. Greek tragedy and Racine's plays are written in verse, as are almost all of Shakespeare's dramas, and Goethe's Faust.

A practical reason to write drama in verse was that verse lines are easier for actors to memorize exactly. In the latter half of the 20th century, verse drama fell almost completely out of favor with English-language dramatists. Christopher Fry and T.S. Eliot may have been its last practitioners in that language.

Lyric Poetry

Lyric poetry is a genre that, unlike epic poetry and dramatic poetry, does not attempt to tell a story but instead is of a more personal nature. Rather than depicting characters and actions, it portrays the poet's own feelings, states of mind, and perceptions. While the genre's name, derived from "lyre," implies that it is intended to be sung, much lyric poetry is meant purely for reading. Though lyric poetry has long celebrated love, many courtly-love poets also wrote lyric poems about war and peace, nature and nostalgia, grief and loss. Notable among these are the 15th-century French lyric poets, Christine de Pizan and Charles, Duke of Orléans. Spiritual and religious themes were addressed by such medieval lyric poets as St. John of the Cross and Teresa of Ávila. The tradition of lyric poetry based on spiritual experience was continued by later poets such as John Donne, Gerard Manley Hopkins and T.S. Eliot. Although the most popular form of western lyric poetry may be the 14-line sonnet-Petrarchan or Shakespearean-lyric poetry has shown a bewildering variety of forms, including increasingly, in the 20th century, unrhymed ones.

Verse Fable

The fable is an ancient and near-ubiquitous literary genre, often (though not invariably) set in verse form. Notable verse fabulists have included Aesop (mid-6th century BCE), Vishnu Sarma (ca. 200 BCE), Phaedrus (15 BCE-50 CE), Marie de France (12th century), Biernat of Lublin (1465-after 1529), Jean de la Fontaine (1621-95), Ignacy Krasicki (1735-1801), Ivan Krylov (1769-1844) and Ambrose Bierce (1842-1914). All of the semi-legendary Aesop's successors, translators and imitators have owed him a fundamental debt. Verse fables have been written in a variety of meter and rhyme patterns. Ignacy Krasicki, for example, in his Fables and Parables, used 13-syllable lines, in couplets rhyming aa, bb...

Prose Poetry

Prose poetry is a hybrid genre that demonstrates attributes of both prose and poetry. It may be indistinguishable from the micro-story (aka the "short short story," "flash fiction"). Most critics argue that it qualifies as poetry because of its conciseness, use of metaphor, and special care for language.

While some examples of earlier prose strike modern readers as poetic, prose poetry is commonly regarded as having originated in 19th-century France, where its practitioners included Aloysius Bertrand, Charles Baudelaire, Arthur Rimbaud and Stéphane Mallarmé. The genre has subsequently found notable exemplars in French (Francis Ponge); English (Oscar Wilde, T.S. Eliot, Gertrude Stein, Sherwood Anderson, Allen Ginsberg, Russell Edson, Charles Simic, Robert Bly, James Wright); Spanish (Octavio Paz, Ángel Crespo); Polish (Boleslaw Prus); Russian; and Japanese.

Since the late 1980s especially, prose poetry has gained increasing popularity, with journals devoted solely to that genre.

PROSODY

Prosody may refer to:

- Prosody (linguistics) includes intonation and vocal stress in speech.
- Meter (poetry) includes the scansion and metrical shape of the lines.
- Prosody (music) refers to the way the composer sets the text of a vocal composition in the assignment of syllables to notes in the melody to which the text is sung; this is particularly a function of rhythm and pitch, and is not to be confused with musical form.

METER (POETRY)

Meter (British English spelling: metre) describes the linguistic sound patterns of a verse. Scansion is the analysis of poetry's metrical and rhythmic patterns. Prosody is sometimes used to describe poetic meter, and indicates the analysis of similar aspects of language in linguistics. Meter is part of many formal verse forms.

Fundamentals

The units of poetic meter, like rhyme, vary from language to any language and between poetic traditions. They can involve arrangements of syllables into repeated patterns called feet within a line. English meter is traditionally conceived as being founded on the patterns of stressed and unstressed syllables. In Latin verse, on the other hand, while the metrical units are similar, not syllable stresses but syllable lengths are the component parts of meter. Old English poetry used alliterative verse, a metrical pattern involving varied numbers of syllables but a fixed number of strong stresses in each line. Meters in English verse, and in the classical Western poetic tradition on which it is founded, are named by the characteristic foot and the number of feet per line. Thus, for example, blank verse is unrhymed "iambic pentameter," a meter composed of five feet per line in which the kind of feet called iambs predominate. This tradition of metrics originated from the ancient Greek poetry of Homer, Pindar, Hesiod, Sappho, and the great tragedians of Athens.

Technical Terms

- caesura: (literally, a cut or cutting) refers to a particular kind of break within a poetic line. In Latin and Greek meter, caesura refers to a break within a foot caused by the end of a word. In English poetry, a caesura refers to a sense of a break within a line. Caesurae play a particularly important role in Old English poetry.
- Inversion: when a foot of poetry is reversed with respect to the general meter of a poem.
- Headless: a meter where the first foot is missing its first syllable.
- Quantitative: Use in prosody and poetry.

Meter in Various Languages

Greek and Latin

The metrical "feet" in the classical languages were based on the length of time taken to pronounce each syllable, which were categorized as either "long" syllables or "short" syllables (also known as "heavy" and "light" syllables, respectively, to distinguish from long and short vowels). The foot is often compared to a musical measure and the long and short syllables to whole notes and half notes. In English poetry, feet are determined by emphasis rather than length, with stressed and unstressed syllables serving the same function as long and short syllables in classical meter. The basic unit in Greek and Latin prosody is a mora, which is defined as a single short syllable. A long syllable is equivalent to two moras. A long syllable contains either a long vowel, a diphthong, or a short vowel followed by two or more consonants. Various rules of elision sometimes prevent a grammatical syllable from making a full syllable, and certain other lengthening and shortening rules (such as correption) can create long or short syllables in contexts where one would expect the opposite.

The most important Classical meter is the dactylic hexameter, the meter of Homer and Virgil. This form uses verses of six feet. The first four feet are dactyls, but can be spondees. The fifth foot is almost always a dactyl. The sixth foot is either a spondee or a trochee. The initial syllable of either foot is called the ictus, the basic "beat" of the verse. There is usually a caesura after the ictus of the third foot. The opening line of the Æneid is a typical line of dactylic hexameter:

Árma virumque cano, // Troi? qui prímus ab óris

("I sing of arms and the man, who first from the shores of Troy... ")

The first and second feet are dactyls; their vowels are grammatically short, but long in poetry because both are followed by two consonants. The third and fourth feet are spondees, with two long vowels, one on either side of the caesura. The fifth foot is a dactyl, as it must be, with the ictus this time falling on a grammatically long vowel. The final foot is a spondee with two grammatically long vowels.

The dactylic hexameter was imitated in English by Henry Wadsworth Longfellow in his poem Evangeline:

This is the forest primeval. The murmuring pines and the hemlocks,

Bearded with moss, and in garments green, indistinct in the twilight,

Stand like Druids of old, with voices sad and prophetic,

Stand like harpers hoar, with beards that rest on their bosoms.

Also important in Greek and Latin poetry is the dactylic pentameter. This was a line of verse, made up of two equal parts, each of which contains two dactyls followed by a long syllable. Spondees can take the place of the dactyls in the first half, but never in the second. The long syllable at the close of the first half of the verse always ends a word, giving rise to a caesura.

Dactylic pentameter is never used in isolation. Rather, a line of dactylic pentameter follows a line of dactylic hexameter in the elegiac distich or elegiac couplet, a form of verse that was used for the composition of elegies and other tragic and solemn verse in the Greek and Latin world, as well as love poetry that was sometimes light and cheerful. An example from Ovid's Tristia:

("I only saw Vergil, greedy Fate gave Tibullus no time for me.")

The Greeks and Romans also used a number of lyric meters, which were typically used for shorter poems than elegiacs or hexameter. One important line was called the hendecasyllabic, a line of eleven syllables. This meter was used most often in the Sapphic stanza, named after the Greek poet Sappho, who wrote many of her poems in the form. A hendecasyllabic is a line with a never-varying structure: two trochees, followed by a dactyl, then two more trochees. In the Sapphic stanza, three hendecasyllabics are followed by an "Adonic" line. made up of a dactyl and a trochee. This is the form of Catullus 51 (itself a translation of Sappho 31):

/ x / x / x x/ x / x

Ille mi par esse deo videtur;

/ x / x / x x / x / x

ille, si fas est, superare divos,

/ x / x / x x / x / x

qui sedens adversus identidem te

/ x x / x

spectat et audit...

("He seems to me to be like a god; if it is permitted, he seems above the gods, he who sitting across from you gazes at you and listens to you.")

The Sapphic stanza was imitated in English by Algernon Charles Swinburne in a poem he simply called Sapphics:

Saw the white implacable Aphrodite,

Saw the hair unbound and the feet unsandalled

Shine as fire of sunset on western waters;

Saw the reluctant...

English

Old English

Old English poetry has a different metrical system from modern English. In Old English poetry, each line must contain four fully stressed syllables, which often alliterate. The unstressed syllables are less important. Old English poetry is an example of the alliterative verse found in most of the older Germanic languages.

Modern English

Most English meter is classified according to the same system as Classical meter with an important difference. English is an accentual language, and therefore beats and offbeats (stressed and unstressed syllables) take the place of the long and short syllables of classical systems. In most English verse, the meter can be considered as a sort of back beat, against which natural speech rhythms vary expressively.

The most common characteristic feet of English verse are the iamb in two syllables and the anapest in three.

Metrical Systems

The number of metrical systems in English is not agreed. The major four types are: accentual verse, accentual-syllabic verse, syllabic verse and quantitative verse. The alliterative verse of Old English could also be added to this list, or included as a special type of accentual verse. Accentual verse focuses on the number of stresses in a line, while ignoring the number of offbeats and syllables; accentual-syllabic verse focuses on regulating both the number of stresses and the total number of syllables in a line; syllabic verse only counts the number of syllables in a line; quantitative verse regulates the patterns of long and short syllables, this sort of verse is often considered alien to English.

It is to be noted, however, that the use of foreign metres in English is all but exceptional.

Frequently-used Meters

The most frequently encountered line of English verse is the iambic pentameter, in which the metrical norm is five iambic feet per line, though metrical substitution is common and rhythmic variations practically inexhaustible. John Milton's Paradise Lost, most sonnets, and much else besides in English are written in iambic pentameter. Lines of unrhymed iambic pentameter are commonly known as blank verse. Blank verse in the English language is most famously represented in the plays of William Shakespeare, although it is also notable in the work of Milton and Tennyson (e.g. Ulysses, The Princess).

A rhymed pair of lines of iambic pentameter make a heroic couplet, a verse form which was used so often in the eighteenth century that it is now used mostly for humorous effect. The most famous writers of heroic couplets are Dryden and Pope.

Another important meter in English is the ballad meter, also called the "common meter", which is a four line stanza, with two pairs of a line of iambic tetrameter followed by a line of iambic trimeter; the rhymes usually fall on the lines of trimeter, although in many instances the tetrameter also rhymes. This is the meter of most of the Border and Scots or English ballads. It is called the "common meter" in hymnody (as it is the most common of the named hymn meters used to pair lyrics with melodies) and provides the meter for a great many hymns, such as Amazing Grace:

Amazing Grace! how sweet the sound

That saved a wretch like me;

I once was lost, but now am found;

Was blind, but now I see.

Emily Dickinson is famous for her frequent use of ballad meter:

Great streets of silence led away
To neighborhoods of pause;
Here was no notice-no dissent-
No universe-no laws.

A number of different Hymn meters are also in use.

French

In French poetry, meter is determined solely by the number of syllables in a line. A silent 'e' counts as a syllable before a consonant, but is elided before a vowel (where "h aspiré" counts as a consonant). At the end of a line, the "e" remains unelided but is hypermetrical (outside the count of syllables, like a feminine ending in English verse). The most frequently encountered meter in French is the alexandrine, composed of two hemistichs of six syllables each. Classical French poetry also had a complex set of rules for rhymes that goes beyond how words merely sound. These are usually taken into account when describing the meter of a poem.

Spanish

In Spanish poetry, meter is determined mainly by the position of the last accent in a line. Interestingly, a line whose last accent falls in the seventh syllable is invariably called an "octosyllable", regardless of whether it contains seven, eight or nine syllables.

Syllables in Spanish metrics are determined by consonant breaks, not word boundaries; thus a single syllable may span multiple words. For example, the line De armas y hombres canto consists of 6 syllables: "Dear" "ma" "syhom" "bres" "can" "to." Note how the vowel sounds in adjacent words combine into a single unit, as in the third syllable of the line: De armas y hombres canto.

Some common meters in Spanish verse are:

- Septenary: A line with the last accent on the sixth syllable.
- Octosyllable: A line with its last accent on the seventh syllable. This meter is commonly used in romances, narrative poems similar to English ballads, and in most proverbs.

- Hendecasyllable: A line with its last accent in the tenth and accents either in the sixth, or the fourth and the eighth. This meter plays a similar role to pentameter in English verse. It is commonly used in sonnets, among other things.
- Alexandrines: A line consisting of two heptasyllables.

Italian

In Italian poetry, meter is determined solely by the position of the last accent in a line. Syllables are enumerated with respect to a verse which ends with a paroxytone, so that a Septenary (literally, 'having seven syllables') is defined as a verse whose last accent falls on the sixth syllable: it may so contain eight syllables (Ei fu. Siccome immobile) or just six (la terra al nunzio sta). Moreover, when a word ends with a vowel and the next one starts with a vowel, they are considered to be in the same syllable: so Gli anni e i giorni consists of only four syllables ("Gli an" "ni e i" "gior" "ni"). Because of the mostly trochaic nature of the Italian language, verses with an even number of syllables are far easier to compose, and the Novenary is usually regarded as the most difficult verse.

Some common meters in Italian verse are:

- Septenary: A line whose last stressed syllable is the sixth one.
- Octosyllable: A line whose last accent falls on the seventh syllable. More often than not, the secondary accents fall on the first, third and fifth syllable, especially in nursery rhymes for which this meter is particularly well-suited.
- Hendecasyllable: A line whose last accent falls on the tenth syllable. It therefore usually consists of eleven syllables; there are various kinds of possible accentations. It is used in sonnets, in ottava rima, and in many other works. The Divine Comedy, in particular, is composed entirely of hendecasyllables.

CONSTRAINED WRITING

Constrained writing is a literary technique in which the writer is bound by some condition that forbids certain things or imposes a pattern. Constraints are very common in poetry, which often requires the writer to use a particular verse form.

The most common constrained forms of writing are strict restrictions in vocabulary, e.g. Basic English, E-Prime, defining vocabulary for dictionaries, and other limited vocabularies for teaching English as a Second Language or to children. This is not generally what is meant by "constrained writing" in the literary sense, which is motivated by more aesthetic concerns. For example:

- Lipogram, a letter (commonly e or o) is outlawed
- Palindromes, such as the word "radar," read the same both ways
- Alliteratives, in which every word must start with the same letter (or subset of letters; see Alphabetical Africa)
- Acrostics
- Reverse-lipograms (each word must contain a particular letter)
- Anglish
- Anagrams
- Aleatory (where the reader supplies a random input)
- Univocalic poetry

The Oulipo group is a gathering of writers who use such techniques. The Outrapo group use theatrical constraints.

Gadsby is an English-language novel consisting of 50,100 words, none of which contain the letter "e."

In 1969, French writer Georges Perec published La Disparition, a novel that did not include the letter "e." It was translated into English in 1995 by Gilbert Adair as "A Void." Perec subsequently joked that he incorporated the "e"s not used in La Disparition in the novella Les Revenentes (1972), which uses no vowels other than "e". Les Revenentes was translated into English by Ian Monk as The Exeter Text: Jewels, Secrets, Sex.

In 2004, a new marvel from France: a novel, entirely without verbs: Le Train de Nulle Part ("The Train from Nowhere") by Michel Thaler.

Experimental Canadian poet Christian Bök's Eunoia is a lipogram that uses only one vowel in each of its five chapters

One famous constrained writing in the Chinese language is the Lion-Eating Poet in the Stone Den which consists of 92 characters, all with the sound shi. Another is the Thousand Character Classic in which all 1000 characters are unique without any repetition. Cadaeic Cadenza is a short book by Mike Keith using the digits of pi as the length of words. Never Again is a novel by Doug Nufer in which no word is used more than once. Ella Minnow Pea is a book by Mark Dunn where certain letters become unusable throughout the novel.

POETICS

Poetics refers generally to the theory of literary discourse and specifically to the theory of poetry, although some speakers use the term so broadly as to denote the concept of "theory" itself. The word originated with Aristotle's Poetics, a work on the definition of poetry that laid the foundation for Western thought on the subject.

History

Leading poetics scholar T.V.F. Brogan identifies three major movements in Western poetics over the past 3000 years, beginning with the formalist, objectivist Aristotelian tradition. During the romantic era, poetics tended toward expressionism and emphasized the perceiving subject. The 20th century witnessed a return to the Aristotelian paradigm, followed by trends toward metacriticality, or the establishment of a theory of poetics.

Eastern poetics developed primarily with reference to the lyric, as opposed to the mimetic.

HISTORY OF POETRY

The poetry as an art form predates literacy.

Early History

Poetry was employed as a means of recording oral history, storytelling (epic poetry), genealogy, and law. Poetry is often closely identified with liturgy in pre-literate societies. Many of the scriptures currently held to be sacred by contemporary religious traditions with their roots in antiquity were composed as poetry rather than prose to aid memorization and help guarantee the accuracy of oral transmission in pre-literate societies. As a result many of the poems surviving from the ancient world are a form of recorded cultural information about the people of the past, and their poems are prayers or stories about religious subject matter, histories about their politics and wars, and the important organizing myths of their societies.

Poetry as an art form may predate literacy Thus many ancient works, from the Vedas (2500-500 BC) to the Odyssey (700-500 BC), appear to have been composed in poetic form to aid memorization and oral transmission, in prehistoric and ancient societies. Poetry appears among the earliest records of most literate cultures, with poetic fragments found on early monoliths, rune stones and stelae.

The oldest surviving poem is the Epic of Gilgamesh, from the 3rd millennium BC in Sumer (in Iraq/Mesopotamia), which was written in cuneiform script on clay tablets and, later, papyrus. The Epic of Gilgamesh is based on the historical king Gilgamesh. The oldest love poem, found on a clay tablet now known as Istanbul #2461, was also a Sumerian poem. It was recited by a bride of the Sumerian king Shu-Sin, who ruled from 2037-2029 BC. The oldest epic poetry besides the Epic of Gilgamesh are the Greek epics Iliad and Odyssey and the Indian Sanskrit epics Ramayana and Mahabharata. The longest epic poems ever written were the Mahabharata and the Tibetan Epic of King Gesar.

Ancient thinkers sought to determine what makes poetry distinctive as a form and what distinguishes good poetry from bad, resulting in the development of "poetics", or the study of the aesthetics of poetry. Some ancient societies, such as the Chinese through the Shi Jing, one of the Five Classics of Confucianism, developed canons of poetic works that had ritual as well as aesthetic importance. More recently, thinkers struggled to find a definition that could encompass formal differences as great as those between Chaucer's The Canterbury Tales and Matsuo Basho's Oku no Hosomichi, as well as differences in context that span from the religious poetry of the Tanakh to love poetry to rap.

Context can be critical to poetics and to the development of poetic genres and forms. For example, poetry employed to record historical events in epics, such as Gilgamesh or Ferdowsi's Shahnameh, will necessarily be lengthy and narrative, while poetry used for liturgical purposes in hymns, psalms, suras and hadiths is likely to have an inspirational tone, whereas elegies and tragedy are intended to invoke deep internal emotional responses. Other contexts include music such as Gregorian chants, and formal or diplomatic speech political rhetoric and invective, light-hearted nursery and nonsense rhymes, and even medical texts. The Polish historian of aesthetics, Wladyslaw Tatarkiewicz, in a paper on "The Concept of Poetry," traces the evolution of what is in fact two concepts of poetry. Tatarkiewicz points out that the term is applied to two distinct things that, as the poet Paul Valéry observes, "at a certain point find union. Poetry [...] is an art based on language. But poetry also has a more general meaning [...] that is difficult to define because it is less determinate: poetry expresses a certain state of mind."

Classical and Early Modern Western Traditions

Classical thinkers employed classification as a way to define and assess the quality of poetry. Notably, Aristotle's Poetics describes the three genres of poetry: the epic, comic, and tragic, and develops rules to distinguish the highest-quality poetry of each genre, based on the underlying purposes of that genre. Later aestheticians identified three major genres: epic poetry, lyric poetry and dramatic poetry, treating comedy and tragedy as subgenres of dramatic poetry. Aristotle's work was influential throughout the Middle East during the Islamic Golden Age, as well as in Europe during the Renaissance. Later poets and aestheticians often distinguished poetry from, and defined it in opposition to, prose, which was generally understood as writing with a proclivity to logical explication and a linear narrative structure.

This does not imply that poetry is illogical or lacks narration, but rather that poetry is an attempt to render the beautiful or sublime without the burden of engaging the logical or narrative thought process. English Romantic poet John Keats termed this escape from logic, "Negative Capability." This "romantic" approach views form as a key element of successful poetry because form is abstract and distinct from the underlying notional logic. This approach remained influential into the twentieth century. During this period, there was also substantially more interaction among the various poetic traditions, in part due to the spread of European colonialism and the attendant rise in global trade. In addition to a boom in translation, during the Romantic period numerous ancient works were rediscovered.

Modern Developments

The use of verse to transmit cultural information continues today. Many Americans know that "in 1492, Columbus sailed the ocean blue". An alphabet song teaches the names and order of the letters of the alphabet; another jingle states the lengths and names of the months in the Gregorian calendar. Some writers believe poetry has its origins in song. Most of the characteristics that distinguish it from other forms of utterance-rhythm, rhyme, compression, intensity of feeling, the use of refrains-appear to have come about from efforts to fit words to musical forms. In the European tradition the earliest surviving poems, the Homeric and Hesiodic epics, identify themselves as poems to be recited or chanted to a musical accompaniment rather than as pure song. Another interpretation is that rhythm, refrains, and kennings are essentially paratactic devices that enable the reciter to reconstruct the poem from memory.

In preliterate societies, these forms of poetry were composed for, and sometimes during, performance. There was a certain degree of fluidity to the exact wording of poems. The introduction of writing fixed the content of a poem to the version that happened to be written down and survive. Written composition meant poets began to compose for an absent reader. The invention of printing accelerated these trends. Poets were now writing more for the eye than for the ear.

- Edwin Arlington Robinson's villanelle "The House on the Hill" was first published in The Globe in September 1894.

  They are all gone away,

  The House is shut and still,

  There is nothing more to say.

  Through broken walls and gray

The winds blow bleak and shrill.
They are all gone away.
Nor is there one to-day
To speak them good or ill:
There is nothing more to say.
Why is it then we stray
Around the sunken sill?
They are all gone away,
And our poor fancy-play
For them is wasted skill:
There is nothing more to say.
There is ruin and decay
In the House on the Hill:
They are all gone away,
There is nothing more to say.

Dylan Thomas's villanelle Do not go Gentle into that Good Night

Do not go gentle into that good night,
Old age should burn and rave at close of day;
Rage, rage against the dying of the light.
Though wise men at their end know dark is right,
Because their words had forked no lightning they
Do not go gentle into that good night.
Good men, the last wave by, crying how bright
Their frail deeds might have danced in a green bay,
Rage, rage against the dying of the light.
Wild men who caught and sang the sun in flight,
And learn, too late, they grieved it on its way,
Do not go gentle into that good night.
Grave men, near death, who see with blinding sight

Blind eyes could blaze like meteors and be gay,
Rage, rage against the dying of the light.
And you, my father, there on the sad height,
Curse, bless me now with your fierce tears, I pray.
Do not go gentle into that good night.
Rage, rage against the dying of the light.

Theodore Roethke's villanelle "The Waking"

I wake to sleep, and take my waking slow.
I feel my fate in what I cannot fear.
I learn by going where I have to go.
We think by feeling. What is there to know?
I hear my being dance from ear to ear.
I wake to sleep, and take my waking slow.
Of those so close beside me, which are you?
God bless the Ground! I shall walk softly there,
And learn by going where I have to go.
Light takes the Tree; but who can tell us how?
The lowly worm climbs up a winding stair;
I wake to sleep, and take my waking slow.
Great Nature has another thing to do
To you and me; so take the lively air,
And, lovely, learn by going where to go.
This shaking keeps me steady. I should know.
What falls away is always. And is near.
I wake to sleep, and take my waking slow.
I learn by going where I have to go.

BLANK VERSE

Blank verse is a type of poetry, distinguished by having a regular meter, but no rhyme. In English, the meter most commonly used with blank verse has been iambic pentameter.

The first known use of blank verse in the English language was by Henry Howard, Earl of Arundel and Surrey in his interpretation of the Æneid (c. 1554). He was possibly inspired by the Latin original, as classical Latin verse (as well as Greek verse) did not use rhyme; he may have been inspired by the Italian verse form of versi sciolti, which also contained no rhyme. The unknown author of Arden of Faversham (circa 1590) is the most interesting example of end-stopped blank verse

Christopher Marlowe was the first English author to make full use of the potential of blank verse, and also established it as the dominant verse form for English drama in the age of Elizabeth I and James I. The major achievements in English blank verse were made by William Shakespeare, who wrote much of the content of his plays in unrhymed iambic pentameter, and Milton, whose Paradise Lost is written in blank verse. After Milton (in fact, during his later life), blank verse went out of fashion and for a century and a half the favored verse form in English was that of couplets. Romantic English poets such as William Wordsworth, Percy Bysshe Shelley, and John Keats revived blank verse as a major form. Following shortly afterwards, Alfred Lord Tennyson became particularly devoted to blank verse, using it for example in his long narrative poem "The Princess", as well as for one of his most famous poems: "Ulysses". Among American poets, Hart Crane and Wallace Stevens are notable for using blank verse in extended compositions at a time when many other poets were turning to free verse.

Russian bylinas are in blank verse.

History of English Blank Verse

The earliest blank verse consisted of end-stopped and regular lines. Gorboduc (1561), the first blank-verse tragedy, illustrates how monotonous such verse could be. Marlowe and then Shakespeare developed its potential greatly in the late 16th century. Marlowe was the first to exploit the potential of blank verse for powerful and involved speech:

You stars that reign'd at my nativity,

Whose influence hath allotted death and hell,

Now draw up Faustus like a foggy mist

Into the entrails of yon labouring clouds,

That when they vomit forth into the air,

My limbs may issue from their smoky mouths,

So that my soul may but ascend to Heaven. (Doctor Faustus)

Shakespeare developed this feature, and also the potential of blank verse for abrupt and irregular speech. The earliest effects were like these:

Death?

My lord?

A grave.

He shall not live. (King John), 3.3

Shakespeare also used enjambment increasingly often in his verse, and in his last plays was given to using feminine endings (in which the last syllable of the line is unstressed, for instance lines 3 and 6 of the following example); all of this made his later blank verse extremely rich and varied.

Ye elves of hills, brooks, standing lakes and groves,

And ye that on the sands with printless foot

Do chase the ebbing Neptune, and do fly him

When he comes back; you demi-puppets that

By moonshine do the green sour ringlets make

Whereof the ewe not bites; and you whose pastime

Is to make midnight mushrooms, that rejoice

To hear the solemn curfew; by whose aid,

Weak masters though ye be, I have bedimmed

The noontide sun, called forth the mutinous winds,

And 'twixt the green sea and the azured vault

Set roaring war-to the dread rattling thunder

Have I given fire, and rifted Jove's stout oak

With his own bolt;... (The Tempest, 5.1)

This very free treatment of blank verse was imitated by Shakespeare's contemporaries, and led to general metrical looseness in the hands of less skilled users. However, Shakespearean blank verse was used with some success by John Webster and Thomas Middleton in their plays. Ben Jonson, meanwhile, used a tighter blank verse with less enjambment in his great comedies Volpone and The Alchemist.

Blank verse was not much used in the non-dramatic poetry of the 17th century until Paradise Lost, in which Milton used it with much licence and tremendous skill. Milton used the flexibility of blank verse, its capacity to support syntactic complexity, to the utmost, in passages such as these:

into what Pit thou seest

From what highth fal'n, so much the stronger provd

He with his Thunder: and till then who knew

The force of those dire Arms? yet not for those

Nor what the Potent Victor in his rage

Can else inflict do I repent or change,

Though chang'd in outward lustre; that fixt mind

And high disdain, from sence of injur'd merit,

That with the mightiest rais'd me to contend,

And to the fierce contention brought along

Innumerable force of Spirits arm'd

That durst dislike his reign, and me preferring,

His utmost power with adverse power oppos'd

In dubious Battel on the Plains of Heav'n,

And shook his throne. What though the field be lost?

All is not lost; the unconquerable Will,

And study of revenge, immortal hate,

And courage never to submit or yield:

(Paradise Lost, Book 1)

Milton also wrote Paradise Regained and parts of Samson Agonistes in blank verse.

In the century after Milton, there are few distinguished uses of either dramatic or non-dramatic blank verse; in keeping with the desire for regularity, most of the blank verse of this period is somewhat stiff. The best examples of blank verse from this time are probably John Dryden's tragedy All For Love and James Thomson's The Seasons. An example notable as much for its failure with the public as for its subsequent influence on the form is John Dyer's The Fleece.

At the close of the eighteenth century, William Cowper ushered in a renewal of blank verse with his volume of kaleidoscopic meditations, "The Task", published in 1784. After Shakespeare and Milton, Cowper was the main influence on the next major poets in blank verse, teenagers when Cowper published his masterpiece. These were the Lake Poets William Wordsworth and Samuel Taylor Coleridge. Wordsworth used the form for many of the Lyrical Ballads (1798 and 1800), and for his longest efforts, The Prelude and The Excursion. Wordsworth's verse recovers some of the freedom of Milton's, but is generally far more regular. It is often tedious and prosaic, but at its best it has a calm resonance that is almost unique to Wordsworth. Coleridge's blank verse is technically dazzling, but he wrote little of it: so-called "conversation Poems" such as "The Aeolian Harp" and "Frost at Midnight" are the best known of his blank verse works. The blank verse of Keats in Hyperion is mainly modelled on that of Milton, but takes fewer liberties with the pentameter and possesses the characteristic beauties of Keats's verse. Shelley's blank verse in The Cenci and Prometheus Unbound is closer to Elizabethan practice than to Milton's.

Of the Victorian writers in blank verse, the most prominent are Tennyson and Robert Browning. Tennyson's blank verse in poems like "Ulysses" and "The Princess" is musical and regular; his lyric "Tears, Idle Tears" is probably the first important example of the blank verse stanzaic poem. Browning's blank verse, in poems like "Fra Lippo Lippi", is more abrupt and conversational. Gilbert and Sullivan's 1884 opera, Princess Ida, is based on Tennyson's "The Princess". Gilbert's dialogue is in blank verse throughout (although the other 13 Savoy operas have prose dialogue). An extract spoken by Princess Ida after singing her entrance aria "Oh, goddess wise".

Women of Adamant, fair neophytes-
Who thirst for such instruction as we give,
Attend, while I unfold a parable.
The elephant is mightier than Man,
Yet Man subdues him. Why? The elephant
Is elephantine everywhere but here (tapping her forehead)
And Man, whose brain is to the elephant's
As Woman's brain to Man's-(that's rule of three),-
Conquers the foolish giant of the woods,
As Woman, in her turn, shall conquer Man.
In Mathematics, Woman leads the way:
The narrow-minded pedant still believes
That two and two make four! Why, we can prove,
We women-household drudges as we are-
That two and two make five-or three-or seven;
Or five-and-twenty, if the case demands!

Blank verse, of varying degrees of regularity, has been used quite frequently throughout the 20th century in original verse and in translations of narrative verse. Most of Robert Frost's narrative and conversational poems are in blank verse; so are other important poems like Wallace Stevens's "The Idea of Order at Key West" and "The Comedian as the Letter C", W. B. Yeats's "The Second Coming", W. H. Auden's "The Watershed", John Betjeman's Summoned by Bells, and so on. A complete listing is impossible, since a sort of loose blank verse has become a staple of lyric poetry, but it would be safe to say that blank verse is as prominent now as it has been any time in the past three hundred years.

FREE VERSE

Free verse (also at times referred to as vers libre) is a term describing various styles of poetry that are not written using strict meter or rhyme, but that still are recognizable as 'poetry' by virtue of complex patterns of one sort or another that readers can perceive to be part of a coherent whole.

History

An early usage of the term appears in 1915 in the anonymous preface to the first Imagist anthology. The main author of this preface was Richard Aldington. The preface states: "We do not insist upon 'free-verse' as the only method of writing poetry. We fight for it as for a principle of liberty."

The ideal of the early practitioners of free verse was well described by Ezra Pound, who wrote: "As regarding rhythm: to compose in the sequence of the musical phrase, not in sequence of a metronome."

D. H. Lawrence wrote that Whitman "pruned away his clichés-perhaps his clichés of rhythm as well as of phrase" and that all one could do with free verse was "get rid of the stereotyped movements and the old hackneyed associations of sound and sense".

Some poets have explained that free verse, despite its freedom, must still display some elements of form. Pound's friend T. S. Eliot wrote: "No verse is free for the man who wants to do a good job." Donald Hall goes as far as to say that "the form of free verse is as binding and as liberating as the form of a rondeau."

Some poets think free verse too limiting. In 1922 Robert Bridges voiced his reservations in the essay 'Humdrum and Harum-Scarum.' Robert Frost later remarked that writing free verse was like "playing tennis without a net".

Precursors

As the name vers libre suggests, this technique of using more irregular cadences is often said to derive from the practices of 19th century French poets like Gustave Kahn and especially Jules Laforgue. However, in English it can be traced back at least as far as the King James Bible. Walt Whitman, who based his verse approach on the Bible, was the major precursor for modern poets writing free verse, though they were reluctant to acknowledge his influence.

Many poets of the Victorian era experimented with form. Christina Rossetti, Coventry Patmore, and T. E. Brown all wrote examples of unpatterned rhymed verse. Matthew Arnold's poem Philomela contains some rhyme but is very free. Poems such as W. E. Henley's 'Discharged' (from his In Hospital sequence), and Robert Louis Stevenson's poems 'The Light-Keeper' and 'The Cruel Mistress' could be counted early examples of free verse.

In France, free verse was occasionally used by symbolist Arthur Rimbaud. In the Netherlands, tachtiger (i.e. member of 1880s generation of innovative poets) Frederik van Eeden also employed the form at least once in his poem Waterlelie "water lily".

12

Literary Theory

Literary theory is the theory (or the philosophy) of the interpretation of literature and literary criticism. Its history begins with classical Greek poetics and rhetoric and includes, since the 18th century, aesthetics and hermeneutics. In the 20th century, "theory" has become an umbrella term for a variety of scholarly approaches to reading texts, most of which are informed by various strands of Continental philosophy.

LITERARY THEORY AND LITERATURE

One of the fundamental questions of literary theory is "What is literature?", though many contemporary theorists and literary scholars believe either that the term "literature" is undefinable or that it can potentially refer to any use of language. Specific theories are distinguished not only by their methods and conclusions, but even by how they define a "text." For some scholars of literature, "texts" means "books belonging to the Western literary canon". But the principles and methods of literary theory have been applied to non-fiction, popular fiction, film, historical documents, law, advertising, etc., in the related field of cultural studies. In fact, some scholars within cultural studies treat cultural events like fashion, football riots, etc. as "texts" to be interpreted. Taken broadly, then, literary theory can be thought of as the general theory of interpretation.

Since theorists of literature often draw on a very heterogeneous tradition of Continental philosophy and the philosophy of language, any classification of their approaches is only an approximation. There are many "schools" or types of literary theory, which take different approaches to understanding texts. Most theorists, even among those listed below, combine methods from more than one of these approaches (for instance, the deconstructive approach of Paul de Man drew on a long tradition of close reading pioneered by the New Critics, and de Man was trained in the European hermeneutic tradition).

Broad schools of theory that have historically been important include the New Criticism, formalism, Russian formalism, and structuralism, post-structuralism, Marxism, feminism and French feminism, new historicism, deconstruction, reader-response criticism, and psychoanalytic criticism or psychocriticism.

HISTORY

The practice of literary theory became a profession in the 20th century, but it has historical roots that run as far back as ancient Greece (Aristotle's Poetics is an often cited early example) and ancient Rome (Longinus' On the Sublime and Horace's Ars Poetica), and the aesthetic theories of philosophers from ancient philosophy through the 18th and 19th centuries are important influences on current literary study. The theory and criticism of literature are, of course, also closely tied to the history of literature.

The modern sense of "literary theory," however, dates only to approximately the 1950s, when the structuralist linguistics of Ferdinand de Saussure began strongly to influence English language literary criticism. The New Critics and various European-influenced formalists (particularly the Russian Formalists) had described some of their more abstract efforts as "theoretical" as well. But it was not until the broad impact of structuralism began to be felt in the English-speaking academic world that "literary theory" was thought of as a unified domain.

In the academic world of the United Kingdom and the United States, literary theory was at its most popular from the late 1960s (when its influence was beginning to spread outward from elite universities like Johns Hopkins and Yale) through the 1980s (by which time it was taught nearly everywhere in some form). During this span of time, literary theory was perceived as academically cutting-edge research, and most university literature departments sought to teach and study theory and incorporate it into their curricula. Because of its meteoric rise in popularity and the difficult language of its key texts, theory was also often criticized as faddish or trendy obscurantism (and many academic satire novels of the period, such as those by David Lodge, feature theory prominently). Some scholars, both theoretical and anti-theoretical, refer to the 1970s and 1980s debates on the academic merits of theory as "the theory wars."

By the early 1990s, the popularity of "theory" as a subject of interest by itself was declining slightly (along with job openings for pure "theorists") even as the texts of literary theory were incorporated into the study of almost all literature. As of 2004, the controversy over the use of theory in literary studies has all but died out, and discussions on the topic within literary and cultural studies tend now to be considerably milder and less acrimonious (though the appearance of volumes such as Theory's Empire: An Anthology of Dissent, edited by Daphne Patai with Will H. Corral, may signal a resurgence of the controversy). Some scholars draw heavily on theory in their work, while others only mention it in passing or not at all; but it is an acknowledged, important part of the study of literature.

DIFFERENCES AMONG SCHOOLS

The intellectual traditions and priorities of the various kinds of literary theory are often radically different. Some differ so strongly that even finding a set of common terms upon which to compare them is not a trivial effort.

For instance, the work of the New Critics often contained an implicit moral dimension, and sometimes even a religious one: a New Critic might read a poem by T.S. Eliot or Gerard Manley Hopkins for its degree of honesty in expressing the torment and contradiction of a serious search for belief in the modern world. Meanwhile a Marxist critic might find such judgments merely ideological rather than critical; the Marxist would say that the New Critical reading did not keep enough critical distance from the poem's religious stance to be able to understand it. Or a post-structuralist critic might simply avoid the issue by understanding the religious meaning of a poem as an allegory of meaning, treating the poem's references to "God" by discussing their referential nature rather than what they refer to.

Such a disagreement cannot be easily resolved, because it is inherent in the radically different terms and goals (that is, the theories) of the critics. Their theories of reading derive from vastly different intellectual traditions: the New Critic bases his work on an East-Coast American scholarly and religious tradition, while the Marxist derives his thought from a body of critical social and economic thought, and the post-structuralist's work emerges from twentieth-century Continental philosophy of language.

To expect such different approaches to have much in common would be naïve; so calling them all "theories of literature" without acknowledging their heterogeneity is itself a reduction of their differences.

In the late 1950s, Canadian literary critic Northrop Frye attempted to establish an approach for reconciling historical criticism and New Criticism while addressing concerns of early reader-response and numerous psychological and social approaches. His approach, laid out in his Anatomy of Criticism, was explicitly structuralist, relying on the assumption of an intertextual "order of words" and universality of certain structural types. His approach held sway in English literature programs for several decades but lost favor during the ascendence of post-structuralism.

For some theories of literature (especially certain kinds of formalism), the distinction between 'literary' and other sorts of texts is of paramount importance. Other schools (particularly post-structuralism in its various forms: new historicism, deconstruction, some strains of Marxism and feminism) have sought to break down distinctions between the two and have applied the tools of textual interpretation to a wide range of 'texts', including film, non-fiction, historical writing, and even cultural events.

Another crucial distinction among the various theories of literary interpretation is intentionality, the amount of weight given to the author's own opinions about and intentions for a work. For most pre-20th century approaches, the author's intentions are a guiding factor and an important determiner of the 'correct' interpretation of texts. The New Criticism was the first school to disavow the role of the author in interpreting texts, preferring to focus on "the text itself" in a close reading. In fact, as much contention as there is between formalism and later schools, they share the tenet that the author's interpretation of a work is no more inherently meaningful than any other.

SCHOOLS OF LITERARY THEORY

Listed below are some of the most commonly identified schools of literary theory, along with their major authors. (In many of these cases, such as those of the historian and philosopher Michel Foucault and the anthropologist Claude Lévi-Strauss, these authors were not literary critics and did not primarily write about literature; but, since their work has been broadly influential in literary theory, they are nonetheless listed here.)

- American pragmatism and other American approaches
  - Harold Bloom, Stanley Fish, Richard Rorty
- Cultural studies-emphasizes the role of literature in everyday life
  - Raymond Williams, Dick Hebdige, and Stuart Hall (British Cultural Studies); Max Horkheimer and Theodor Adorno; Michel de Certeau; also Paul Gilroy, John Guillory
- Comparative Literature-considers literatures from different languages, nations and cultures
- Darwinian literary studies-situates literature in the context of evolution and natural selection
- Deconstruction-seeks to blow apart conventional meaning and definitions by analyzing the qualities that are absent in a textual component and then defining them by that absence. This school is well known for calling into question many accepted literary theories and has even gone on to question existence itself.
  - Jacques Derrida, Paul de Man, J. Hillis Miller, Philippe Lacoue-Labarthe, Gayatri Spivak, Avital Ronell
- Feminism-which emphasizes themes of gender relations
  - Luce Irigaray, Héléne Cixous, Elaine Showalter

- Formalism
- German hermeneutics and philology
    - o Friedrich Schleiermacher, Wilhelm Dilthey, Hans-Georg Gadamer, Erich Auerbach
- Marxism (see Marxist literary criticism)-which emphasizes themes of class conflict
    - o Georg Lukács, Valentin Voloshinov, Raymond Williams, Terry Eagleton, Fredric Jameson, Theodor Adorno, Walter Benjamin,
- New Criticism-which looked at literary works on the basis of what is written, and not at the goals of the author or biographical issues
    - o W.K. Wimsatt, F.R. Leavis, John Crowe Ransom, Cleanth Brooks, Robert Penn Warren
- New historicism-which examines a text by also examining other texts of the time period
    - o Stephen Greenblatt, Louis Montrose, Jonathan Goldberg, H. Aram Vesser
- Postcolonialism-focuses on the influences of colonialism in literature, especially regarding the historical conflict resulting from the exploitation of less developed countries and indigenous peoples by western nations
    - o Edward Said, Gayatri Chakravorty Spivak, Homi Bhabha and Declan Kiberd
- Post-structuralism-criticism of structuralism
    - o Michel Foucault, Julia Kristeva, later Roland Barthes, Gilles Deleuze and Félix Guattari, Maurice Blanchot
- Psychoanalysis (see psychoanalytic literary criticism)-Explores the role of the subconscious in literature including that of the author, reader, and characters in the text
    - o Sigmund Freud, Jacques Lacan, Slavoj □i□ek, Viktor Tausk
- Queer theory-examines, questions, and criticizes the role of gender identity and sexuality in literature
    - o Judith Butler, Eve Sedgewick, Michel Foucault

- Reader Response-focuses upon the active response of the reader to a text
    - o Louise Rosenblatt, Wolfgang Iser, Norman Holland, Hans-Robert Jauss, Stuart Hall
- Russian Formalism
    - o Victor Shklovsky, Vladimir Propp
- Structuralism and semiotics (see semiotic literary criticism)--examined the underlying structures in the content of a text (plot, for example)
    - o Roman Jakobson, Claude Lévi-Strauss, early Roland Barthes, Mikhail Bakhtin, Jurij Lotman, Antti Aarne, and morphology of folklore
- Other theorists: Robert Graves, Alamgir Hashmi, John Sutherland, Northrop Frye, Leslie Fiedler, Kenneth Burke, Barbara Johnson

13

Fiction and Non-fiction

Fiction (from the Latin fingere, "to form, create") is storytelling of imagined events and stands in contrast to non-fiction, which makes factual claims about reality.

Fictional works-novels, short stories, fables, fairy tales, films, comics, interactive fiction, animation, video games-may include or reference factual occurrences. The term is also often used synonymously with literature and more specifically fictional prose. In this sense, fiction refers only to novels or short stories and is often divided into two categories, popular fiction (e.g., science fiction or mystery fiction) and literary fiction (e.g., Marcel Proust or William Faulkner).

An Overview

Fiction is largely perceived as a form of art and/or entertainment, although not all fiction is necessarily artistic. Fiction may be created for the purpose of educating, such as fictional examples used in school textbooks. Fiction is also frequently instrumentalized by propaganda and advertising. Fiction may be propagated by parents to their children out of tradition (e.g. Santa Claus) or in order to instill certain beliefs and values. Fables with an explicit moral goal are not necessarily targeted at children, however.

Fiction may over time blend with factual accounts and develop into mythology. Many atheists perceive religion as no different from any fictional tale, whereas members of religious groups typically explain their beliefs with faith and/or historical figures/events; and claim they are fundamentally different from fictional tales (although they may call other religious views fictional). The sociological school of constructivism argues that every view of reality is fundamentally a construction of the self and that a safe distinction between fact and fiction is impossible, whereas the philosophy of naturalism holds that reality can be approximated and truth can be demonstrated through usefulness, allowing the distinction from fiction.

Fiction has often been the target of censorship or boycotts, escalating into book burnings or bans. Extremist regimes like the Taliban have been even more prohibitive, restricting all reading to religious texts. There is an ongoing debate regarding sexual content in fiction and whether or not juveniles can be safely exposed to it; opponents of fiction with sexual content typically label it pornography. On the other hand fiction is also used to express religion.

The Internet has had a massive impact on the distribution of fiction, calling into question the feasibility of copyright as a means to ensure royalties are paid to copyright holders. Also digital libraries such as Project Gutenberg have come into being which make public domain texts more readily available. The combination of inexpensive home computers, the Internet and the creativity of its users has also led to new forms of fiction, such as interactive computer games or computer-generated comics. Countless forums for fan fiction can be found online, where loyal followers of specific fictional realms create and distribute derivative stories. The Internet is also used for the development of collaborative fiction, where a story is written sequentially by different authors, or the entire text can be revised by anyone using wiki.

Fiction is a fundamental part of human culture, and the ability to create fiction and other artistic works is frequently cited as one of the defining characteristics of humanity.

CATEGORIES OF FICTION

Types of fiction prose:

- Flash fiction: A work of fewer than 2,000 words. (1,000 by some definitions)
- Short story: A work of at least 2,000 words but under 7,500 words.

- Novelette: A work of at least 7,500 words but under 17,500 words.
- Novella: A work of at least 17,500 words but under 60,000 words.
- Novel: A work of 60,000 words or more.
- Epic: A work of 200,000 words or more.

Novel

A novel (from French nouvelle Italian "novella", "New") is an extended fictional narrative in prose. Until the eighteenth century, the word referred specifically to short fictions of love and intrigue as opposed to romances, which were epic-length works about love and adventure. During the 18th century the novel adopted features of the old romance and became one of the major literary genres. It is today defined mostly by its ability to become the object of literary criticism demanding artistic merit, a specific 'literary' style and a deeper meaning than a true story of the same content could claim to have.

ELEMENTS OF FICTION

The fiction writer might use the following to create artistic effects in his or her story:

Narratology is the theory and study of narrative and narrative structure and the way they affect our perception. The term was coined in French, narratologie, by Tzvetan Todorov in his 1969 Grammaire du Décaméron (Prince). Its objects of study are all kinds of narrated texts-both fiction (literature, poetry, etc.) and non-fiction (historiography, academic publishing, etc.),-as well as the dramatic structures, plot devices, characterization, settings, genres, and literary techniques. Usually, the term "narratology" is used in connection with fictional texts, which doesn't imply that non-fictional texts or other forms of fiction (theater, films, electronic entertainment, etc.) are not included in the studies' field.

- antagonist: the character that stands in opposition to the protagonist
- character: a participant in the story, usually a person

- conflict: a character or problem with which the protagonist must contend
- climax: the story's highest point of tension or drama
- dialogue: the speech of characters as opposed to that of the narrator
- plot: a related series of events revealed in narrative
- point of view: the perspective of the narrator; usually refers to the voice, first or third person.
- protagonist: the central character of a story
- resolution: the plot component in which the result of the conflict is revealed
- scene: a piece of the story showing the action of one event
- setting: the locale and time of a story that creates mood and atmosphere
- structure: the organization of story elements
- subplot: a plot that is part of or subordinate to another plot
- suspension of disbelief: the reader's temporary acceptance of story elements as believable, usually necessary for enjoyment
- theme: a conceptual distillation of the story; what the story is about
- tone: the tone of "voice" that the author uses.

NON-FICTION

Non-fiction is an account or representation of a subject which is presented as fact. This presentation may be accurate or not; that is, it can give either a true or a false account of the subject in question. However, it is generally assumed that the authors of such accounts believe them to be truthful at the time of their composition. Non-fiction is one of the two main divisions in writing, particularly used in libraries, the other being fiction. However, non-fiction need not be written text necessarily, since pictures and film can also purport to present a factual account of a subject.

Types

Essays, journals, documentaries, scientific papers, photographs, biographies, textbooks, blueprints, technical documentation, user manuals, diagrams and journalism are all common examples of non-fiction works, and fiction within any of these works is usually regarded as dishonest. Other works can legitimately be either fiction or non-fiction, such as letters, magazine articles, histories, websites, speeches and travelogues. Although they are mostly either one or the other it is not uncommon for there to be a blend of both, particularly non-fiction with a dash of fiction for added spice.

Distinctions

The numerous literary and creative devices used within fiction are generally thought inappropriate for use in non-fiction. They are still present particularly in older works but they are often muted so as not to overshadow the information within the work. Simplicity, clarity and directness are some of the most important considerations when producing non-fiction. Audience is important in any artistic or descriptive endeavour but it is perhaps most important in non-fiction. In fiction, the writer believes that readers will make an effort to follow and interpret an indirectly or abstractly presented progression of theme, whereas the production of non-fiction has more to do with the direct provision of information. Understanding of the potential readers' use for the work and their existing knowledge of a subject are both fundamental for effective non-fiction. Despite the truth of non-fiction it is often necessary to persuade the reader to agree with the ideas and so a balanced, coherent and informed argument is also vital. Mark Twain said, paraphrased: "The difference between fiction and non-fiction is that fiction must be absolutely believable."

History

Cave paintings, from 40,000 years ago, are one of the oldest forms of human expression and could be either a record of what prehistoric man caught on hunting trips, i.e. non-fiction, or alternately a story expressing what they would like to catch on future occasions, i.e. fiction. If cave art is ambiguous on this matter, cuneiform inscriptions which hold the earliest writings seem to have been initially for non-fiction. Some of the most important symbols in cuneiform represent goods such as oxen and barley and the earliest texts in existence deal with the buying and selling of these items and other economic matters, although fiction was not far behind.

Much of the non-fiction produced throughout history is of a mundane and everyday variety such as records and legal documents which were only ever seen by a few and are of little interest except to the historian. It probably easily outweighs fiction in the amount that has been produced but fiction generally has a longer lasting appeal as it is designed for entertainment and even rather mediocre fiction survives a few generations. The non-fiction that transcends its original time tends to be viewed as either exceptionally well made or perfectly embodying the ideas, manners and attitudes of the time it was produced, even if it was not actually created as history.

At any one time in history there is the body of non-fiction work which represents the currently accepted truths of the period. Although these non-fiction works may be contradictory they form a corpus that is regularly being altered with better explanations of ideas or with new facts. A good example of this are the non-fiction scientific books and papers which explain the science of the day but are then superseded by better representations. Textbooks for explaining and teaching the current state of scientific and historical knowledge are regularly updated and manuals for operating new technology are also produced.

SHORT STORY

A short story is a form of short fictional narrative prose. Short stories tend to be more concise and to the point than longer works of fiction, such as novellas (in the modern sense of this term) and novels.

Short stories have their origins in oral story-telling traditions and the prose anecdote, a swiftly-sketched situation that comes rapidly to its point. With the rise of the comparatively realistic novel, the short story evolved as a miniature, with some of its first perfectly independent examples in the tales of E.T.A. Hoffmann and Anton Chekhov.

Many authors today release compilations of their short stories in short story collections.

History.

Origins

Short stories date back to the (oral) story-telling traditions which produced such notable tales as Homer's the Iliad and the Odyssey. Tales such as these were told in a rhyming, poetic format, with the rhymes acting as a mnemonic tool for people to remember the story. Short sections of these tales focused on individual narratives that could be told at one sitting. The overall arch of the story would only emerge through the telling of multiple sections of the tale.

Fables, which tend to be folk tales with an explicitly expressed moral, were said by the Greek historian Herodotus to have been invented by a Greek slave named Aesop in the 6th century BCE (although other times and nationalities are also given for Aesop). These ancient fables are known today as Aesop's Fables.

The other ancient form of short story, anecdotes, were popular during the years of the Roman Empire. Anecdotes functioned as a sort of parable, a brief realistic narration that embodies a point. Many of the surviving Roman anecdotes were later collected in the Gesta Romanorum in the 13th or 14th century. Anecdotes remained popular in Europe well into the 18th century, when the fictional anecdotal letters of Sir Roger de Coverley were published.

In Europe, the oral story-telling tradition began to develop into written stories in the early 14th century, most notably with Geoffrey Chaucer's Canterbury Tales and Giovanni Boccaccio's Decameron. Both of these books are composed of individual short stories (which range from farce or humorous anecdotes to well-crafted literary fictions) set within a larger narrative story (a frame story), although the frame tale device was not adopted by all writers.

At the end of the 16th century, some of the most popular short stories in Europe were the darkly tragic "novella" of Matteo Bandello (especially in their French translation). During the Renaissance, the term novella was used when referring to short stories.

The mid 17th century in France saw the development of a refined short novel, the "nouvelle", by such authors as Madame de Lafayette. In the 1690s, traditional fairy tales began to be published (one of the most famous collections was by Charles Perrault). The appearance of Antoine Galland's first modern translation of the Thousand and One Nights (or Arabian Nights) (from 1704; another translation appeared in 1710-12) would have an enormous influence on the 18th century European short stories of Voltaire, Diderot and others.

Modern Short Stories

Modern short stories emerged as their own genre in the early 19th century. Early examples of short story and short story collections include the Brothers Grimm Fairy Tales (1824-1826), Nikolai Gogol's Evenings on a Farm Near Dikanka (1831-1832), Edgar Allan Poe's The Gold Bug (1843), about a cryptographic treasure map and Nathaniel Hawthorne's Twice Told Tales (1842). In the later part of the 19th century, the growth of print magazines and journals created a strong market demand for short fiction between 3,000 and 15,000 words in length. Among the famous short stories to come out of this time period was "Ward No. 6" by Anton Chekhov.

In the first half of the 20th century, a number of high-profile magazines, such as The Atlantic Monthly, Scribner's, and The Saturday Evening Post, all published short stories in each issue. The demand for quality short stories was so great, and the money paid for them so high, that F. Scott Fitzgerald repeatedly turned to short story writing to pay off his numerous debts. The demand for short stories by print magazines hit its peak in the middle of the 20th century, when in 1952 Life magazine published Ernest Hemingway's long short story (or novella) The Old Man and the Sea. The issue containing this story sold 5,300,000 copies in only two days.

Since then, the number of commercial magazines that publish short stories has declined, even though several well-known magazines like The New Yorker continue to feature them. Literary magazines also provide a showcase for short stories. In addition, short stories have recently found a new life online, where they can be found in online magazines, in collections organized by author or theme, and on blogs.

ELEMENTS AND CHARACTERISTICS

Short stories tend to be less complex than novels. Usually, a short story will focus on only one incident, has a single plot, a single setting, a limited number of characters, and covers a short period of time.

In longer forms of fiction, stories tend to contain certain core elements of dramatic structure: exposition (the introduction of setting, situation and main characters); complication (the event of the story that introduces the conflict); rising action, crisis (the decisive moment for the protagonist and their commitment to a course of action); climax (the point of highest interest in terms of the conflict and the point of the story with the most action); resolution (the point of the story when the conflict is resolved); and moral.

Because of their short length, short stories may or may not follow this pattern. For example, modern short stories only occasionally have an exposition. More typical, though, is an abrupt beginning, with the story starting in the middle of the action. As with longer stories, plots of short stories also have a climax, crisis, or turning-point. However, the endings of many short stories are abrupt and open and may or may not have a moral or practical lesson.

Of course, as with any art form, the exact characteristics of a short story will vary by author.

Length

Determining what exactly separates a short story from longer fictional formats is problematic. A classic definition of a short story is that one should be able to read it in one sitting, a point most notably made in Edgar Allan Poe's essay "The Philosophy of Composition" (1846). Other definitions place the maximum word length at 7,500 words. In contemporary usage, the term short story most often refers to a work of fiction no longer than 20,000 words and no shorter than 1,000.

NOVELLA

A novella is a narrative work of prose fiction somewhat longer than a short story but shorter than a novel. A common length is about 50 to 100 pages, or around 20,000 to 40,000 words. The extra length is generally used for more character development than is possible in a short story, but without the much greater character and plot development of a novel.

Although the novella is a common literary genre in several European languages, it is less common in English. English-speaking readers would be most familiar with the novellas of Franz Kafka, particularly The Metamorphosis and In the Penal Colony, or George Orwell's Animal Farm and Joseph Conrad's Heart of Darkness.

Like the English word "novel", the English word "novella" derives from the Italian word "novella" (plural: "novelle"), for a tale, a piece of news. As the etymology suggests, novellas originally were news of town and country life worth repeating for amusement and edification.

History

As a literary genre, the novella's origin lay in the early Renaissance literary work of the Italians and the French. Principally, by Giovanni Boccaccio (1313-1375), author of The Decameron (1353)-one hundred novelle told by ten people, seven women and three men, fleeing the Black Death by escaping from Florence to the Fiesole hills, in 1348; and by the French Queen, Marguerite de Navarre (1492-1549), [aka Marguerite de Valois, et. alii.], author of Heptaméron (1559)-seventy-two original French tales (structured like The Decameron). Her psychological acuity and didactic purpose outweigh the unfinished collection's weak literary style.

Not until the late eighteenth-and early nineteenth-centuries did writers fashion the novella into a literary genre structured by precepts and rules. Contemporaneously, the Germans were the most active writers of the Novelle (German: "Novelle"; plural: "Novellen"). For the German writer, a novella is a fictional narrative of indeterminate length-a few pages to hundreds-restricted to a single, suspenseful event, situation, or conflict leading to an unexpected turning point (Wendepunkt), provoking a logical, but surprising end; Novellen tend to contain a concrete symbol, which is the narration's steady point.

Novella versus Novel

In German and Dutch, the word for "novella" is Novelle (German) and novelle (Dutch), and the word for "novel" is Roman (German) and roman (Dutch). In French "novella" is nouvelle and "novel" is roman. In Swedish "novella" (and "short story") is novell and "novel" is roman. This etymological distinction avoids confusion of the literatures and the forms, with the novel being the more important, established fictional form. The Austrian writer Stefan Zweig's (1881-1942) Die Schachnovelle (1942) (literally, "The Chess Novella", but translated in 1944 as The Royal Game) is an example of a title naming its genre.

Commonly, longer novellas are referred to as novels; Dr. Jekyll and Mr. Hyde and Heart of Darkness are sometimes called novels, as are many science fiction works such as The War of the Worlds and Armageddon 2419 A.D.. Occasionally, longer works are referred to as novellas, with some academics positing 100,000 words as the novella?novel threshold. In the science fiction genre, the Hugo and Nebula literary awards define the novella as: "A... story of between seventeen thousand, five hundred (17,500) and forty thousand (40,000) words."

Stephen King, in his introduction to Different Seasons, an anthology of four of his novellas, has called the novella "an ill-defined and disreputable literary banana republic"; King notes the difficulties of selling a novella in the commercial publishing world, since it does not fit the typical length requirements of either magazine or book publishers. Despite these problems, however, the novella's length provides unique advantages; in the introduction to a novella anthology titled Sailing to Byzantium, Robert Silverberg writes:

The novella is one of the richest and most rewarding of literary forms...it allows for more extended development of theme and character than does the short story, without making the elaborate structural demands of the full-length book. Thus it provides an intense, detailed exploration of its subject, providing to some degree both the concentrated focus of the short story and the broad scope of the novel. (Silverberg, vii)

In his essay 'Briefly, the Case for the Novella,' Canadian author George Fetherling (who wrote the novella Tales of Two

Cities) said that to reduce the novella to nothing more than a short novel is like "saying a pony is a baby horse."

ESSAY

An essay is a short work of writing that treats a topic from an author's personal point of view. Essays are non-fictional but often subjective; while expository, they can also include narrative. Essays can be literary criticism, political manifestos, learned arguments, observations of daily life, recollections, and reflections of the author.

The definition of an essay is vague, overlapping with those of an article and a short story. Almost all modern essays are written in prose, but works in verse have been dubbed essays (Alexander Pope's An Essay on Criticism and An Essay on Man). While brevity usually defines an essay, voluminous works like John Locke's An Essay Concerning Human Understanding and Thomas Malthus's An Essay on the Principle of Population provide counter-examples.

The Essay as Literary Genre

The word essay derives from the French infinitive essayer, 'to try' or 'to attempt'. The first author to describe his works as essays was the Frenchman Michel de Montaigne (1533-1592). Inspired in particular by the works of Plutarch, a translation of whose Oeuvres morales (Moral works) into French had just been published by Jacques Amyot, Montaigne began to compose his essays in 1572; the first edition, entitled Essais, was published in two volumes in 1580. For the rest of his life he continued revising previously published essays and composing new ones.

Francis Bacon's essays, published in book form in 1597, 1612, and 1625, were the first works in English that described themselves as essays. Ben Jonson first used the word essayist in English in 1609, according to the Oxford English Dictionary.

Notable essayists are legion. They include Virginia Woolf, Adrienne Rich, Alamgir Hashmi, Joan Didion, Susan Sontag, Natalia Ginzburg, Sara Suleri, Annie Dillard, Joseph Addison, Richard Steele, Charles Lamb, William Hazlitt, Thomas Babington Macaulay, Ralph Waldo Emerson, Walter Bagehot, George Orwell,

John D'Agata, and E.B. White. It is very difficult to define the genre into which essays fall. The following remarks by Aldous Huxley, a leading essayist, may help:

"Like the novel, the essay is a literary device for saying almost everything about almost anything. By tradition, almost by definition, the essay is a short piece, and it is therefore impossible to give all things full play within the limits of a single essay. But a collection of essays can cover almost as much ground, and cover it almost as thoroughly, as can a long novel. Montaigne's Third Book is the equivalent, very nearly, of a good slice of the Comédie Humaine. Essays belong to a literary species whose extreme variability can be studied most effectively within a three-poled frame of reference. There is the pole of the personal and the autobiographical; there is the pole of the objective, the factual, the concrete-particular; and there is the pole of the abstract-universal. Most essayists are at home and at their best in the neighborhood of only one of the essay's three poles, or at the most only in the neighborhood of two of them. There are the predominantly personal essayists, who write fragments of reflective autobiography and who look at the world through the keyhole of anecdote and description. There are the predominantly objective essayists who do not speak directly of themselves, but turn their attention outward to some literary or scientific or political theme. ... And how splendid, how truly oracular are the utterances of the great generalizers! ... The most richly satisfying essays are those which make the best not of one, not of two, but of all the three worlds in which it is possible for the essay to exist" (Collected Essays, "Preface").

The Essay as a Pedagogical Tool

In recent times, essays have become a major part of a formal education. Secondary students are taught structured essay formats to improve their writing skills, and essays are often used by universities in selecting applicants. In both secondary and tertiary education, essays are used to judge the mastery and comprehension of material. Students are asked to explain, comment on, or assess a topic of study in the form of an essay.

Academic essays are usually more formal than literary ones. They may still allow the presentation of the writer's own views, but this is done in a logical and factual manner, with the use of the first person often discouraged.

The Five-paragraph Essay

Many students' first exposure to the genre is the five paragraph essay, a highly structured form requiring an introduction presenting the thesis statement; three body paragraphs, each of which presents an idea to support the thesis together with supporting evidence and quotations; and a conclusion, which restates the thesis and summarizes the supporting points. The use of this format is controversial. Proponents argue that it teaches students how to organize their thoughts clearly in writing; opponents characterize its structure as rigid and repetitive.

Academic Essays

Longer academic essays (often with a word limit of between 2,000 to 5,000 words) are often more discursive. They sometimes begin with a short summary analysis of what has previously been written on a topic, which is often called a literature review. Longer essays may also contain an introductory page in which words and phrases from the title are tightly defined. Most academic institutions will require that all substantial facts, quotations, and other supporting material used in an essay be referenced in a bibliography at the end of the text. This scholarly convention allows others (whether teachers or fellow scholars) to understand the basis of the facts and quotations used to support the essay's argument, and thereby help to evaluate to what extent the argument is supported by evidence, and to evaluate the quality of that evidence. The academic essay tests the student's ability to present their thoughts in an organized way and tests their intellectual capabilities. Some types of essays are

Descriptive Essays: The aim of descriptive essays is to provide a vivid picture of a person, location, object, event, or debate. It will offer details that will enable the reader to imagine the item described.

Narrative Essays: The aim of a narrative essay is to describe a course of events from a subjective vantage point, and may be written in first-person present or first person past tense. Though not always chronological, narrative essays do follow the development of a person through a series of experiences and reflections. The focus of the essay is often to more clearly identify the point of view of the narrator, and to express common features of subjectivity.

Compare and Contrast Essays: The aim of a compare and contrast essay is to develop the relationship between two or more things. Generally, the goal is to show that superficial differences or similarities are inadequate, and that closer examination reveals their unobvious, yet significant, relations or differences.

Persuasive Essays: In a persuasive essay, the writer tries to persuade the reader to accept an idea or agree with an opinion. The writer's purpose is to convince the reader that her or his point of view is a reasonable one. The persuasive essay should be written in a style that grabs and holds the reader's attention, and the writer's opinion should be backed up by strong supporting details. Argumentative Essays: Argumentative essays are most often used to address controversial issues-i.e. serious issue over which there is some evident disagreement. An argument is a position combined with its supporting reasons. Argumentative papers thus set out a main claim and then provide reasons for thinking that the claim is true.

Imitation

Imitation essays are essays in which the writer pulls out the main thesis and outline of a particular paper, and then writes an essay in his or her own style.

Non-literary Essays

Art

In the visual arts, an essay is a preliminary drawing or sketch upon which a final painting or sculpture is based, made as a test of the work's composition (this meaning of the term, like several of those following, comes from the word essay's meaning of "attempt" or "trial").

Music

In the realm of music, composer Samuel Barber wrote a set of "Essays for Orchestra," relying on the form and content of the music to guide the listener's ear, rather than any extra-musical plot or story.

Film

Film essays are cinematic forms of the essay, with the film consisting of the evolution of a theme or an idea rather than a plot per se; or the film literally being a cinematic accompaniment to a narrator reading an essay. The genre is not well-defined but might include works of early Soviet documentarians like Dziga Vertov, or present-day filmmakers like Michael Moore or Errol Morris.

Photography

A photographic essay is an attempt to cover a topic with a linked series of photographs.

Bibliography

Abandon: *A Romance/Pico Iyer*, New Delhi, Penguin, 2003.

Abercrombie, D.: *Elements of General Ponetics*, Edinburgh, Edinburgh University Press, 1967.

Ailsby, Christopher: *Roll of Infamy*, Osceola, MBI, 1997.

Alexander, Yonah: *Combating Terrorism: Strategies of Ten Countries*, Mich., University of Michigan Press, 2002.

Allen, Ernst: *The English Novel: a Short Critical History*, London: Phoenix House, 1954.

Amitav Ghosh's: *The Shadow Lines: Critical Essays*, New Delhi, Atlantic, 2002.

Anita Desai: *Vision and Technique in Her Novels*, New Delhi, B.R., 2001.

Arthur Miller: *As a Critic of Drama*, New Delhi, Anmol, 2004.

Authors, Texts, Issues: *Essays on Indian Literature*, Delhi, Pencraft International, 2003.

Ayoni and Other Stories: *A Collection of Telugu Short Stories*, New Delhi, Stree Katha, 2001.

Ball, M. J. : *Phonetics: The Science of Speech*, London, Arnold, 1999.

Barter, James: *The Ganges*, San Diego, Lucent Books, 2003.

Bennett, J. A. W.: *Middle English Literature*, Oxford, Clarendon Press, 1986.

Bentley, Eades: *The Jacobean and Caroline Stage*, Oxford, Clarendon Press, 1941.

Beyond Borders: *An Anthology of SAARC Poetry*, Noida, Rainbow, 2002.

Bhattacharyya, Nath: *Indian Religious Historiography*, New Delhi, Munshiram Manoharlal Publishers, 1996.

Brown, G.: *Listening to Spoken English*, Harlow, Longman, 1990.

Brown, J. M.: *Ireland in Fiction; a Guide to Irish Novels, Tales, Romances, and Folk-lore*, London: Maunsel, 1919.

Bush, Douglas: *English Literature in the Earlier Seventeenth Century, 1600-1660*, Oxford, Clarendon Press, 1962.

Cahalan, M.: *The Irish Novel: a Critical History*, Boston, Twayne Publishers, 1988.

Caidin, Martin: *The Tigers are Burning*, NY, Hawthorn Books, 1974.

Cavanagh, John: *British Theatre: a Bibliography, 1901 to 1985*, Hampshire, Motley, 1989.

Chambers, Kerchever: *English Literature at the Close of the Middle Ages*, New York: Oxford University Press, 1947.

Classe, A.: *The Rhythm of English Prose*, Oxford, Blackwell, 1939.

Couper-Kuhlen, E.: *An Introduction to English Prosody*, London, Edward Arnold, 1986.

Courthope, John: *A History of English Poetry*, London, MacMillan and Co., 1903.

Crane, Salmon: *A Census of British Newspapers and Periodicals, 1620-1800*, London, Cambridge University Press, 1927.

Crystal, D.: *Prosodic Systems and Intonation in English*, Cambridge, Cambridge University Press, 1969.

Davis, Brian L. : *Uniforms and Insignia of the Luftwaffe*, London, Arms and Armor, 1999.

Davis, Gwenn: *Drama by Women to 1900: a Bibliography of American and British Writers*, London, Mansell, 1992.

Derek, Albert: *Old English and Middle English Poetry*, London, Routledge & K. Paul, 1977.

Dobree, Bonamy: *English Literature in the Early Eighteenth Century, 1700-1740*, Oxford, Clarendon Press, 1959.

Edmund Spenser: *A Critical Study*, New Delhi, Anmol Pub., 2005.

Edmund, Kerchever: *English Literature at the Close of the Middle Ages*, New York: Oxford University Press, 1947.

Eliot, T.S. : *A Twenty-First Century View*, New Delhi, Atlantic, 2005.

Ferrence, G.: *Deadly Fashion: the Rise and Fall of Cigarette Smoking in North America*, New York, Garland, 1989.

Francis, Russell: *The Scottish Novel: from Smollett to Spark*, Cambridge, Harvard University Press, 1978.

Gerald, Eades: *The Jacobean and Caroline Stage*, Oxford, Clarendon Press, 1941.

Grimes, Janet: *Novels in English by Women, 1891-1920: a Preliminary Checklist*, New York, Garland Publishing, 1981.

Halliday, M. A. K.: *Intonation and Grammar in British English*, The Hague, Mouton, 1967.

Harivansh R.B.: *In the Afternoon of Time: An Autobiography*, New Delhi, Penguin, 2001.

Hart, Russell: *The Scottish Novel: from Smollett to Spark*, Cambridge, Harvard University Press, 1978.

Hogan, Robert Goode: *The Modern Irish Drama: a Documentary History*, NJ: Humanities Press, 1975.

Horsman, E. A.: *The Victorian Novel*, Oxford, Clarendon Press, 1990.

Jack, Ian Robert James: *English Literature, 1815-1832*, Oxford, Clarendon Press, 1963.

James Baldwin: *Protest and Beyond: A Study of Afro-American Fiction*, New Delhi, Rajat Pub., 2005.

James, Ernest: *Principles of Textual Criticism*, San Marino, Huntington Library, 1972.

James, M.: *The Irish Novel: a Critical History*, Boston, Twayne Publishers, 1988.

James, Runcieman: *English Literature of the Late Seventeenth Century*, New York, Oxford University Press, 1969.

Jhumpa Lahiri: *The Master Storyteller: A Critical Response to Interpreter of Maladies*, New Delhi, KPH, 2002.

John Milton: *A Critical Study*, New Delhi, Anmol, 2005.

Knowles, G.: *Patterns of Spoken English: An Introduction to English Phonetics*, London, Longman, 1987.

Koehl, Lewis: *The Black Corps*, Madison, University of Wisconsin Press, 1983.

Laver, J.: *Principles of Phonetics*, Cambridge, Cambridge University Press, 1994.

Logan, P.: *The Later Jacobean and Caroline Dramatists*, Lincoln, University of Nebraska Press, 1978.

Matricardi, Paolo: *Complete Book of World War II Combat Aircraft*, NY, Military Press, 1988

Milhous, Judith: *A Register of English Theatrical Documents, 1660-1737*, Carbondale, Southern Illinois University, 1991.

Naipaul, V.S. : *A House for Mr. Biswas: With an Introduction by Ian Buruma*, New Delhi, Penguin, 1992.

Nath, Narendra: *Indian Religious Historiography*, New Delhi, Munshiram Manoharlal Publishers, 1996.

Neil Bissoondath: *Indo-Caribbean-Canadian Diaspora*, New Delhi, Rawat, 2005.

Nicoll, Allardyce: *A History of English Drama, 1660-1900*, Cambridge, University Press, 1952-65.

Pearsall, Albert: *Old English and Middle English Poetry*, London, Routledge & K. Paul, 1977.

Perkins, David: *A History of Modern Poetry*, Cambridge, Belknap Press of Harvard University Press, 1976.

Philip Roth: *A Novelist in Crisis*, New Delhi, Classical Publishing, 2001.

Pierre, Turner: *Uniforms and Insignia of the Luftwaffe*, London, Arms and Armor, 1999.

Rahilly, J.: *Phonetics: The Science of Speech*, London, Arnold, 1999.

Raja Rao: *The Fictionist*, Delhi, B.R. Publishing, 2003.

Richard, L.: *A Microfiche Concordance to Old English*, Newark, University of Delaware, 1980.

Robert, Lewis: *The Black Corps*, Madison, University of Wisconsin Press, 1983.

Roberta, G.: *Deadly Fashion: the Rise and Fall of Cigarette Smoking in North America*, New York, Garland, 1989.

Rogers, H.: *The Sounds of Language: An Introduction to Phonetics*, Harlow, Longman, 2000.

Royle, Trevor: *The Macmillan Companion to Scottish Literature*, London, MacMillan Reference Books, 1983.

Salman Rushdie: *New Critical Insights*, New Delhi, Atlantic Pub., 2003.

Salzman, Paul: *English Prose Fiction, 1558-1700: a Critical History*, Oxford, Clarendon Press, 1985.

Seidlhofer, B.: *Pronunciation, Oxford*, Oxford University Press, 1994.

Stephen, J. M.: *Ireland in Fiction; a Guide to Irish Novels, Tales, Romances, and Folk-lore*, London: Maunsel, 1919.

Stevenson, Lionel: *Victorian Fiction: a Guide to Research*, Cambridge, Harvard University Press, 1966.

Sutherland, John: *The Stanford Companion to Victorian Fiction*, Stanford, Stanford University Press, 1989.

Sydney, J.: *Brands, Consumers, Symbols and Research*, Thousand Oaks, Sage Publications, 1999.

Terence, P.: *The Later Jacobean and Caroline Dramatists*, Lincoln, University of Nebraska Press, 1978.

Thorpe, Ernest: *Principles of Textual Criticism*, San Marino, Huntington Library, 1972.

Underhill, A.: *Sound Foundations*, London, Heineman, 1994.

Vann, J. Don: *Victorian Novels in Serial*, New York, Modern Language Association of America, 1985.

Venezky, L.: *A Microfiche Concordance to Old English*, Newark, University of Delaware, 1980.

Vikram Seth: *Multiple Locations, Multiple Affiliation*, New Delhi, Rawat, 2001.

Walter, Ernest: *Tradition and Dream : the English and American Novel from the Twenties to Our Time*, London: Hogarth Press, 1986.

Walter, Ernst: *The English Novel: a Short Critical History*, London: Phoenix House, 1954.

Wearing, J. P.: *The London Stage, 1890-1899: a Calendar of Plays and Players*, NJ, Scarecrow Press, 1976.

Wickham, Glynne William Gladstone: *Early English Stages, 1300 to 1660*, London, Routledge and Paul; 1959.

William Blake: *A Critical Study*, New Delhi, Anmol, 2005.

William, John: *A History of English Poetry*, London, MacMillan and Co., 1903.

Yeats, W.B. : *Poetry and Plays*, New Delhi, Atlantic, 2002.

Index

R

S

T

U

V

W